take a hint from the heavens ...

1986 is packed with promise. Make the most of it with the predictions, insights, clues and suggestions America's most popular astrologer, Sydney Omarr, has prepared for you!

Learn about the "geometry" of relationships—who you get along with, and why ... pore over celebrity sun signs and personality profiles ... discover how and why the movements of the zodiac affect men and women so differently ... and much, much more. Whatever your desire, whatever your dilemma, let Sydney Omarr's time-tested wisdom guide you through 1986, and watch your dreams become exciting realities!

For Expanding Your Personal Knowledge of Astrology, SIGNET Brings to You

SYDNEY OMARR'S ASTROLOGICAL GUIDES FOR YOU IN 1986

- [ ] **ARIES** .... (136764—$2.75)*
- [ ] **TAURUS** .... (136772—$2.75)*
- [ ] **GEMINI** .... (136780—$2.75)*
- [ ] **CANCER** .... (136799—$2.75)*
- [ ] **LEO** .... (136802—$2.75)*
- [ ] **VIRGO** .... (136810—$2.75)*
- [ ] **LIBRA** .... (136829—$2.75)*
- [ ] **SCORPIO** .... (136837—$2.75)*
- [ ] **SAGITTARIUS** .... (136845—$2.75)*
- [ ] **CAPRICORN** .... (136853—$2.75)*
- [ ] **AQUARIUS** .... (136861—$2.75)*
- [ ] **PISCES** .... (136888—$2.75)*

*Price is $3.25 in Canada

Buy them at your local bookstore or use this convenient coupon for ordering.

NEW AMERICAN LIBRARY
P.O. Box 999, Bergenfield, New Jersey 07621

Please send me the books I have checked above. I am enclosing $_____
(please add $1.00 to this order to cover postage and handling). Send check or money order—no cash or C.O.D.'s. Prices and numbers are subject to change without notice.

Name_____

Address_____

City _____ State _____ Zip Code _____

Allow 4-6 weeks for delivery.
This offer is subject to withdrawal without notice.

SYDNEY OMARR'S
DAY-BY-DAY ASTROLOGICAL GUIDE FOR

Capricorn
(DECEMBER 22–JANUARY 19)

1986

A SIGNET BOOK

NEW AMERICAN LIBRARY

NAL BOOKS ARE AVAILABLE AT QUANTITY DISCOUNTS
WHEN USED TO PROMOTE PRODUCTS OR SERVICES.
FOR INFORMATION PLEASE WRITE TO PREMIUM MARKETING DIVISION,
NEW AMERICAN LIBRARY, 1633 BROADWAY,
NEW YORK, NEW YORK 10019.

Copyright © 1985 by Sydney Omarr

All rights reserved

Sydney Omarr is syndicated worldwide by Los Angeles Times Syndicate.

SIGNET TRADEMARK REG. U.S. PAT. OFF. AND FOREIGN COUNTRIES
REGISTERED TRADEMARK—MARCA REGISTRADA
HECHO EN CHICAGO, U.S.A.

SIGNET, SIGNET CLASSIC, MENTOR, PLUME, MERIDIAN and NAL BOOKS
are published by New American Library,
1633 Broadway, New York, New York 10019

First Printing, July 1985

1 2 3 4 5 6 7 8 9

PRINTED IN THE UNITED STATES OF AMERICA

CONTENTS

1 **Defining Terms**   7
   - *Astrology*   7
   - *The Zodiac*   8
   - *Sun Sign*   9
   - *Element*   9
   - *Quality*   11
   - *Element and Quality Together*   12
   - *Planet*   13
   - *House*   15
   - *Rising Sign*   16
   - *Horoscope*   17
   - *Aspect*   18
   - *Transiting Planet*   19

2 **Your House of the Sun**   21
   Your "Piece of the Pie"

3 **The Geometry of Relationships**   32
   What Signs You Get Along with—and Why

4 **Twelve Places at the Table**   35
   Personality Profiles of the Signs

5 **Moods of the Moon**   44
   Day-by-Day Changes

6 **Venus and Mars**   55
   Love and Sex ... Peace and War ...
   Cooperating and Competing

7	Venus Sign Position Chart 1910–1975	70
8	Mars Sign Position Chart 1910–1975	76
9	The Planets As "Stars" Astrological Cast of Characters	80
10	Astrotrivia—Rating Yourself in the Best Game in Town	95
	I Sun Signs of the Rich and Famous	95
	II More Celebrity Sun Sign Lore	97
	III Fascinating Facts About the Signs	99
	IV Where Do You Belong?	100
	V Which Animal Best Suits You?	102
11	Sun Sign Changes 1920–1975	105
12	CAPRICORN: The Big Picture	113
13	CAPRICORN: Objectives and Obstacles A Game Plan for Being the Most Successful CAPRICORN Under the Sun	116
14	Pairing Off with CAPRICORN Your Compatability with Other Signs of the Zodiac	121
15	The CAPRICORN Sex Role Dilemma	125
16	The CAPRICORN Female Child ... Young Woman ... Mate ... Mother	128
17	The CAPRICORN Male Child ... Young Man ... Mate ... Father	132
18	CAPRICORN Help Wanted Selecting a Career/Your On-the-Job Style	136
19	How "Pure" a CAPRICORN Are You? Your Moon Sign ... Your Rising Sign	139
20	Find Your Rising Sign	144
21	CAPRICORN Astro-Outlook for 1986	147
22	Fifteen Months of Day-by-Day Predictions	149

1

Defining Terms

What Are Those Astrologers Talking About?

Everyone knows it is more fun to visit another country if you know a bit of the language, and it's a lot easier to find your way around, too. The same idea applies to astrology, which is still foreign territory to many people. Astrology has its very own language, but it really isn't difficult to get a handle on it as long as you understand a few important terms. What follows is a kind of "Astrological Phrase Book," a brief compendium of the most basic words and concepts in the astrological language. Once you've learned them, you'll find you know a lot more about the why of your sun sign as well as information that will help you understand other astrological factors that make you what you are. Best of all, your new language can help you enjoy and explore one of the most exciting, underdeveloped territories under the sun—modern astrology!

Astrology Is an Ancient and Practical "Science"
The first definition of astrology in the standard dictionary is "astronomy," and at one time in history the two studies were synonymous. The word astrology derives from Greek and literally means "the science (or study) of the stars." However, even in earliest times astrology has had much less to do with the "fixed" stars, which appear to remain in one place, than the planets, which move. (The word "planet" means wanderer.) Early man noticed that, as these heavenly bodies moved, their movements coincided with certain earthly events—mainly the changing of the seasons. Gradually, the movement

of the planets was observed to coincide with other important worldly events, such as wars, and the science of "divination" (prediction) by the planets was born. Astronomy and astrology lived happily together until the Christian church banned the latter in about 1550, condemning it as mere superstition. Astrology bounced back in the 1700s, when it came into use as an indicator of human personality, as well as a way to foretell future events. However, this so-called modern astrology is based on the same premise the ancients set down thousands of years ago: "As above, so below." Simply put, what it means is that the positions of the planets, which represent the cosmic order, are related in a significant and observable way to both human behavior and events in human life.

The Zodiac Is a "Circle of Signs"

The zodiac ("circle of animals") is an invisible band in the sky which corresponds to the apparent yearly path of the sun, moon, and the major planets around the earth. It is the "apparent" path in the sense that it is what we *observe* from here on earth. Obviously we know that the earth and other planets revolve around the sun, but the study of astrology (and astronomy) takes earth as the reference point.

The 360-degree circle of the zodiac around the earth is divided into twelve thirty-degree segments—the twelve astrological signs. Throughout the year, as the sun appears to move, it passes through each of these segments in about thirty days. Zero degrees Aries, the vernal equinox or beginning of spring, is the beginning of the zodiac and the start of the seasonal year. It is at that point, on or about March 22, that the sun crosses or intersects with the *ecliptic*—another imaginary band that is (in the mind's eye) the extension of the earth's equator. Another major intersection of the sun's path and the ecliptic takes place at the fall equinox about September 22, the beginning of the seventh sign of the zodiac, Libra. (Equinox means equal days and nights, which is what we experience briefly in the early spring and early fall.) The zodiac "finishes" with the end of the twelfth sign Pisces, about March 21, then begins again with Aries.

Though the segments of the zodiac (the astrological signs) are *named* for the constellations of stars in the sky, they do not correspond with them. The constellations served as convenient visual markers for the ancient astrologer/priests, but the zodiac—and astrology—has always been based on the seasonal year, which never changes. The position of the constellations have changed with reference to our point of view here on earth, however, due to the slipping of the earth's axis. The constellations return a couple of degrees every year and have been doing so for centuries. That's why when the modern *astronomer* says "Aries," he is referring to a group of stars that is in a different position in the sky than the segment of the zodiac the *astrologer* calls "Aries."

Your Sun Sign is Determined by the Month and Day You Were Born

The twelve segments of the zodiac are the twelve astrological signs, from Aries through Pisces, and it takes the sun exactly one year to pass through all twelve signs. A person born when the sun is passing through a particular segment of the zodiac is said to be born under that sign, and it is his/her sun sign. For example, a person born October 14 is said to be born under the sign of Libra. Your sun sign is the most important component of your astrological personality, it is the "real you." However, there are nine other planets besides the sun, and at the moment of a person's birth, those planets are passing through certain segments of the zodiac, or signs, as well. You will learn about some of these lesser influences on your personality in this book later on.

An Element Is Part of a Sign

Obviously your sun sign is a lot more than simply a piece of the sky, or it wouldn't have any meaning. The meaning it has is based on two ancient astrological concepts, the *four elements* and the *three modes*. When these two factors are combined they form the basis of all astrological descriptions of human personality. You can't *see* an element or a quality; they are only to be understood in terms of analogy, but they are fundamental to everything else in astrology, so it is important to understand them.

The four elements, defined by ancient philosophers as the basic components of everything and everybody, are *fire, earth, air,* and *water.* It is doubtful that even in earliest times this breakdown was to be taken as a physical reality: The elements are really four different ways we experience both things and people. For instance, if a thing or a person was experienced as hot rather than cold, sharp rather than dull, active rather than passive, it was said to partake of the *fire* element. And it's easy to see the connection.

Later on, during the Renaissance, the four elements were called "humors," starting a whole new way of typing people. *Fire was the humor choler,* and people who were said to have too much of it were those angry, impatient types who are subject to modern-day diseases like high blood pressure and heart attacks. *The earth element was called black bile* and could cause extreme melancholia (depression) in a person who had too much of it. *Air was the sanguine or rosy humor* and meant a lighter personality. *The water element was the humor phlegm,* and people with too much of it had rather "soggy" personalities and tended to be fat, as well. If the relationship between the elements (or humors) and the signs of the zodiac is beginning to ring a bell, it should. Here's the way the twelve signs break down into elements:

Fire signs: Aries, Leo, Sagittarius
Earth signs: Taurus, Virgo, Capricorn
Air signs: Gemini, Libra, Aquarius
Water signs: Cancer, Scorpio, Pisces

The four elements as four primal types of being exist today in the way many psychologists categorize people's thought processes. Once again, the relationship to the ways in which the twelve astrological signs really do perceive and react to the world is uncannily correct:

The fire signs are instant reactors who put it all together very quickly; things rarely have to be spelled out for a fire sign. These types of people also see the future possibilities inherent in the present and want to bring them about *now*. Obviously, fire signs tend to be impatient, but they have strong wills. Fire is the principle of *action*.

The earth signs are more pragmatic and slower to react. If they can't literally see something or touch it, they have difficulty visualizing it. They operate out of *sense perceptions* and are the realists of the zodiac—the builders who provide stability and continuity. Earth is the principle of *sustenance*.

The air signs see everything as connected to everything else. They are sequential thinkers for whom there must be a beginning, a middle, and an end to everything. For the most part these people operate on *logic* and act only when they can see the sense of their actions. The air signs are endlessly curious and represent the principle of *connecting and reasoning*.

The water signs tend to feel their way through life. What is most real to them is what their emotions tell them; they do what their emotions tell them to do as well. They are imaginative thinkers, the poets and artists of the zodiac. The water principle is that of *caring, nurturing, and protecting*.

A Quality Is Part of a Sign

There are only four elements, but there are twelve signs. In astrological arithmetic, the *three qualities* which divide the *four elements* make up the difference. It isn't easy to grasp the concept of the elements, but the qualities (or "modes" as they are sometimes called) help a lot, because they make the elements a lot more tangible. Called *cardinal*, *fixed*, and *mutable*, the three modes can best be understood as *kinds of motion*.

Cardinal motion is start-up movement. It is the principle of bringing into being. Cardinal goes forward, so, the cardinal signs are *initiators*.

The four cardinal signs are those that start the four seasons:
  Aries (*spring*)
  Cancer (*summer*)

Libra (*fall*)
Capricorn (*Winter*)

Fixed motion means staying in place. Fixed things have come into being, and now simply are. The fixed signs represent stability, and are difficult to move. The four fixed signs represent the middle of each season:
Tarus (*spring*)
Leo (*summer*)
Scorpio (*fall*)
Aquarius (*winter*)

Mutable motion means flexible motion. Things that are mutable are changing, able to turn into something else. The mutable signs represent the *ability to adjust, and to accept change.* The four mutable signs are those that end the seasons:
Gemini (*spring*)
Virgo (*summer*)
Sagittarius (*fall*)
Pisces (*winter*)

Elements and Qualities Together Add Up to Signs
When you put elements and qualities together you begin to get a picture of what they add up to—the twelve astrological signs. Here is how each quality modifies each element.

Fire element/Cardinal quality = Aries
This get-up-and-go sign has all the flash and dash of fire plus an added dose of a pioneering spirit by virtue of its cardinal quality.

Fire element/Fixed quality = Leo
Leo burns with the ardor and enthusiasms of fire, but gives off very steady heat due to its fixed quality.

Fire element/Mutable quality = Sagittarius
Sagittarius represents the kind of fire that spreads, igniting everything and everybody in its path—which is rather erratic because of Sagittarius's mutable quality.

Earth element /Cardinal quality = Capricorn
Capricorn is the most active builder of the earth signs because of its cardinal quality. Capricorn's brand

of reality demands that something be brought into being.

***Earth element/Fixed quality* = Taurus**
This strong sign stands and waits, holding things and people together. Taurus is the warmest and most nurturing of the earth signs, and is always "there."

***Earth element/Mutable quality* = Virgo**
Virgo's practical sense knows that all things must change. This mutable sign represents the principle of stability with flux; that is, permanence in the face of change.

***Air element/Cardinal quality* = Libra**
Libra's air nature moves forward, actively connecting people and things into partnerships via its cardinal quality of initiation.

***Air element/Fixed quality* = Aquarius**
Aquarius is the most immovable of the air signs, representing the permanance of ideas and their practical application.

***Air element/Mutable quality* = Gemini**
This very movable sign represents changing thoughts and opinions, the breaking up of static ideas so that new ones can come about.

***Water element/Cardinal quality* = Cancer**
Cancer is the most initiating of the water signs because of the cardinal quality. Though shy, Cancer generally moves quietly but effectively to the forefront.

***Water element/Fixed quality* = Scorpio**
Scorpio's powerful self-control comes from the emotional water element that is contained and compressed because of this sign's fixed quality.

***Water element/Mutable quality* = Pisces**
Pisces extreme emotionalism—as well as this sign's creativity—comes from feelings that constantly change and move into new areas, creating new outlets.

Planets Are the Most Important Factor in Astrology
"Planet" is probably an even more important word in the astrological language than "sign." How can that be?

Because it is the placement of the planets in various signs which indicates personality and it is the movement of the planets through the zodiac that indicates events. In other words, without the planets the signs would have no application to people and what happens to them.

As early man noticed that the planets moved in fairly regular patterns, he began to associate certain characteristics with each of the planets, and each planet gradually took on a "personality." In a number of different cultures, certain planets were hooked up with certain gods, because it was the gods who really controlled life on earth. The moon was virtually always a female god—like Diana or Artemis. Jupiter, always a "good guy" planet, was known as Vishnu, the preserver, to the Hindus. Before he got his Roman name of Jupiter, the Greeks knew him as Zeus, a lusty fellow who had a heart of gold. (You'll get a complete rundown on each of the planets in Chapter 9, "The Planets As Stars.")

From these planetary "personalities" came the idea that each planet caused a certain kind of behavior or event by virtue of its own nature. For instance, Mars, always the war god, is still regarded by modern astrologers as an indicator of strife and conflict. When predicting events, the astrologer looks at what sign and what house Mars will be passing through at a certain point in time to see what kind of influence it is most likely to bring into a person's life.

When looking at personality, the astrologer determines which sign a person's Mars is in at the time of the person's birth to see how that individual is most likely to assert him-/herself. The sun, the most important planet makes us what we are in totality according to which sign the sun is placed in at our birth; i.e., our sun sign's Venus is the planet of relationships, and its placement in a specific sign shows how a person is likely to relate to others.

In short, planets indicate *action*, and the signs in which the planets are placed indicate *the kind of action*.

Since ancient times, astrologers have recognized seven planets. The sun (which is really a star), the moon (which is really a satellite of our own planet, earth) Mercury, Venus, Mars, Jupiter, and Saturn.

With the development of the telescope, three more planets were discovered (although there is some evidence that early astrologer/priests divined their existence). Uranus was first spotted in 1781, Neptune in 1846, and Pluto as late as 1930. Some astrologers/astronomers anticipate that there are two more to be found, so that there would be twelve planets instead of the current ten.

A House Is an Area of Life—and a Planet's "Home"
Just as there is a great circle in the sky called the zodiac, and it is divided into twelve equal units of *space*, there is another circle which is based on units of *time*. As we all know, the earth makes one complete rotation on its own axis every twenty-four hours. Imagine yourself standing in one place during a twenty-four-hour period and making a mark on the sky every two hours while that sky appears to pass by you as the earth turns. At the end of twenty-four hours, you will have marked off twelve different units of sky. A "house" is simply one of those pieces of sky that has passed by during your day-long vigil. Toward the end of your day of skywatching, twelve houses will have gone by, and "house one" will be coming up again.

When an astrologer draws up a natal horoscope—which is simply a map of the sky when you were born—he/she does it by drawing a picture of the sky as it appeared from the exact place of birth, at the exact time of your birth. What happens is that the twelve houses are lined up in a very specific way—a very different way than if you had been born *in another place at the same time* or *at the same time in another place*.

What is most important about the particular lineup of the houses is that each house represents a different area of human life, and how those areas are positioned *for you* has a tremendous effect on your astrological makeup. For instance, the second house is the house of income and personal possessions and has a lot to do with attitude toward money and how easy or how difficult it will be to come by in your lifetime. The seventh house is the house of partnership and offers clues about who you are likely to marry. If you know the time of your birth within one hour or so, you can add a very important dimension to your astrological self-knowledge by reading the chapter "Your House of the Sun—Your 'Piece of the Pie,' " because the house of the horoscope into which the sun falls in your horoscope usually indicates what area of life will absorb you during your lifetime.

Your Rising Sign Is the One that Starts the First House

Your rising sign is sometimes called the ascendant, because it is the sign of the zodiac that was "ascending" on the eastern horizon at the time of your birth, no matter what time your birth occured. It is the "sunrise sign," corresponding to the nine o'clock position on the face of an ordinary clock. The astrologer's "clock" starts at this position and is read counter-clockwise around the circle of the face. If you were born around sundown, your rising sign will be the one 180 degrees *opposite* the sign you were born under. For instance, if you are an Aries born at sundown, your rising sign will be Libra. If you are an Aries born at sunrise, your rising sign is probably Aries as well.

Why is your rising sign so important? Because it starts the first house of personality, or your very individual way of presenting yourself to the world. No matter what your sun sign is, your rising sign will cover it to a greater or lesser degree (which is why it is so difficult to guess someone's Sun Sign when you first meet them). The rising sign has to do with appearances and can actually influence your physical looks.

If you don't know the time of day you were born, you can't determine your rising sign (although some astrologers can by doing what is called a "rectification," based on the events in your life so far). However, even those who do not know their rising sign can have their horoscopes read; what the astrologer does is put your sun sign on the first house, and do an analysis of what is called a solar horoscope. If you *do* know your birthtime within an hour or so, you can use the rising sign chart in this book to determine yours.

Planets in Signs in Houses Make Up a Horoscope

The whole basis of astrology is that anyone born in a particular moment in time partakes of the qualities of that moment in time. Actually, the same applies for things; for instance, a business that has its beginnings at a precise astrological moment also has a horoscope which can be read, and tells a lot about its potential for success or failure.

An astrologer looks at the particular moment in drawing up a horoscope—or "picture of the hour." A horoscope is basically a map of the sky, showing exactly where the planets were in relation to the signs and the houses, to each other, and from the particular reference point of your birthplace. It is also called a "natal chart" or "natal map."

Everyone's horoscope has ten planets and twelve houses. Those ten planets can be in a variety of signs, and in a variety of houses. Each planet means something different according to its own nature, how that nature operates in a particular sign, and what area of life the planet is most likely to affect by virtue of which house of the horoscope it falls into. Sound complicated? It is, and only a highly trained astrologer can interpret the many factors and put them together for you in a meaningful way. The most exciting part of astrology is the fact that *no two individuals are ever exactly alike*—not even twins, who are born a few minutes apart.

Although you can find out a lot about your astrological personality right in this book, many people like to take the next step and have a personalized horoscope drawn up for them and interpreted by a professional astrologer. There are a number of ways to find a good person to do this for you; in astrology, as in every other profession, there are variations in the level of competence. Two places you can start your search are:

National Astrological Society
62 West 39th St.
New York, NY 10018

American Federation of Astrologers
Tempe, AZ 85282

An Aspect Is the Distance Between Planets

Among the more sophisticated factors an astrologer looks for in your horoscope are the *aspects*. Within the 360-degree circle of the horoscope (and the zodiac), planets form certain aspects to each other by virtue of the distance between them. Some distances are considered harmonious, and some are inharmonious, in terms of how those two (or more) planets work together. It's all a matter of mathematics. The soft or harmonious aspects are the sextile (60 degrees apart) and the trine (120 degrees apart). The hard or inharmonious aspects are formed when planets are in square to each other (90 degrees apart) or in opposition, 180 degrees or exactly half a circle apart. These are only the major aspects, and there are lots and lots of minor ones between, but you can get a good picture of interplanetary relationships with only these few.

For example, if your sun sign is Aries, and at the time of your birth the planet Saturn was in the sign of Libra, or 180 degrees away from Aries, you are likely to have a more serious (Saturnine) disposition than the typical "happy" Aries. Depending on your point of view, this can be a positive note in your horoscope, because you will have greater powers of concentration than many an Aries—or a negative note, because you will be less happy-go-lucky. In another example, a person with a Capricorn sun sign may have a horoscope in which Jupiter, the planet of expansiveness, is 120 degrees away from the sun—either in the sign of Virgo or Taurus—and therefore in "trine" aspect to his/her sun. The result: a much more outgoing, giving Capricorn than the run-of-the-mill type. On the other hand, such an easy aspect could expand Capricorn's acquisitive nature too much, and make for a megalomanic (someone who craves worldly goods and power).

The ancients separated aspects into "favorable" and "unfavorable," but psychologically-thinking modern astrologers know that it is not that simple; it all depends on the total horoscope, plus the individual's reactions to the particular vibrations of the planets in that horoscope.

A Transiting Planet Affects Your Life Now

When someone goes to an astrologer for the first time, he/she usually has *two* readings—separate, but interrelated. The first will be an interpretation of your natal chart or birth horoscope. This tells you about your given personality—the traits, problems, abilities, and advantages you are most likely to have by virtue of the placement of the planets in the sky at the time of your birth. The second reading will have to do with what you can expect in your life at the present time and the near future. Your birth horoscope always remains the same, but the planets in the sky keep changing their relationships to your birth horoscope throughout your lifetime. The astrologer will acquaint you with the current "transit"—or movements—of the planets and how you, the individual, can expect them to affect you. For instance, if an astrologer notes that Uranus, the "earthquake planet," is approaching your fourth house (the house of emotional security, the place where we really live), the astrologer might alert you to the fact that big changes are in the offing: even a total shaking of the foundations, or a pulling up of roots. This is a major transit, and many people change their residence, partners, or jobs when it occurs. Similarly, but on a less critical note, the astrologer may notice that the planet Venus is going to make a transit over the place in the zodiac occupied by Mars in your birthchart. This could indicate a firey romantic interlude or the rekindling of an old flame.

There are two important things to keep in mind about astrological predictions. The first is that your natal horoscope—your "birth imprint"—really determines how you will react to life's events. To put it even more strongly, your innate personality will really *create* the events of your life, because "character is destiny." There is no doubt that the planets create conditions, but we must take responsibility for how we cooperate with those conditions. The second thing is that *there are very few hard and fast rules*. There are guidelines, to be sure, and most of them have ancient roots; a lot of astrological prediction is based on the case history technique. However, since no two sets of conditions—

the one in the sky and the one in an individual birthchart—are ever *exactly* the same, it is virtually impossible for any astrologer to tell you specifically what is going to happen.

2

Your House of the Sun

Your "Piece of the Pie"

The prime symbol in the very symbolic language of astrology is the perfect circle; it represents the sky around us, the cosmic atmosphere into which we are all born. All astro-math is based on division of the 360-degree figure, which since ancient times has been regarded as having mystical qualities. When thinking about the houses of the horoscope, however, it helps to use a very down-to-earth analogy. Look at that circle as a great "pie in the sky," which is divided into twelve cosmic slices—each slice representing one house and a different facet of human experience.

Just as there are ten planets in everyone's horoscope, there are twelve houses. However, not all those houses may be occupied by a planet; it all depends on where the planets were in the sky at the moment of your birth. The placement of any planet in a specific house is a *very* important factor in your individual horoscope, but the most important is the placement of the sun. No matter what your sun sign, your House of the Sun has a lot to tell you about the life you've been "given" to live on this earth. As your sun sign is the prime indicator of *character and personality*, your house of the sun points to the *area of human affairs* that you are most likely to find yourself concentrating on in your lifetime.

In the sense that it helps define the boundaries of your life, your house of the sun is your "piece of the pie"—that slice of life within which you will live. Does your house of the sun totally box you in? In a way it does, but it is more productive to think of the dimensions of your house of the sun as *guidelines* about where you can most profitably focus your energies.

Here's the way it works:

- The *sun* is the most important planet in your horoscope. It is the planets that do the "acting," and the sun plays the leading role.
- Your sun sign determines *how* your sun (the real you) acts, i.e., the characteristics of the character you play.
- Your house of the sun is the "stage" on which you will play out your role.

For instance, if your sun sign is Scorpio (the great investigator) and your house of the sun is the twelfth (hidden things), you find yourself drawn to some kind of career in which you must "dig" to do your investigating. Ergo, you might make a good psychoanalyst, archeologist, or genetic researcher. Or, your greatest pleasure in life might be reading mystery novels or spy thrillers—or writing or editing them.

In order to figure out which piece of the pie you've been served, you have to know your birth-time within an hour or so. If you were born during Daylight Savings Time or War Time, you have to subtract one hour from your birth time to determine the "real sun time."

Each house is described here from three different angles:

- The matters or principles connected with it
- The people/places/things related to it
- The problems and the possibilities of having your sun in that house.

Birth time, 4 to 6 a.m.: **Sun in First House**

- *First house matters:* Exploration ... use of the physical body ... being on the scene ... breaking new ground ... independent action ... emergencies ... conquest ... controversy ... strategy ... competition ... being in the vanguard.

- *First house people/places/things:* Entrepreneurs ... acrobats ... cutting instruments ... rock music ... metals ... satire ... hardware ... the head and face ... opticians ... adrenalin ... new products ... commodities ... salesmen ... fighters ... firemen.
- *Problems and possibilities:* With your sun in the first house, your sun sign personality is quite strong. Regardless of what your sun sign is, you should be able to make clear-cut decisions and have a good sense of your own identity. If you are to gain control over your life, you are going to have to banish fear from it and develop both the moral and the physical courage that is available to you. Though your will should be strong, you will have to keep yourself from a tendency to tyrannize others. When you feel most defeated is the time your first house sun will come to your rescue. The one thing that could keep you from living out the very vivid life this house placement gives you is inflexibility and intolerance. Be willing to listen.

Birth time, 2 to 4 a.m.: **Sun in Second House**

- *Second house matters:* Calmness ... conservation ... ability to make grow ... eroticism ... collecting ... comforting ... administrating ... luxury ... stabilizing ... building up ... perpetuating ... patience ... using ... making stronger ... indulging.
- *Second house people/places/things:* Possessions ... money ... the voice ... landscape gardeners ... brokers and bankers ... love/passion ... personal adornment ... life-sustaining skills ... buying and selling ... security needs ... nurses ... food and shelter ... good music ... creature comforts.
- *Problems and possibilities:* You should be able to establish yourself firmly and securely in whatever you choose to do; self-adjustment should come easily to you. Your economic life could be relatively worry-free but you must resist valuing money and

possessions for their own sake and becoming overly materialistic. You must develop the will that is given you and turn it into willpower, or you could lose self-respect. You are a good manager, but if you allow yourself to become too settled, you will fear to take the necessary risks to make your life less limited. Though things come to you fairly easily, do not let yourself over-indulge in any of them, including rich food.

Birth time midnight to 2 a.m.: **Sun in Third House**

- *Third house matters:* Connecting ... associating ... verbalizing ... dexterity ... inquisitiveness ... distribution ... novelty ... thinking and reasoning ... cause and effect ... exchanging ... bringing the news ... being responsive ... "here today, gone tomorrow."
- *Third house people/places/things:* Short journeys ... realatives (especially siblings) ... speech/languages ... high school teachers ... role-playing/entertaining ... computers ... graphic arts ... handwork ... transportation ... the nervous system ... handwriting .. repair men ... gossip ... comedy ... ventriloquists.
- *Problems and possibilities:* You should be an excellent communicator who reports things clearly and accurately. In your desire for information, however, you could become rather superficial and a bit of a talebearer. If you don't focus your mental energies carefully, you may waste the gift of curiosity your third house sun gives you. You must also learn to live with uncertainty, and to keep your opinions flexible. If life scares you, you are likely to become very defensive and locked in to your ideas. Develop your capacity for listening as well as your talent for talking.

Birth time 10 p.m. to 12 a.m.: **Sun in Fourth House**

- *Fourth house matters:* Adaptability ... change ... instinctiveness ... fluctuation ... protecting ...

imagination ... softness ... the subconscious ... survival ... enveloping ... integrating ... fertility ... mothering.
- *Fourth house people/places/things:* Dreams ... the past ... roots ... home and family ... physical sensation ... museums ... caterers ... water and other liquid ... introverts ... obstetrics ... boats ... domestics ... imagination.
- *Problems and possibilities:* Via your fourth house sun, you are given the possibility of understanding yourself and your motivations quite thoroughly. If you handle your life in a mature way, you will establish a warm and comfortable home for you and your family. However, you must strive for real self-knowledge if you are not to become simply self-absorbed and self-centered. Your imagination is considerable, and you could be highly creative; the down side is that you could develop irrational fears that verge on paranoia. Work to see the world clearly at all times and try to conquer your tendency to play the introvert. No mater what your sun sign, the placement of that sun in the fourth house will make you instinctively avoid the limelight. Get out there and shine!

Birth time 8 to 10 p.m.: **Sun in Fifth House**

- *Fifth house matters:* Being at the heart of things ... pleasures ... power ... ambition ... generosity/giving ... "gilding the lily" ... showmanship ... stability ... management ... territorial rights ... self-expression ... autocracy ... organization.
- *Fifth house people/places/things:* Philanthropy ... corporations ... impresarios ... holidays and vacations ... romantic love ... children ... gamblers ... gold ... circuses ... nursery teachers ... fashion and fashion designers ... public life.
- *Problems and possibilities:* Even if you have a "shy" sun sign, your fifth house placement of the sun will force you into some form of self-expression that is possibly very creative. You also have a capability

for approaching life with a joyful, expectant manner; however, your pursuit of pleasure and play could become extreme. Consciously avoid any pleasure that threatens to get out of control. Your affairs of the heart could be many, but it is important to keep alert for anything that smacks of an abusive partner; it's possible you could enjoy the drama of an unhappy situation. Develop your capacity for warmly accepting others.

Birth time 6 to 8 p.m.: **Sun in Sixth House**

- *Sixth house matters:* Competence/skill ... specialization ... refining ... categorizing ... analyzing ... obedience ... realism ... responsibility ... purifying ... invention ... making things work ... ministering ... discriminating.
- *Sixth house people/places/things:* Service ... critics ... crafts ... libraries ... closets ... public health ... the harvest ... small animals ... dependents ... dental hygienists ... research ... diagnosing ... numbers work ... chemists.
- *Problems and possibilities:* With your sun in the sixth house you have the potential of becoming a true master at something; however, if you allow yourself to get bogged down in life's details, you could possibly end up being a wage slave. No matter what your sun sign, your instincts tell you to be of service to others. While you are capable of great self-sacrifice, you must avoid the temptation to be overly humble and to assume the servant role. You are mentally very keen, and can break things and jobs down into smaller parts in order to accomplish them. Do not let the state of your own health become an obsession. With the sun is the sixth house, your basic constitution should be quite strong. Don't worry!

Birth time 4 to 6 p.m.: **Sun in Seventh House**

- *Seventh house matters:* Sharing ... comparing ... give-and-take ... peacemaking ... negotiation ...

making things beautiful ... creating balance ... fairness ... sociability ... gratification ... advocacy ... diplomacy ... aestheticism.

- *Seventh house people/places/things:* Divorce lawyers ... love poetry ... marriage brokers ... the kidneys and lower back ... illustration ... resort managers ... public relations ... fine arts ... receptionists ... boutiques ... jugglers ... tailors ... pianos.
- Possibilities and problems: You have a great need to identify with others, and can create a wonderful rapport with them easily. However, your need for a life partner could make you overly dependent. If you have an independent sun sign, this could create a serious life conflict. With this placement, you are able to adjust to new people and new situations easily, but you must avoid a tendency not to stick with a position when you really believe in it. You have the potential of forming very warm, balanced and intimate relationships; however, if you do not handle this gift in a mature manner, you could develop a fear of intimacy, and shy away from it or become an outrageous and insincere flirt.

Birth time 2 to 4 p.m.: **Sun in Eighth House**

- *Eighth house matters:* Release of blockages ... probing ... anonymity ... procreation ... rejuvenation ... willpower ... endurance ... controlling ... investigation ... aloneness ... demolishing and rebuilding ... crisis ... elimination.
- *Eighth house people/places/things:* Puzzles ... generals ... political parties ... labor lawyers ... the healing arts ... death and dying ... taxes ... spies ... superathletes ... crime detection ... statesmen ... sex symbols ... geologists ... explorers ... mating instinct ... sanitation engineers.
- *Problems and possibilities:* A light sun sign (like Gemini or Libra), the placement of the sun in this house will add depth to your character. You will feel compelled to investigate things that are hidden or

even dangerous. While it is good to probe, you must beware of a tendency to concentrate on what is morbid. All things being equal, you will be highly sexed; however, with insufficient self-knowledge, your healthy sexual instincts could turn into obsession with the subject—or a total advoidance of it. Learn to live with your dynamic physical body and you will live with others quite happily. Also, encourage your religious or mystical feelings, which are quite real. You have the potential of totally transforming your life at one point or another.

Birth time noon to 2 p.m.: **Sun in Ninth House**

- *Ninth house matters:* Anticipating ... aspiring ... moving around ... expanding things ... speculating ... idealism ... advising ... unpredictability ... search for truth ... search for opportunity ... taking aim ... magnanimity ... excess.
- *Ninth house people/places/things* Casinos ... ambassadors ... passport offices ... luck ... international transportation ... trading/high finance ... dancers ... aristocrats ... large animals ... higher studies ... lawmaking ... profiteers ... veterinarians.
- *Problems and possibilities:* Even if you have a routine-loving sun sign (like Virgo), this placement of the sun will give you the desire and the ability to constantly renew your life, and to adapt to new patterns of behavior. You will feel strongly about one religious or ethical system or another, or at least have a very strong personal philosophy. However, you could become rather dogmatic and rigid in your opinions. Your adaptability is admirable, but a desire for the new and novel could be the "downside" of your openness to new experience. Exercise control. With certain sun signs, there may be a tendency toward inner battles between opportunity-seeking and a firm set of principles. You are a spender—of both your money and your physical resources.

Birth time 10 a.m. to 12 a.m.: **Sun in Tenth House**

- *Tenth house matters:* Realism ... structure ... ambition ... rigidity ... integrating ... limitation ... disciplining ... reputation ... social position ... creating the useful ... contraction ... coolness ... convention.
- *Tenth house people/places/things:* Figures ... fame ... common sense ... property ... correctional systems and facilities ... ceramics ... money lenders ... efficiency experts ... the bones ... the elderly ... sculptors ... watches and clocks.
- *Problems and possibilities:* You have the capacity of becoming a respected member of whatever group you move in, because your public image is very important to you. If you play your cards right, you can arrive at a sense that you are fulfilling your destiny. However, if you become obsessed with power and appearances, you could end up living a shallow, meaningless life behind your strong facade. It is most important with this placement of the sun to find the right outlet for you to express yourself and get positive feedback from others. You won't be happy starving in a garret, because both money and recognition are too important to you. This position of the sun often brings fame.

Birth time 8 to 10 a.m.: **Sun in Eleventh House**

- *Eleventh house matters:* Helping ... experimentation ... humanitarianism ... association ... liberalism .. freedom ... suddenness ... awakenings ... combining ... freethinking ... rationality ... caring ... breaking through ... observing coolly ... predicting.
- *Eleventh house people/places/things:* Paradoxes ... stunt men ... electricity ... zealots ... divorce ... fireworks ... the social sciences ... reform ... geniuses ... aviation ... weathermen ... brotherly love ... magnetism ... groups ... friends ... causes.
- *Problems and possibilities:* If you are a very personal

sun sign (like Cancer), you will gain a lot of objectivity with the placement of the sun in this house. You should have very high aims and goals, and some of them will undoubtedly involve helping the less fortunate in some way or another. Though this is admirable, if you don't set yourself on a definite path in life and stick to a definite plan, you could simply drift along, with only vague ideas about where you can shine. It is important to be quite realistic with the sun in this house. Your own crowd is important to you, but you must avoid becoming such a part of the group that you lose a sense of your own individuality—which is potentially very great. Some people with the sun in the 11th house are downright wacky, but often very achieving people.

Birth Time 6 to 8 a.m.: **Sun in Twelfth House**

- *Twelfth house matters:* Dissolving ... ambiguity ... disguising ... retreating ... sensualism ... enchantment ... paying dues ... healing spiritually ... insubstantiality ... confinement ... persuading ... comprehending the incomprehensible ... merging ... pretending.
- *Twelfth house people/places/things:* Makeup ... escapism ... alcohol and drugs ... drama and dramatic actors ... films ... advertising ... pastoral work ... fishing ... astrophysics ... con men ... magicians ... hospitals ... alibis ... myths ... prisons.
- *Problems and possibilities:* Yours is not an easy house of the sun to have—especially if you are a very self-expressive sun sign type like Leo. You may feel that life is confining you in some way or another; what you are really sensing is your gift of the ability to transcend self to a much higher spiritual level. You should be an expert at coping with intangibles and sensing the nuances of any situation. In a sense, you have a kind of ESP which can be developed for life success. However, the real down side of the twelfth house sun is that it

can lead to a very confused, unfocussed attitude toward life. It is essential that you give yourself a definite structure to work within if you are to free yourself from the worries and cares of life. By all means avoid any form of escapism that is dangerous.

3

The Geometry of Relationships

What Signs You Get Along with—and Why

The first thing most people want to know about their sun sign is what other signs they are compatible with. It's a natural question, and a good one to ask an astrologer, because one aspect of astrology, called "synastry" (literally, "stars together") concentrates on the subject of relationships. When practising synastry, the astrologer compares the two birth charts of the two people involved to find what connections there are between them. It is a complicated process, but it provides excellent clues about how two people will relate to each other. What chart comparison does is *describe the nature of the relationship*. Actually, to an astrologer there are no "bad" or "good" relationships; there are just a lot of different kinds and each has a special character. Of course it is true that some relationships end up on the rocks, sometimes devastating one or both parties involved. But, even in such cases, the astrologer looks at it as a "karmic" relationship—one in which people *had* to come together in order to learn some life lessons.

While comparing two complete horoscopes is the ideal way to look at a relationship, there is a very simple method of looking at two sun signs, and coming up with an overall prediction of how two people will relate to each other. This method goes back to the great circle of the zodiac and to the division of the twelve signs into four elements: fire, earth, air, and water.

Here's the lineup of signs in each element:

Fire: Aries, Leo, Sagittarius

Earth: Taurus, Virgo, Capricorn
Air: Gemini, Libra, Aquarius
Water: Cancer, Scorpio, Pisces

The general rules of thumb for element-mixing are as follows:

Great	Good	Semi-tough or Difficult
Fire and air	Fire and fire	Fire and water
Water and earth	Earth and earth	Earth and air
	Air and air	Fire and earth
	Water and water	Air and water

Here's the way it looks mathmatically:

If you divide the 360-degree circle of the zodiac by the twelve signs, you find that each sign is 30 degrees away from the next.

- Signs that are 30 degrees apart—or next to each other—are semi-tough.
- Signs that are 60 degrees (two signs) or 180 degrees (six signs) away from each other are the best combinations. (The latter, 180 degrees away from each other, makes these signs polar opposites, and in astrology polar opposites attract.)
- Signs that are 120 degrees apart—four signs away from each other—are in the same element, and their relationship is good, but far from perfect.
- Signs that are 90 degrees or three signs away from each other have the most difficult relationships of all. They are said to be in "square aspect" to each other.

When you look at the four elements in terms of what they signify in the physical world, you get a good idea why some elements get along more easily.

Fire turns water into steam (hot air).
Water puts fire out.
Fire scorches earth.

Earth smothers fire.
Air fans fire and makes it brighter.
Fire warms up cool air.
Water softens up hard earth.
Earth makes water keep its shape.
Water and air do nothing (unless you add heat).
Air blows earth around.

What about combinations of the same element, such as fire with fire? In effect, they tend to neutralize or cancel each other out. Or, they can simply be too much of one element for comfort.

- Two fire signs together could experience "burn out" fairly quickly.
- Two air signs might analyze each other to the death of the relationship.
- Two earth signs could depress each other a lot.
- Two water signs could make for an overly "heavy" relationship.

4

Twelve Places at the Table

A Mini Astrodrama in Which the Twelve Signs Play Themselves

No matter how accurate or colorful any description of a zodiac sign may be, it is still a description—not the real thing. A sign is simply an abstract concept until it takes form in a living, breathing human being. There are obviously as many different types of people as there are individual horoscopes, and no two are exactly alike. However, the twelve signs of the zodiac are still the best guidelines we have for sorting out human behavior into broad but meaningful categories. There are even fiction writers who use the zodiac signs as prototypes for characters they create because it makes them more realistic, i.e., more like people you are likely to meet.

What follows is fiction, but it gets closer to the truth about each zodiacal sign than a general description ever can. The twelve characters in this docudrama are obviously caricatures, because their behavior is highly exaggerated. But it is exaggeration for emphasis, and for the purpose of bringing to life the twelve signs of the zodiac, which don't really exist except as real people. Like real people, these twelve characters have foibles; but they have fine points too. As you read this drama, you may find yourself drawn to some signs and put off by others. Make mental notes of which signs you find yourself most sympathetic with and check out your findings in the parts of this book about astrological compatibility. It could prove very interesting—

and very revealing. As each sign of the zodiac has a sex or gender, they are portrayed here as male or female accordingly. But the basic behavior pattern is applicable to both sexes.

The twelve signs of the zodiac are invited to dinner at that great dining room in the sky. When they arrive, they find that their host (who shall remain signless) has slipped up, and there are only eleven places set at the table. Since it is a fancy affair, each sign is trying to be on his/her best behavior. However, the situation is a bit unsettling, so in the course of trying to resolve it, they all relapse into their natural zodiacal characteristics.

Aries An energetic young man, he comes bounding into the room, almost tripping on an untied shoelace. He is dressed rather casually for the occasion, and looks as if he got dressed rather quickly. When he realizes what the situation is, there's no doubt in his mind how to handle it.

"Only eleven places? Don't worry; Pisces will probably never show anyway. But, I got here before anybody else (the doorman will prove it) so I should definitely get a seat. In fact, I should sit down *first*. No, I don't need to wash my hands or anything. I'm *starved*, so I hope you aren't having anything like the gooey mess with the French name you had before. A hamburger will do just fine. And don't serve it cold like you did the last time. Hey, there's a great-looking dish over there, ha ha! Seat me next to her, will you Cancer? Well, she looks like a nice warm type, so I think I'll go let her warm me up. By the way, I'm organizing a sky-diving club. Want to join? Seriously, if you can't afford the membership fee, I'll put it up for you, because I'd love to have you join. Oh, you're doing okay now? Glad to hear you're off the rack. Got any pretzels?"

Taurus An attractive young woman with faint dimples in her roundish cheeks and a slightly unruly but pretty mass of curly hair comes sauntering into the room. She is dressed in a soft and pretty outfit that looks expensive, and has her handbag clutched tightly under her arm. She looks around the room with moderate curiosity. As the host walks up to her, she gives him a warm smile; when she speaks, her voice is low and melodious—but firm.

"Only eleven places? You mean, only eleven *chairs*. All you have to do is set another place and give me a pillow to sit on. I don't mind, as long as I'm comfortable. And I smell something wonderful, so I know the food is going to be delicious. To be honest with you, that's really why I came. I don't like to go out much, you know. What I really like is curling up in my warm and comfy bed—with someone warm and comfy, of course. (Are you busy later on?) But, now that I'm *here*, there's no way I'm not going to eat. What's for dessert? Who's that nervous-looking lady over there? Virgo? I'll go try to make her feel comfortable."

Gemini It's hard to tell just how old this fellow is as he springs in the door; he could be any age, though he looks about eighteen. He is dressed in the very latest style, though nothing he has on is really extreme. His eyes dart all over the room, and he is carrying a notebook under his arm. When the host tells him about the eleven places, he is so busy listening to another conversation, he almost misses it. When he reacts, it is in a typically casual way.

"Don't worry about me; I don't need a place. I'll just float around the room, because what I really came here for is the conversation. I'm writing a book, you know—it's called *1001 Opening Conversational Gambits* and tonight I'm researching. I see you've got some really fascinating types here. How did you make up the guest list? Are they all married? Why did they come alone? What's the menu? Who's the chef? Can I see the wine list? Who's that blowsy-looking type over there? Taurus? I'll bet *she's* got a story. Where's the telephone? I've got to make a call."

Cancer A sexy, voluptuous woman of indeterminate age pauses at the door; she seems shy, but conscious of the impression she is making. Her clothes are a bit unusual, and some things are from the thrift shop. However, her antique jewelry is genuine, and the whole effect is glamorous. When she discovers there are only eleven places, she is visibly upset, and there is a touch of a whine in her voice as she speaks.

"I wish I'd known; I could have stayed home with the children. They have colds, you know. If you want, I'll simply leave; but I really don't want to go home by myself; I'll get scared and have bad dreams. Upset? Yes, I am upset, and when I get upset I can't eat. Unless it's really soothing and nourishing. Did you know that a touch of heavy cream in mashed potatoes is simply heavenly? Chicken soup? I make it by the gallon. Say, you look as if you could stand a little fattening up. Well, all right. I *guess* I'll stay—unless I change my mind, of course."

Leo   This is a fine figure of a man—fairly tall, rather muscular, and with a thick crop of curly hair that is somewhere between blond and red. He is elegantly dressed and his gold cufflinks probably put a real drain on Fort Knox. His grand entrance is smooth and practised, and his handshake is hearty and warm. When his host tells him the news, he takes it very personally.

"Well, let me tell you, this is embarrassing! I mean, all these people here to see me, and I may have to stand? I've given bigger parties than this, and they've always gone off without a hitch. Let me handle things for you the next time. For now, just get that chair over there and squeeze someone in—Virgo won't mind. No, *here*; not *there!* While we're all waiting I guess I can entertain everyone with my tantrum act. What? No, I'm only kidding—though I am mad. I'll do my Hamlet number instead. Like my cufflinks? They match my Gold Card. I've ordered another pair with sapphires, too."

Virgo   A rather prim woman stands quietly at the door looking as if she would like to blend into the woodwork. She is dressed very neatly, but conservatively, with flat-heeled sensible shoes. In her handbag she carries a surgical mask to wear in case any of the other guests has a cold. Her reaction to the news that there are only eleven places is swift and shrill.

"Well, it certainly isn't *my* fault. I answered the invitation the minute I got it. I *always* do! Why didn't you check on things more carefully? If you had, this wouldn't have happened, and you wouldn't have all these people standing around thinking terrible things about you. I don't mind for myself, you understand, I don't eat much anyway; you never know what you're going to get. I'll stay in the kitchen and help the cook clean up. You can't be too careful about these things, you know. You wouldn't believe the sanitary conditions I've found in *some* kitchens. Not mentioning any names, of course. Oh, *why* did you mess things up this way; you are simply impossible. . . ."

Intermission: Our host walks away as Virgo continues to complain. As he checks on the guests, he discovers that Libra has just arrived. Sagittarius and Pisces are nowhere to be found, but Scorpio, Capricorn, and Aquarius are waiting to greet him. Because he looks like he's a bit uncomfortable, the host talks to Libra first.

Libra A very attractive male, wearing all the right things, walks tentatively into the room, looking as if he is searching for someone. He is visibly uncomfortable alone. His gaze scans the room, quietly appraising everything and everybody in it. He seems to approve, but in his nervousness, he approaches the table, and starts rearranging one of the settings, then rearranging it again. All this is done very tactfully and gracefully. In fact, he looks as if he couldn't make an awkward gesture if he tried. His host approaches him and breaks the news. Libra's reaction is smooth and unruffled.

"Oh, how *clever* of you to arrange this little puzzle for us. It will make things so much more fun. Of course, we've got to make things absolutely fair; we wouldn't want to hurt anyone's feelings. I could leave if it would help, but . . . Oh, how nice of you to tell me I'll definitely have a place; it makes me feel a lot less awkward. I rarely go places alone, you know. Who would I like to sit next to? Well, the Capricorn lady looks like a sturdy and sensible type. But on the other hand, Scorpio is a *knockout*. Is she attached? Hmmm, Taurus looks like she'd like to chat, but oh, that Cancer! Decisions, decisions; I'll make up my mind later on. Where did you get that *great* painting?

Scorpio   A slim and sexy woman dressed totally in black comes slinking into the room. Her style and movement are absolutely magnetic, and every eye turns to look at her. But she gives no visible response that she is aware of it. She doesn't seem to be feeling anything at all, but when her host approaches and tells her what is going on, she is seething with quiet rage.

"Do you really think you are going to get away with this? I suspected something when I got that weird invitation. Who in the world would ever come as they are and let everybody else know what they're really like? No matter how many times you tell me it was an innocent mistake to set only eleven places, I'll never believe it. Nothing in this world is innocent. And when it comes to drawing straws, just remember you owe me one from the last time. You know, the *last* time! Who's that wimpy looking guy over there? Gemini? Maybe I'll amuse myself with him for a while. I need a new conquest; I'm getting out of practice."

Sagittarius   While Scorpio has been talking with the host, a tall rather rangy male has come loping into the room carrying a suitcase. He is a bit disheveled because his flight was late. He throws the suitcase in a corner and starts putting himself back together—a bit absentmindedly because he is looking around the room with a big smile and a lot of anticipation. He moves toward the host and gives a slap on his back that is almost *too* hearty.

"Only eleven places? Why worry? We'll work it out somehow. Life's too short to get uptight anyway. Had the greatest trip, and I'm turning right around tomorrow and going to the Orient so I can practice my Chinese. Say, are you serving Chinese food? I love Chinese food—and a good beer to go with it. At least I hope you're serving better wine than you did last time. You're looking a little pale . . . been partying too much lately? Ha ha, only kidding. Who's that guy over there with the flashy cufflinks? And the mouse with the sensible shoes? Think I'll see if I can loosen her up a bit. Did you hear I'm going to win the lottery again? What do you mean, how do I know? I just *know*. And I've got a great idea for an international fast food chain I'm going to bankroll with my winnings. I'm gonna call it 'The Great Gobler' and serve only turkey sandwiches. Hey, I'm thirsty. Where's the bar?"

Aquarius An intellectual-looking gentleman—sort of an absentminded professor type—has been standing in the doorway quietly puffing his pipe and scrutinizing the crowd. His jacket and pants don't match, but he isn't aware of it. An even stranger—but typical—sartorial note is his electric blue tie with orange stripes. He's got his earphones with him; if things get too dull, he'll listen to some hard rock or electronic music and be in seventh heaven. When he finds out about the missing place, he gives a thoughtful answer and makes an impractical suggestion.

"Oh, well, rather than make anyone feel left out, we could cancel the whole dinner and bring the food to the local shelter for the homeless. Ah, you don't care for that idea. Too bad; I'm becoming more and more concerned about poverty in our own backyard. Of course, I'm no bleeding heart like Pisces, but fair's fair. Want to hear about a new invention I'm working on? It's an electronic stamp sorter that will revolutionize the whole philatelic world. Huh? Oh, that's stamp collecting. Glad you asked me to come alone, since I'm free as a bird now. My last attachment got so *sticky!* I've sworn off. At least off those emotional types who want you to get so involved. No, I never get lonely—I've got too many friends for that. By the way, I can just sit on the floor in the lotus position, and get some meditating in at the same time."

Capricorn A rather handsome, perfectly put together woman has been quietly observing the crowd and the room, mentally putting a price tag on everything. What she has on is very expensive, but understated and in excellent taste. In her handbag she carries a petition with her name on it. She wants to run for local office, and is hoping to pick up some supporters tonight. If they are "her kind of people," that is. Her reaction to the host's situation is sober but logical.

"Well, it's obvious someone will have to go, but I

trust your judgment to decide who is most important—if you know what I mean. Your appointments are in excellent taste; I see you like Tiffany as much as I do. Who's that rather tacky looking type over there? Cancer? Where *does* she get her clothes? I have little sympathy for people who can't get their act together and run their lives successfully. She's probably a poet. Ah, well, different strokes for different folks; fantasy has no place in *my* life, you know. By the way, I have some excellent ideas about how to shape things up in the community; will you sign my petition? At dinner, are we going to discuss great books? I just bought a whole series . . . all leather-bound, of course. They look smashing in my living room."

Pisces Meanwhile, a rather wispy but very pretty woman has been wandering in and out of the doorway, looking as if she isn't quite sure she is in the right place. She is dressed in a misty fabric of very pale colors; there doesn't seem to be a clear-cut edge anywhere. In fact, if you don't rub your eyes, you might think you are seeing an apparition. The host knows it's Pisces and catches her just as she's about to drift out the door again. He doesn't bother telling her about the missing place, because he knows she wouldn't understand why that was important.

"Late? Am I late? I lost my watch two weeks ago. Or was it three? Oh well, what's time anyway in the larger scheme of things? Hungry? Not really, though I can't remember the last time I ate. *Love*—it's *love* that's food for the soul, and that's what I care about nourishing. I wonder if any of these people have had any *real* soul food lately. No, don't worry, I won't try to convert anyone tonight. I'm too, too drained because of my current work. What kind? Well, it really isn't a job-job, I mean where you make money, and all. I've started a shelter for homeless animals in my apartment; I cry so much when I see a stray that I can't stand it. Who? Ho, he left some time ago. Something about there being 'other fish in the sea.' What in the world do you suppose he meant by that? By the way, I'm a little short of cash. Do you think you could lend me . . .?"

At this point, things are at a stalemate, but the situation will quickly resolve itself in one of twelve ways. Take your pick: This time *you* can choose the ending you like—and the one you think makes best astrological sense.

A. Aries gets in a fight with Leo and has to go to the emergency room.
B. Taurus gets really tired and hungry and decides to go home, cook a hamburger, and go to bed early.
C. Gemini runs out of note paper and gets laryngitis at the same time.
D. Cancer gets a call from the babysitter and is so worried she goes home to take care of her children.
E. Leo gets so irritated that no one is paying attention to the bruises Aries gave him that he leaves in a huff.
F. Virgo gets a stomach ache and decides to leave. Besides, it's time for her mineral bath.
G. Libra isn't able to make up his mind and gets a headache in the process.
H. Scorpio decides it's definitely a plot to humiliate her, and bows out less than graciously.
I. Sagittarius gets a little drunk and leaves early to get the plane.
J. Capricorn leaves as soon as she gets her petition filled up because there isn't anyone there *really* worth knowing.
K. Aquarius decides to go teach people at the shelter to use his stamp-sorting machine so they can get jobs.
L. Pisces remembers she has a date with her spiritual advisor and that she forgot to feed the animals.

5

Moods of the Moon

How to Successfully Navigate Its Day-by-Day Changes

Never underestimate the power of the moon. It is the closest planet to earth, and the only one whose effect on human life can actually be measured. Even the most skeptical antiastrology person has to admit that the moon rules the tides. If you stand on the beach for even a half hour or so, you can literally *see* how the moon works its magic as the water flows higher or lower, according to the time of day. There are places in the world where the tide rises as much as forty feet from its lowest to its highest point—that's *power*. If you think about the fact that humans are about 98 percent water in our chemical makeup, it's much easier to accept the fact that the moon has the same powerful effect on us as it does on the tides.

Like the "female" she symbolically is, the moon also changes her mind—or her sign—more quickly than any other planet. If you look at the day-by-day predictions in this book, which gives the position of the moon for every day, you will see that this changeable planet moves into a different sign about every two days.

As it moves from sign to sign, the moon brings a different kind of energy to the earth's atmosphere. Those who are particularly sensitive—like Cancers—feel it most strongly. But even the most stolid types are often moved by the effect of the particular sign the moon occupies on any given day, though they may not want to admit it.

Are we then slaves to the moods of the moon? Not if we understand its energies and cooperate with them. If you work *with* the moon and not against her, you can actually make life a lot easier for yourself. For instance, there are certain activities that go more smoothly when the moon is in a particular sign, just as other activities are more difficult to accomplish. Scheduling things accordingly could prevent a lot of frustration. You don't have to become a complete "lunatic" (ancient meaning, "one ruled by the moon") to benefit from its positive vibes, but simply go with the flow. Keep in mind, however, that the moon's effect will be *modified* by your sun sign, so be sure to check out your individual daily prediction. For instance, for *any* sun sign, the days when the moon is in that sign should bring a surge of energy. Whether you handle that energy positively or negatively is up to you.

Here's a rundown of the moods of the moon and the human activities that go with them.

When the Moon Is in Aries   There is a very *physical* tone to this day. People may be throwing their weight around in more ways than one. Impatience, independent action, and quick tempers can sprout up all over the place. The good news is that most people will be feeling rather decisive, so some things can be completed. The bad news is that decisions may be totally unilateral; what *you* want may be exactly what someone else *doesn't* want. Similarly, people may be invading each other's territories; "keep off the grass" signs won't mean much today. Rule-breaking is the order of the day, and so are the consequences that go along with it. However, if there's a big mountain to scale, today's the day to begin the climb. If there's a formidable task that requires a lot of get-up-and-go to accomplish, today's the day to plunge in with both feet. If there's something you've been hesitating to tell someone, today you'll get the nerve to say it, but it may be difficult to be tactful. Try, anyway. On the up side, people will be feeling in the mood for some fun and frolic—practical jokes are very "moon in Aries." Even the boss may get in the spirit of things. It's a good day to:

Make a sale	Sharpen knives
Do heavy housework	Stop worrying
Do some baking	Make a clean break
Start a diet	Start an exercise class
Buy a lottery ticket	Do something on your own
Get a haircut	Try a new recipe
Have your eyes checked	Throw a last-minute party

When the Moon Is in Taurus Today, the amber light goes on, and people start to proceed with more caution. Rather than being adventurous, most people will feel like sticking with routine tasks. It is not a good day to try something new. In this more conservative mood, people will tend to hold on to what they have; don't try to borrow money from a friend today. Concentrate on making your own money grow, instead. Speaking of increase, this is an excellent day to "make your garden grow" in every sense of the phrase. Along with a quieter mood of the day, you may feel like pampering yourself a bit; allow yourself at least one luxury. Chocoholics, beware, however; this is a day for food binges and all forms of dietary excess. Creature comforts are a lot on everyone's mind; in fact, it may be difficult to crawl out of that comfortable bed in the morning. And more than a few people will be crawling back into it fairly early—with their favorite person. Sexual cravings are high on the list of "moon moods" today. Enjoy!

It's a good day to:

Put something off until tomorrow	Put up preserves
Buy clothes or jewelry	Have a massage
Get your teeth filled	Start singing lessons
Start a savings account	Sell high on the market
Stick to your guns	Buy a plant
Buy candy	Buy real estate
Stay home and watch television	Hug somebody

When the Moon Is in Gemini There's a touch more energy in the air today, and people will begin moving around a lot more. For some, there will be a lot of nervous energy and the scattery feeling that goes along with it; don't force yourself to concentrate if you can avoid it. It's a day to make connections—call, write, or bump into both new and old friends. Wits are generally sharp today, and people could be cracking jokes all around you. On the other hand, they may also be spilling some secrets. Gossip is easy to start today, and it could spread like wildfire. Mind your mouth! Anything requiring manual dexterity can easily get done today; even those who are usually clumsy may find they have nimble fingers. The tendency today is to do things quickly, if a bit superficially. If there are a couple of things that require a once-over-lightly treatment, get them out of the way now. If you haven't been invited to a party, give your own—or at least plan to get together with some buddies for a little socializing; the time is definitely right.

It's a good day to:

Get your hair cut	Use your hands
Join a club	Pay bills
Have a tooth pulled	Eat out
Sign up for a new course	Take a walk/drive
Send a letter	Call your brother/sister
Try something new	Tell a fib
Learn a language	Do two things at once

When the Moon Is in Cancer In Cancer, the moon is in her very own sign—and you'll know it. All those "moon" characteristics—like changeableness, sensitivity, and the desire for security—will be heightened. Cancers, of course, will feel it most strongly; and the other water signs, Scorpio and Pisces, may be even moodier than usual. The general tendency today is to do things that make you feel comfortable and feel good. For some, that means eating a lot of food; for others, it could be hitting the bottle a bit. People tend to feel a bit sorry for themselves during the transit of the moon through Cancer. When two people who live together are both feeling that way, the result can be a rather touchy day—and evening. As much as you want the comfort of others, you are better off on your own and working off those anxious feelings by yourself. Not for safety, but for comfort's sake, the best place to go today is no farther than your own backyard. You'll probably be feeling very stay-at-home anyway. However, it's an excellent day for memories. Reminisce with somebody you love, or get out that old photo album by yourself. You might find yourself shedding a tear or two, but it's all in a good cause.

It's a good day to:

Bake something delicious	Hug your children
Buy something old	Take care of somebody
Put up preserves	Go without makeup
Buy property	Call your mother
Start a habit	Buy something for the house
Plant something	Entertain at home
Pamper yourself	Give your hair a treatment

When the Moon Is in Leo Today, everyone feels like "coming out of the woodwork." Just as Cancer moon makes you want to hide, Leo moon makes you want to get out there and be seen. Nothing but the best will do on this day, so it could be a rather expensive one. Most people will be more generous than usual—both with their money and their affections; many a new romance has started under a Leo moon. Leo is also one of the more playful signs, so a lot of you will be in the mood for fun and games. Eating out is very Leo moon—and so is picking up the check. Today, you may have to fight for it. However, the boss may be a lot stricter than usual, and even those with nobody to "boss" will try to push somebody around. If you've got children, today you will appreciate them very much—no matter what they do. Most people find themselves reaching for the newest thing in the closet under this transit of the moon. If they don't have anything new to wear, they'll probably go out and buy it—on credit. No matter what time of the year it is, you'll be looking for a little sunshine or at least a warm place. On the beaches or by the fireplaces are where most people would like to be today—wishing life were one long vacation.

It's a good day to:

Borrow money	Buy jewelry
Get a new hairstyle	Invest in the market
Start building something	Do something creative

Follow a hunch Prepare a gourmet meal
Steal the spotlight Dress up
Be brave Kiss somebody new
Be waited on

When the Moon Is in Virgo   Now it's back to work, and back to reality. There's a sharp distinction between the Virgo moon mood and what precedes it, so you may shock yourself. Perhaps by deciding it's really time to get organized and then actually *doing* it. On the home front it's a great day to rearrange all those sloppy closets and cupboards. On the job, you couldn't pick a better time to wrestle with that nasty detail work you've been avoiding. However, all is not good news under Virgo moon. For one thing, by contrast to Leo moon's generosity, people will be positively stingy today—both with their money and their love. Even the best of situations could deteriorate today when one or the other of the involved parties decides to point out the other's flaws. Your best course under the Virgo moon is to check that impulse to criticize. People can become highly self-critical during this transit, too. One extreme example of the going-over some people can give themselves during a Virgo moon is to develop mysterious maladies or to discover aches and pains they never felt before. Not to worry; they'll be all better by the time the moon moves into the next sign. Virgo moon is also inspection time, so the boss may be particularly sensitive to messy desks today and sloppiness in general. Keep things buttoned up and tidy for best results.

It's a good time to:

Start a diet Start a new job
Get a physical Sew or mend something
Bake bread Read a good book
Quit smoking Get a complete makeover
Buy a pet Call your maiden aunt
Try to do without something Feel like a martyr
Buy health food Do a puzzle

When the Moon Is in Libra   Now it's time to kiss and make up. Any relationships that suffered from the ragged nerves of Virgo moon time can be nicely patched up today. Pleasantries should be easy for one and all. In fact, even people who are normally rather gruff should smile a bit more today. Libra moon is one of the most social of moon periods; meeting and greeting should be prevalent activities. Most people will want to put their best foot forward, too, so the impulse to dress up and look your best may come upon you. You may feel rather self-indulgent as well; hard work is not as compatible with the Libra moon period as rest and relaxation are. It's definitely a time of togetherness, so even habitual loners may be looking for company. Most people will feel they need people—possibly one special person. Romance blossoms under the Libra moon in its purest form. It's not so much sex people want now as romantic love and companionship. No one's actually made a count, but it's a fair bet that more flowers get sent under the Libra moon than at any other time. Physical beauty is also highly important, so Libra moon is a great one under which to get yourself a whole new look or to redo anything that needs it. Something that's off-balance will bother you more at this time.

It's a good day to:

Be tactful	Forgive and forget
Redecorate	Add color to your life
Give a party	Luxuriate
Fall in love	Sign up for a dance class
Join a singing group	Buy a stereo
Buy something beautiful	Buy a down comforter
Try a new makeup	Learn about wine

When the Moon Is in Scorpio Things could easily get heavy today, and the tendency will be to go to extremes. Haters will hate more; lovers will love more passionately and physically. The sex drive is stimulated in many people during this transit of the moon. With all those intense emotions flying around, it's not surprising that people easily get hot under the collar—and/or imagine that somebody is out to get them. However, there is an up side to the Scorpio moon, and that is the extra jot of will power it gives the most weak-willed people. If you've got to dig in your heels and clench your teeth to get something done, today's the day you will be able to do it. People *endure* a lot under the Scorpio moon. The only problem is that they may develop some resentment toward those they believe should be enduring with them. However, the tendency is to keep silent. In spite of the intense emotionalism of the Scorpio moon, there isn't a lot of outright complaining. People will let the pressure build up inside of them and then burst out into violent rages. If your temper isn't good under the best of circumstances, control it during the Scorpio moon, by all means. It's also a time when people tend to feel a bit claustrophobic; a good walk in the fresh air can work wonders at this time.

It's a good day to:

See a psychiatrist	Have good sex
Buy a house	Face up to a crisis
Open a secret bank account	Read a good mystery
Make a firm decision	Take body-building
Do your taxes	Get a prescription filled
Throw away what you don't need	Buy life insurance
Do some strenuous exercise	Change your life

When the Moon Is in Sagittarius Things definitely lighten up when the moon moves into Sagittarius—and people loosen up, too. In fact, one danger under this moon is getting too relaxed—with your diet, your money, or your generous spirits. Moderation is not the mood of the day, so you may have to force it on yourself. It is not a good time to try to stop smoking—or to stop doing anything self-indulgent. There's definitely a "live and let live" attitude in the air when the moon is in Sagittarius, so bad relations should be easily improved. A spirit of good will is pervasive, as well as a lighthearted attitude. One thing that means is that even normally conservative people will be willing to take chances; those for whom a more liberal outlook is a natural state of affairs could really go too far out on a limb. If you gamble, bet *only* what you can afford to lose today. The place everyone will want to be today is outdoors. In fact, more than one person will simply disappear from the scene to do something either adventurous or relaxing. It's an excellent day to think big, but you may find the follow-through a bit difficult. The big picture is what's easiest to see right now; leave the fine brush strokes for another time. Enjoy the spirit of fun and generosity that should be in the air.

It's a good day to:

- Make a long-distance call
- Plan a trip
- Buy a dog (or a horse)
- Contribute to a wildlife-foundation
- Try a new approach
- Sell anything to anybody
- Try your luck/feel lucky
- Go to church
- Enjoy a hobby
- Learn a new language
- Do something charitable
- Borrow money
- Run away from it all
- Get a bigger place

When the Moon Is in Capricorn In sharp contrast to the "easy come, easy go" feeling of the Sagittarius moon, the moon in Capricorn brings on a much more serious mood. You could call it the "workaholic's moon," and even those whose work style is less intense will find themselves wanting to get a lot done. It's important to *accomplish something* when the moon is in Capricorn, if you are to feel comfortable. Most people want to tread only on solid ground at this time, so there could be a bit of distrust in the air. No one wants to waste time—and least of all on things or people from whom they are not likely to derive some kind of benefit. Another curious facet of the Capricorn moon mood is a tendency to feel older and more serious; some lighter types dislike the feeling so much they will go out of their way to look young. It's the kind of day that matronly secretary in the office is likely to appear in something rather frilly. People can really handle things under the Capricorn moon too; endurance is *very* Capricorn. That means those who exercise will work out harder and longer; those who normally do not push themselves will do at least a little self-prodding. A good image is paramount to many people when the moon is in this sign, and the tendency is for people to be quite status conscious. Self-control is the order of the day, in every respect.

It's a good day to:

- Start a new job
- Buy antiques
- Make a list
- Keep your money

Buy anything for investment	Go to the dentist
Wear anything with a good label on it	Start a diet
	Work late
Bet on a favorite	Ask for repayment of a debt
Go to the chiropractor	
Buy insurance	Clean house

When the Moon Is in Aquarius When the moon moves into the sign of Aquarius from the sign of Capricorn, it's as if somebody took the cork out of the bottle. Suddenly, the rather repressed mood bursts into a desire for change—a *need* for change. This is one of those days when people tend to make rash moves like quit a dull job, call it quits with a clinging person, throw out everything in their closet and start all over again. Reaching this point is easy to do under the Aquarian moon. However, it's usually very positive. What's important at this time is to try something new, not just get rid of something old. Some people decide to experiment with a new recipe, a new lover, or a new hair style. It's the kind of day when a woman with long hair will decide to get a crew cut. On the relationship side, the mood now is one of brotherly love and friendship rather than highly charged sexual encounters. Wanting to be with friends and feeling like part of a group is what's important now. No one is a stranger under the Aquarian moon, and talking to people on the street is very common. The thing to be careful of under this moon is doing something irreparable—like finally telling the boss what you really think of him. He/she could easily decide that it's time for a change of personnel.

It's a good day to:

Do something kinky	Buy/wear something crazy
Try a new food	Color your hair
Do something friendly	Contribute to a charity
Start flying lessons	Move to a new place
Do something impulsive	Buy a television/stereo
Join a club	Make a new friend
Make a speculative investment	Be fair

When the Moon Is in Pisces This is a time when people wear their hearts on their sleeves and feel *very* vulnerable. There's a lot of ultrasensitivity under the Pisces moon, and a lot of crying on shoulders—if you can find one that isn't already occupied. Mixed in with the emotionalism is a real feeling of empathy with others; now's the time people feel that everyone is in the same boat. However, it may be a bit difficult to keep things afloat today, because there isn't a lot of firm direction from anyone or anything. It's confusion time, and even the clearest of messages can get a little garbled. Indecisiveness will spread like the plague, so don't expect to get any clear-cut answers today. Creative people get more creative under the Pisces moon, and anyone could feel just a bit poetic. Romantic relationships are heavenly under the Pisces moon as long as they don't get out of control. Keeping certain other things under control—like drinking and other forms of escapism—is a wise precaution, too. The most satisfying and least dangerous escape is to hold hands with someone you love while you watch a real tearjerker movie. Lots of people call in sick under the Pisces moon, and there's a good reason: Most people don't like to cry in public.

It's a good day to:

Put on weight
Fall in love
Develop ESP
Find God
Buy flowers or perfume
Swear off something
Get hooked on something

Write a poem
Take in a stray dog or cat
Visit the sick
See a therapist
Stay home and read
Pamper yourself
Buy a camera

6

Venus and Mars

Love and Sex
Peace and War
Cooperating and Competing

Next to your sun sign, your moon sign, and your rising sign, the positions of Venus and Mars in your horoscope are probably the most important indicators of your personal psychology. This is because Venus shows your affectional nature and Mars shows your sexual nature. To put it another way, *Venus shows your wants and needs in romantic love while Mars shows your sexual style and your manner of expressing it.*

In a broader sense, Venus and Mars are the principles of peace and war. Venus wants to cooperate and relate to others, to share life experiences. Mars is totally concerned with self and getting what you want. Everybody's got a Venus and Mars in their horoscope because every human being has to both live with others and assert him-/herself. It's all a matter of degree. If you want to, you can think of Venus as the "higher" side of human relationships; Mars the "lower." However, you've got to keep in mind that—like all other opposites in the universe—both *cooperating* and *competing* are necessary if the world is to continue going round.

Because Venus has to do with the need to share, the sign in which it is placed will tell a lot about how you attract people you want to share with. It will also show what attracts you to others. Beyond the love arena, the position of Venus in your horoscope shows your attitudes toward money and personal possessions, creature comforts, and things of beauty. Venus is "feminine" in nature, and women tend to relate to their Venus sign more than men. But for *both* sexes, it is an available energy.

The good side of Venus is:
Sharing, beautifying, peacemaking
The bad side is:
acquisitiveness, self-indulgence, laziness

Because the position of Mars shows how you go about getting what you want, it will tell a lot about your personal drive—how *much* you want what you want. It is the desire principle, and will indicate just how passionate your passions are. Ambition, assertiveness, and anger are just a few steps away from each other, so Mars will also reveal what makes you angry or what gets you going. The planet Mars is "masculine" in nature—highly so—and men will find it easier to get in touch with their Mars energy. However, every woman's got a Mars too, and sooner or later a woman's Mars energy will present itself.

The "good" side of Mars is:
Dynamic energy, courage, sexual drive
The "bad" side is:
manipulation, cowardice, sexual abuse

No matter what area of life you are relating these planets to, it is useful to think of them in sexual terms, and of our human sexual organs. Venus is open and receptive; Mars thrusts forward and penetrates. Because we normally attract someone or are attracted to someone before we get sexually involved, Venus energy precedes Mars energy. In other words, Venus shows how *receptive* you are; Mars shows how *active* you are. Venus also has a lot to do with our ideas and images of romance, our romantic fantasies, while Mars is an indicator of sexual fantasies—which may or may not be acted out, depending on the individual's degree of inhibition.

Just as some combinations of people can coexist in constant harmony while others are in constant conflict,

Venus and Mars in an individual person can work well together, or at cross-purposes. When your Venus doesn't get along well with your Mars, you've got a problem. Sometimes a sexual problem, but always an inner conflict. How can you tell if your Venus and Mars are "friends" or "foes"? First, by looking up the positions of your personal Mars and Venus in the charts provided at the end of this chapter, reading the descriptions of those planets in the signs they fall in for you. But, just to make things a bit clearer, here's a rundown of easy Mars/Venus relationships and difficult ones. (By the way, you can also apply this principle in comparing your Venus/Mars positions to those of someone else, as well.)

Venus and Mars are "at war" when:

- One is in a fire sign, and one is in an earth sign. Here you've got a conflict between the practical and the experimental sides of yourself.
- One is in a fire sign and one is in a water sign. One part of you says "let's do it"; the other side says, "I might get hurt," so you might be stalled.
- One is in an earth sign and one is in an air sign. Air likes to think about things a little; earth needs to know it will work. Once again, it may hold you back.
- One is in an air sign and one is in a water sign. Yours is a conflict between the mental relationship and the emotional one; you may find it hard to decide what you want.

Venus and Mars are on good terms when:

- One is in a fire sign, one is in an air sign.
- One is in an earth sign and one is in a water sign.
- Both are in the same element.

Venus and Mars in The Signs

Venus in Aries (fire element)

While this position of Venus in a man or a woman indicates the kind of person who falls in love impulsively, both sexes want to be conquered, when they have Venus in Aries. They may be outrageously flirtatious, but can lead others on a merry chase before they give in. There is a tendency to look for trouble when Venus is in ths position; actually, it is excitement Venus in Aries people crave. Their personal likes and dislikes will be quite clearly defined, and they will be vocal about them. In matters of taste, there is less refinement than when Venus is in a softer sign. Both the males and the females may play up their sexuality in the way they dress; they like very loud things like rock music and bright colors. There is also an impish charm in these people and a tendency to play love games. The *real* goal is to be swept away by a romantic lover who lives up to a mediaeval code of chivalry and/or chastity.

Mars in Aries (fire element)

This is a highly competitive position for Mars; people with Mars in Aries leave no doubt about the fact that they want it, and they want it *now*—whatever "it" is. Mars in Aries can cut through a lot of life's red tape. When it comes to courtship, Mars in Aries people are equally able to disregard the small talk and get right down to business. However, this position of Mars often makes for a rather selfish lover—one who is so concerned with getting that he/she doesn't do an awful lot of giving. Mars in Aries people are likely to turn off as quickly as they turn on. Passion burns brightly, but is often short-lived. They are highly independent and likely to leave if a romantic partner gets too possessive or demanding. Mars in Aries is also always ready for a fight, so relationships are a bit stormy.

Venus in Taurus (earth element)

This is a highly sensual position for Venus to be in. People with Venus in Taurus are turned on by sweet words and soft music—and any form of touching. They like all kinds of nice and beautiful things, and will be attracted by someone who dresses well and has expensive taste. Venus in Taurus people can be a little self-indulgent, but in the main their desire is to make the object of their affection comfortable. And they will do it in very tangible ways; Venus in Taurus people of both sexes like to do things for others. When someone with Venus in Taurus is attracted, he/she is loyal. Love does not come in a flash, as it does with Venus in Aries people, but when it comes, it usually stays. At least as far as the person with Venus in Taurus is concerned. These people are generally so devoted that a breakup is extremely unsettling. You can always make a Venus in Taurus person happy with candy or flowers. The best kind of love feels good, tastes good, looks good, and smells good.

Mars in Taurus (earth element)

This Mars can express itself as ambition with a definite direction—or as controlled sexuality. Mars in Taurus people of both sexes can appear rather lazy, but actually their slow movements are usually on a deliberate course. Some people with Mars in Taurus are really looking for a safe position in a job or with a partner. Their manner of sexuality is highly sensual though they may be slow to get aroused. When a Mars in Taurus person enters into an affair, however, there is usually the intention to make it a long and serious one. These people are certainly capable of quick affairs, but they generally prefer a comfortable relationship where they do not constantly have to keep proving their love. There is a certain giving quality to Mars in Taurus, and the men are exceptionally considerate lovers. The women are fairly passive, but passionate and giving when they get going.

Venus in Gemini

Venus in Gemini people of both sexes tend to be turned on more by *talk* than by physical stimulation. Relationships have to have a mental dimension in order for them to get involved. In fact, Venus in Gemini people are likely to make better friends than lovers. When their affections *are* engaged, the connection is likely to be a little tenuous, and the Venus in Gemini's feelings may not run as deep as his/her partner's. Fickleness is a reality with these people— they like a lot of changes, and that goes for people as well as environments. Job-hopping is a trait of Venus in Gemini, and so is a constant changing of the guard in their romantic lives. However, Venus in Gemini people make wonderful romantic partners, because they are really *interested* in the people they get involved with. Never tell a Venus in Gemini person to "shut up and make love"; he/she will be very likely to shut the door on the relationship.

Mars in Gemini

Mars in Gemini people assert themselves rather erratically; there isn't a lot of staying power, in jobs or in relationships. The "alternating current" of Mars in Gemini energy makes for a rather on again, off again sexual life. People with Mars in this position are capable of having a number of purely mental relationships in between their sexual ones. These are the kind of people who talk their way into things, including a job and someone's bed. Their approach is a bit on the delicate side, and one may wonder when the Mars in Gemini person is really going to get started. However, once their passion is aroused, Mars in Gemini people like a lot of variety; sex can get quite original with these people. The tendency to bore easily goes both for their attitudes toward their sexual partners and the manner in which they have sex. Both sexes are real charmers, however, and sometimes get their way in a rather devious manner.

Venus in Cancer (water element)

The overriding thing that people with Venus in Cancer want is *security*, really the emotional kind, but since a secure home base goes along with their needs, the material kind is important too. Venus in Cancer people can be highly traditional in their romantic values— home, mother, and apple pie are symbols of the things that turn these people on. If you want to engage the emotions of a Venus in Cancer person, all you have to do is look as if you *need* somebody— preferably a mother. Venus in Cancer people need to be needed, but sometimes can go overboard by totally taking over the other person's life. With Venus in this sign, people respond strongly to all kinds of romantic things, from the card that says "I love you" to a little token of affection for no special occasion. However, Venus in Cancer people are highly self-protective, so you first have to break down their natural reserve and fear of getting hurt. Once you do, you won't find a more faithful lover. Except perhaps Taurus.

Mars in Cancer (water element)

Mars in Cancer people can sneak up on you when they've decided they want you; their approach is a bit sideways, like the locomotion of the crab that is the Cancer symbol. They are soft and subtle lovers and said by some to be among the best sexual partners in the zodiac. However, as sensitive and understanding as they tend to be in the sexual area, they can be overly possessive with people they love, and even turn rather cruel when they are rejected. Cancer is a water sign, and it is as if that water starts boiling—invisibly—then the lid totally pops off when the explosion comes. Mars in Cancer people tend to be a little blind to their sexual/ambition drive and can even pretend to themselves that it doesn't exist. For this reason, they make formidable enemies, because while they look as if they are asking for peace they are really preparing for battle.

Venus in Leo (fire element)

There's a pretty simple way to get a Venus in Leo person to like you. Give him/her a lot of attention—*positive* attention. Venus in Leo people do want love, but they want admiration and adulation to come along with it. A bit like Venus in Aries, Venus in Leo wants a *courtly* lover—someone who will swear absolute loyalty. When it's a Leo sun sign person who also has Venus in Leo, you've got the absolute monarch of them all. Venus in Leo also goes only for the best, and is attracted to what looks expensive or rewarding—in both jobs and people. Venus in Leo expects you to dress and look your best, no matter what the circumstances. It is not a "casual" Venus. Demonstrations of love are very important, too. Words are great, of course, and so is a lot of hugging and the rest of the physical love spectrum. However, candy—or some other tangible token of affection—is expected. Venus in Leo has fierce pride, so if you even slip once and appear not to *respect* this person, he/she is likely to brush you off—with a very grand gesture of course.

Mars in Leo (fire element)

Speaking of grand gestures, Mars in Leo wrote the book. This kind of person is the one who will lavish the object of his/her affection with all kinds of luxurious things. Mars in Leo is a real showy person and expects to be appreciated for it. Both the males and the females are aggressive about going after what they want, and once they are happily ensconced—with a lover or a job—they are loyal and steady. However, the down side of the Mars in Leo position is a violent temper: a *really* violent temper. Both sexes can get quite physical in expressing anger. This is the position of the female who throws plates and the man who slaps his faithless lover on the cheek. Mars in Leo is unrelentingly honest—and will expect you to be too. One devious move, and it's over

Venus in Virgo (earth element)

Venus in Virgo wants a love that *works*. Pure sex or romance may appeal to Virgo's desire for the unadulterated, but there's got to be an element of the practical in it too. People with Venus in Virgo often actually fall in love with their jobs faster than they do with people. When Venus is in the sign, you often find the dedicated, loyal, "number two" person who spends a lifetime catering to the needs of a powerful boss. He/she is likely to be just a little bit in love with that boss too. As for sex, the Venus in Virgo person has a very healthy attitude toward it—possibly too healthy in the sense that it is sometimes regarded as an excellent form of exercise. Venus in Virgo people are not really cold—in fact, when they love someone they can't do enough for them, particularly in attending to their physical comfort. The problem is that this position of Venus makes a person overly analytical in determining what he/she wants. If the Venus in Virgo person keeps his/her mouth shut, and doesn't openly criticize, there is a much better possibility that he/she will make good, solid relationships.

Mars in Virgo (earth element)

Virgo's inventive sexuality is one of the best-kept secrets in the zodiac; Mars in Virgo turns out some of the most experimental and skillful lovers of all. That is, if you can attract one of these people in the first place. Mars in Virgo people are far from promiscuous; in fact, their standards are likely to be a bit too high. They are constantly questioning their *own* desires and drives, picking them apart instead of acting upon them. Mars in Virgo is ideal for success in just about any job or profession. With any sun sign, it adds to the ability to cooly analyze problems and solve them with a reasonable amount of dispatch. When it comes to romantic involvement, this is not one of the more "romantic" Mars positions (unless the sun sign is Libra). You may feel as if your Mars in Virgo lover is checking you over first for anything that might turn him/her off. This is the sign that usually says "let's shower together" before he/she says "let's go to bed."

Venus in Libra (air element)

First off, remember that when the planet Venus is in Libra, it's in its "home sign." When it comes to beauty, harmony, and balance, Venus in Libra people want it all. When Venus is in Libra, the most attractive things in life are the *nicest*—people, places, jobs, clothes, you name it. Venus in Libra people want it nice, but they also want it *easy*. In fact, this sometimes "cold" position of Venus can make for a person who marries for status or money. If you look comfortable in every sense of the word, you've got a shot at attracting that Venus in Libra person who catches your eye. And he/she will, because this position of Venus usually confers a great-looking body. Even if the Venus in Libra person loves or marries for convenience, he/she gives an awful lot in return. Once you've engaged his/her love the Venus in Libra person considers you the best, the most beautiful/handsome, and the brightest person in the universe and will treat you accordingly.

Mars in Libra (air element)

This position of Mars often makes for a passive/aggressive type of individual—a specific psychological pattern. The Mars in Libra person rarely goes directly after what he/she wants, but more or less lingers in front of it, waiting for the other person to make the right move. Mars in Libra people don't get hired as quickly as other types because they don't seem to *care* enough about whether or not they get the job. When it comes to love, Mars in Libra can be quite frustrating. You really don't know what's going on here—does or doesn't he/she want to get involved? This is also a rather "refined" position for brash Mars. Mars in Libra people usually have excellent manners, and never appear to get ruffled. They will just sit and smile while you rant and rave. Suddenly, however, they can turn on their heel and walk out the door. The technique Mars in Libra people use to go about making their subtle conquests is *talk*—but it can easily fool you because it seems so casual.

Venus in Scorpio (water element)

A lot of people with sun sign Scorpio have Venus in Scorpio too; (one's Venus sign is often one's sun sign because Venus is so close to the sun in the solar system). These double-whammy Scorpios are extraordinarily intense in all their emotional needs, but anyone with Venus in Scorpio is going to be touched by the madness of this intense sign. The curious paradox is that Venus in Scorpio people are either totally *turned on* by someone or something—or totally *turned off*. There are very few halfway deals in their lives. Venus in Scorpio can also be highly manipulative, adjusting his/her emotions to suit other needs—like money. When Venus is in Scorpio, people are attracted to what seems mysterious, dangerous, or hard-to-get. They love puzzles, and can be a bit of a puzzle themselves to prospective romantic partners. When they do get involved, however, they have a great deal of staying power—emotionally at least. They can fairly easily separate their physical *actions* from their mental states, however.

Mars in Scorpio (water element)

People with Mars in Scorpio have a very strong "energy field" surrounding them; you can almost see it and feel it. What they want, they want passionately—and will seek in no uncertain terms. They are equally positive about what they *don't* want—so you will know whether you've got a shot with them right away. No waiting with *this* aggressive sign. The legendary supersexuality of Scorpio is real with Mars in Scorpio people. However, they may use their sexual power to control other people and situations. And, if they are rejected against their will (which doesn't happen too often) they are capable of the worst kind of venomous reactions, Jealous lovers who are violent to their former partners are a parody of the Mars in Scorpio type of intensity. One way Mars in Scorpio people can hurt or simply tease others is by withholding their love—and their physical passion. They have great powers of self-control.

Venus in Sagittarius (fire element)

People with Venus in the restless, mobile sign of the Centaur often get the reputation for being fickle, and there is more than a grain of truth in that label. But the reason a Venus in Sagittarius person may move around or not become committed is that he/she is so vulnerable to deceit and dishonesty. As the saying goes, "once burned, twice shy," and openhearted, friendly Sagittarius is likely to get burned very early in life. When Venus in Sagittarius people do get involved, they are absolutely delightful to love. Broadminded, unpossessive, full of fun, they really want to enjoy romance. Sagittarius is also a very intellectual sign, so in order to get Venus in Sagittarius people to stick with you for a while, you've got to keep them interested. Sex is great, but sex with talk is even greater for these people. Venus in Sagittarius is also highly idealistic, so you've got to be a higher type to appeal to someone with Venus in this sign. Love is gallantry and honor and all those things that are so hard to find in life.

Mars in Sagittarius (fire element)

Sagittarius is a sign that thinks in global terms, so when Mars is in the sign of Sagittarius, you find a person who wants it all—and often has to be satisfied with nothing. People with Mars in Sagittarius assert themselves bluntly and get right to the point. However, they tend to be so optimistic in their expectations that they may just as quickly decide they have made a mistake. Better luck next love. Mars in Sagittarius doesn't deliberately hurt people; this sign is kind to all—both animals and humans. Their sexual nature can also be rather "animalistic" because this is a lusty sign, and so fond of all outdoor sports that they often want to do it anywhere, anytime. One way Mars in Sagittarius people get to your heart is through your sense of humor; they really know how to make people laugh. It is a powerful weapon in their professional lives too; it's hard to fire someone who is such a delight to have around—even if he/she isn't around that much. The big problem with Mars in Sagittarius people is that they sometimes don't want to take responsibility for their own actions, and lay things on other people. Even if Mars in Sagittarius is the one to break things up, he/she will somehow or other get you to believe that it's *your* fault.

Venus in Capricorn (earth element)

Appearances count a lot to Venus in Capricorn people—in every sense of the word. In order to appeal to them, you've got to look solid and substantial—and fairly rich as well. Because there is a natural reserve to Capricorn, people with Venus in this sign will dislike public displays of affection; the cooler you are in your approach, the better. Their public image and their private one are not too far apart, either. Not that Venus in Capricorn isn't normal; he/she can be quite passionate in bed. But very, very *serious*, too. If you mistake this sign's sober approach to life for coldness, you will not be the first person who has. Once again, like those with Venus in Virgo, Venus in Capricorn is attracted to *practical* people—people who can really work for them in one way or another. While some do actually consciously go after a financially comfortable marital situation, what the vast majority will settle for is someone who is willing to help handle a lot of the more serious aspects of life. Male or female, Venus in Capricorn people want you to be *useful*. Unfortunately, some people with Venus in this sign have such a low sense of self-worth, that they will try to buy love—or sell it—because they don't feel anyone will accept them for what they are.

Mars in Capricorn (earth element)

Mars in Capricorn people always want to know the rules before they enter the game; they assert themselves with extreme caution. However, when they *know* what they want, they have incredible powers to help them get it. One is patience; Mars in Capricorn can wait very well. Another thing they have going for them is self-control; their timing is excellent because they can hold themselves back when they want to. All this makes for a rather sexually confusing type, and sometimes one who is sexually confused. Mars in Capricorn people can go without sex for amazing lengths of time if nothing seems worth the effort. When they do go for it, their approach can be extremely lusty and earthy, as befits the earth element of Capricorn. Even more than someone with Mars in Scorpio, the person with Mars in Capricorn can be a user. In love or business, he/she can easily fake it to get the carrot on the end of the stick. Then, before you know it, the person who seemed so hot for you has now turned stone cold. Sad, but true.

Venus in Aquarius (air element)

The best way to attract someone with Venus in Aquarius is to be a bit unconventional; these people love anyone or anything that is off-beat. However, you may find that you are considered a specimen rather than a romantic partner—or at least that's how it's likely to feel. People with Venus in Aquarius seem to have a real problem with deep involvement; often they really *want* it, but somehow or other their deepest wells of emotion are very difficult to tap.

Their habitual reaction to love is often "easy come, easy go." Are they cruel people? Generally not, and often Venus in Aquarius people suffer a lot from their difficulty with feeling. They will rarely tell you, however, because there is a real need for distance there. And distance is what they seek in one-on-one relationships. If you become possessive with, or jealous of a person with Venus in Aquarius, you will lose him/her very quickly. As with some of the other mental signs like Gemini and Libra, you have got to keep the affair or the marriage *interesting* in one way or another. This is a Venus position that often likes kinky sex, porno movies, and other forms of artificial stimulation. However, they usually don't care enough about sex-for-the-sake-of-sex to be unfaithful.

Mars in Aquarius (air element)

When Mars is in this erratic sign, people tend to go through periods of feast and famine, largely because they can fluctuate between being extremely assertive and sure about what they want or totally inactive. During the latter periods you could actually call the Mars in Aquarius person lazy. In love, the Mars in Aquarius person tends to go after the unusual or difficult; involvements with people who are already attached are quite common. In many cases it is because the Mars in Aquarius person really is terribly afraid of deep involvement. There is a detachment about Mars in Aquarius people that sometimes works against permanent attachment to people or professional situations. Mars in Aquarius really prefers to go it alone. Perhaps the reason is that they always want to be free to experiment with the new. In sex, the Mars in Aquarius person is hung up on technique; he/she likes intelligent sex, and sometimes wants to prove how clever he/she is via this rather bizarre route.

Venus in Pisces (water element)

For people with Venus in Pisces, what's attractive is often bound up with some kind of sacrifice. This is the position of Venus that leads to martyrdom of all kinds. Some Venus in Pisces people find it impossible to get involved with anything or anyone normal and healthy; their instinctive need is to care for the lame and needy. Therefore, many Venus in Pisces people are rather easily taken advantage of by unscrupulous types who use them or take them for all they're worth. By the same token, Venus in Pisces people can put a real *drain* on the object of their affections—demanding more and more proofs of undying love, soulful demonstrations, sometimes even more tangible support. However, in the broadest, most universal sense of the word, Pisces is the "best" position for Venus as it represents the principle of *true love*. True love is totally unselfish, totally self-sacrificing. Though few normal mortals are capable of such "divine" love, Venus in Pisces people come closest to being able to make it. On the more mundane side, people wth Venus in Pisces are attracted by all kinds of sentimental and often impractical things. They will love you most if you spend your last penny on a bouquet of violets rather than bread for the table. So what? You'll just live on love.

Mars in Pisces (water element)

Mars in Pisces people can easily lose their way; the sign of Pisces is not stable enough for the aggressive energy of Mars, so Mars in Pisces people tend to scatter their energies in too many places. On the other hand, they are the most subtle and devious people in the zodiac when it comes to going after what they really *do* want. Their come-on is usually to be rather weak and helpless. Both the males and the females snare you by making you think they really *need* you. There's a lot of poetry to Mars in Pisces people, so the start of an affair is likely to be all moonlight and roses. However, you may find that once you are entangled, you can't get yourself out when you want out. Mars in Pisces people have a way of snarling you up in their webs of erratic energy. Just when they've agreed that you should go, they'll become helpless again and make you feel you have to stay. However, Mars in Pisces people do offer a very wonderful kind of love—soft, sensitive, and caring. The object of their desires is often someone similar or someone involved with art or music in some way. However, Pisces types are best off hooking up with a strong partner—someone who can keep their Mars energy on a straight and even course. The best part of Mars in Pisces people is that they are rarely, if ever, cold.

VENUS SIGN 1910–1975

	Aries	Taurus	Gemini	Cancer	Leo	Virgo
1910	5/7-6/3	6/4-6/29	6/30-7/24	7/25-8/18	8/19-9/12	9/13-10/6
1911	2/28-3/23	3/24-4/17	4/18-5/12	5/13-6/8	6/9-7/7	7/8-11/8
1912	4/13-5/6	5/7-5/31	6/1-6/24	6/24-7/18	7/19-8/12	8/13-9/5
1913	2/3-3/6	3/7-5/1	7/8-8/5	8/6-8/31	9/1-9/26	9/27-10/20
	5/2-5/30	5/31-7/7				
1914	3/14-4/6	4/7-5/1	5/2-5/25	5/26-6/19	6/20-7/15	7/16-8/10
1915	4/27-5/21	5/22-6/15	6/16-7/10	7/11-8/3	8/4-8/28	8/29-9/21
1916	2/14-3/9	3/10-4/5	4/6-5/5	5/6-9/8	9/9-10/7	10/8-11/2
1917	3/29-4/21	4/22-5/15	5/16-6/9	6/10-7/3	7/4-7/28	7/29-8/21
1918	5/7-6/2	6/3-6/28	6/29-7/24	7/25-8/18	8/19-9/11	9/12-10/5
1919	2/27-3/22	3/23-4/16	4/17-5/12	5/13-6/7	6/8-7/7	7/8-11/8
1920	4/12-5/6	5/7-5/30	5/31-6/23	6/24-7/18	7/19-8/11	8/12-9/4
1921	2/3-3/6	3/7-4/25	7/8-8/5	8/6-8/31	9/1-9/25	9/26-10/20
	4/26-6/1	6/2-7/7				
1922	3/13-4/6	4/7-4/30	5/1-5/25	5/26-6/19	6/20-7/14	7/15-8/9
1923	4/27-5/21	5/22-6/14	6/15-7/9	7/10-8/3	8/4-8/27	8/28-9/20
1924	2/13-3/8	3/9-4/4	4/5-5/5	5/6-9/8	9/9-10/7	10/8-11/12
1925	3/28-4/20	4/21-5/15	5/16-6/8	6/9-7/3	7/4-7/27	7/28-8/21
1926	5/7-6/2	6/3-6/28	6/29-7/23	7/24-8/17	8/18-9/11	9/12-10/5
1927	2/27-3/22	3/23-4/16	4/17-5/11	5/12-6/7	6/8-7/7	7/8-11/9
1928	4/12-5/5	5/6-5/29	5/30-6/23	6/24-7/17	7/18-8/11	8/12-9/4
1929	2/3-3/7	3/8-4/19	7/8-8/4	8/5-8/30	8/31-9/25	9/26-10/19
	4/20-6/2	6/3-7/7				
1930	3/13-4/5	4/6-4/30	5/1-5/24	5/25-6/18	6/19-7/14	7/15-8/9
1931	4/26-5/20	5/21-6/13	6/14-7/8	7/9-8/2	8/3-8/26	8/27-9/19

VENUS SIGN 1910–1975

Libra	Scorpio	Sagittarius	Capricorn	Aquarius	Pisces
10/7-10/30	10/31-11/23	11/24-12/17	12/18-12/31	1/1-1/15	1/16-1/28
				1/29-4/4	4/5-5/6
11/19-12/8	12/9-12/31		1/1-1/10	1/11-2/2	2/3-2/27
9/6-9/30	1/1-1/4	1/5-1/29	1/30-2/23	2/24-3/18	3/19-4/12
	10/1-10/24	10/25-11/17	11/18-12/12	12/13-12/31	
10/21-11/13	11/14-12/7	12/8-12/31		1/1-1/6	1/7-2/2
8/11-9/6	9/7-10/9	10/10-12/5	1/1-1/24	1/25-2/17	2/18-3/13
	12/6-12/30	12/31			
9/22-10/15	10/16-11/8	1/1-2/6	2/7-3/6	3/7-4/1	4/2-4/26
		11/9-12/2	12/3-12/26	12/27-12/31	
11/3-11/27	11/28-12/21	12/22-12/31		1/1-1/19	1/20-2/13
8/22-9/16	9/17-10/11	1/1-1/14	1/15-2/7	2/8-3/4	3/5-3/28
		10/12-11/6	11/7-12/5	12/6-12/31	
10/6-10/29	10/30-11/22	11/23-12/16	12/17-12/31	1/1-4/5	4/6-5/6
11/9-12/8	12/9-12/31		1/1-1/9	1/10-2/2	2/3-2/26
9/5-9/30	1/1-1/3	1/4-1/28	1/29-2/22	2/23-3/18	3/19-4/11
	9/31-10/23	10/24-11/17	11/18-12/11	12/12-12/31	
10/21-11/13	11/14-12/7	12/8-12/31		1/1-1/6	1/7-2/2
8/10-9/6	9/7-10/10	10/11-11/28	1/1-1/24	1/25-2/16	2/17-3/12
	11/29-12/31				
9/21-10/14	1/1	1/2-2/6	2/7-3/5	3/6-3/31	4/1-4/26
	10/15-11/7	11/8-12/1	12/2-12/25	12/26-12/31	
11/3-11/26	11/27-12/21	12/22-12/31		1/1-1/19	1/20-2/12
8/22-9/15	9/16-10/11	1/1-1/14	1/15-2/7	2/8-3/3	3/4-3/27
		10-12/11-6	11/7-12/5	12/6-12/31	
10/6-10/29	10/30-11/22	11/23-12/16	12/17-12/31	1/1-4/5	4/6-5/6
11/10-12/8	12/9-12/31	1/1-1/7	1/8	1/9-2/1	2/2-2/26
9/5-9/28	1/1-1/3	1/4-1/28	1/29-2/22	2/23-3/17	3/18-4/11
	9/29-10/23	10/24-11/16	11/17-12/11	12/12-12/31	
10/20-11/12	11/13-12/6	12/7-12/30	12/31	1/1-1/5	1/6-2/2
8/10-9/6	9/7-10/11	10/12-11/21	1/1-1/23	1/24-2/16	2/17-3/12
	11/22-12/31				
9/20-10/13	1/1-1/3	1/4-2/6	2/7-3/4	3/5-3/31	4/1-4/25
	10/14-11/6	11/7-11/30	12/1-12/24	12/25-12/31	

VENUS SIGN 1910–1975

	Aries	Taurus	Gemini	Cancer	Leo	Virgo
1932	2/12-3/8	3/9-4/3	4/4-5/5 7/13-7/27	5/6-7/12 7/28-9/8	9/9-10/6	10/7-11/1
1933	3/27-4/19	4/20-5/28	5/29-6/8	6/9-7/2	7/3-7/26	7/27-8/20
1934	5/6-6/1	6/2-6/27	6/28-7/22	7/23-8/16	8/17-9/10	9/11-10/4
1935	2/26-3/21	3/22-4/15	4/16-5/10	5/11-6/6	6/7-7/6	7/7-11/8
1936	4/11-5/4	5/5-5/28	5/29-6/22	6/23-7/16	7/17-8/10	8/11-9/4
1937	2/2-3/8 4/14-6/3	3/9-4/17 6/4-7/6	7/7-8/3	8/4-8/29	8/30-9/24	9/25-10/18
1938	3/12-4/4	4/5-4/28	4/29-5/23	5/24-6/18	6/19-7/13	7/14-8/8
1939	4-25/5/19	5/20-6/13	6/14-7/8	7/9-8/1	8/2-8/25	8/26-9/19
1940	2/12-3/7	3/8-4/3	4/4-5/5 7/5-7/31	5/6-7/4 8/1-9/8	9/9-10/5	10/6-10/31
1941	3/27-4/19	4/20-5/13	5/14-6/6	6/7-6/1	7/2-7/26	7/27-8/20
1942	5/6-6/1	6/2-6/26	6/27-7/22	7/23-8/16	8/17-9/9	9/10-10/3
1943	2/25-3/20	3/21-4/14	4/15-5/10	5/11-6/6	6/7-7/6	7/7-11/8
1944	4-10/5-3	5/4-5/28	5/29-6/21	6/22-7/16	7/17-8/9	8/10-9/2
1945	2/2-3/10 4/7-6/3	3/11-4/6 6/4-7/6	7/7-8/3	8/4-8/29	8/30-9/23	9/24-10/18
1946	3/11-4/4	4/5-4/28	4/29-5/23	5/24-6/17	6/18-7/12	7/13-8/8
1947	4/25-5/19	5/20-6/12	6/13-7/7	7/8-8/1	8/2-8/25	8/26-9/18
1948	2/11-3/7	3/8-4/3	4/4-5/6 6/29-8/2	5/7-6/28 8/3-9/7	9/8-10/5	10/6-10/31
1949	3/26-4/19	4/20-5/13	5/14-6/6	6/7-6/30	7/1-7/25	7/26-8/19
1950	5/5-5/31	6/1-6/26	6/27-7/21	7/22-8/15	8/16-9/9	9/10-10/3
1951	2/25-3/21	3/22-4/15	4/16-5/10	5/11-6/6	6/7-7/7	7/8-11/9
1952	4/10-5/4	5/5-5/28	5/29-6/21	6/22-7/16	7/17-8/9	8/10-9/3
1953	2/2-3/13 4/1-6/5	3/4-3/31 6/6-7/7	7/8-8/3	8/4-8/29	8/30-9/24	9/25-10/18

VENUS SIGN 1910–1975

Libra	Scorpio	Sagittarius	Capricorn	Aquarius	Pisces
11/2-11/25	11/26-12/20	12/21-12/31		1/1-1/18	1/19-2/11
8/21-9/14	9/15-10/10	1/1-1/13	1/14-2/6	2/7-3/2	3/3-3/26
		10/11-11/5	11/6-12/4	12/5-12/31	
10/5-10/28	10/29-11/21	11/22-12/15	12/16-12/31	1/1-4/5	4/6-5/5
11/9-12/7	12/8-12/31		1/1-1/7	1/8-1/31	2/1-2/25
9/5-9/27	1/1-1/2	1/3-1/27	1/28-2/21	2/22-3/16	3/17-4/10
	9/28-10/22	10/23-11/15	11/16-12/10	12/11-12/31	
10/19-11/11	11/12-12/5	12/6-12/29	12/30-12/31	1/1-1/5	1/6-2/1
8/9-9/6	9/7-10/13	10/14-11/14	1/1-1/22	1/23-2/15	2/16-3/11
	11/15-12/31				
9/20-10/13	1/1-1/3	1/4-2/5	2/6-3/4	3/5-3/30	3/31-4/24
	10/14-11/6	11/7-11/30	12/1-12/24	12/25-12/31	
11/1-11/25	11/26-12/19	12/20-12/31		1/1-1/18	1/19-2/11
8/21-9/14	9/15-10/9	1/1-1/12	1/13-2/5	2/6-3/1	3/2-3/26
		10/10-11/5	11/6-12/4	12/5-12/31	
10/4-10/27	10/28-11/20	11/21-12/14	12/15-12/31	1/1-4/4	4/6-5/5
11/9-12/7	12/8-12/31		1/1-1/7	1/8-1/31	2/1-2/24
9/3-9/27	1/1-1/2	1/3-1/27	1/28-2/20	2/21-3/16	3/17-4/9
	9/28-10/21	10/22-11/15	11/16-12/10	12/11-12/31	
10/19-11/11	11/12-12/5	12/6-12/29	12/30-12/31	1/1-1/4	1/5-2/1
8/9-9/6	9/7-10/15	10/16-11/7	1/1-1/21	1/22-2/14	2/15-3/10
	11/8-12/31				
9/19-10/12	1/1-1/4	1/5-2/5	2/6-3/4	3/5-3/29	3/30-4/24
	10/13-11/5	11/6-11/29	11/30-12/23	12/24-12/31	
11/1-1/25	11/26-12/19	12/20-12/31		1/1-1/17	1/18-2/10
8/20-9/14	9/15-10/9	1/1-1/12	1/13-2/5	2/6-3/1	3/2-3/25
		10/10-11/5	11/6-12/5	12/6-12/31	
10/4-10/27	10/28-11/20	11/21-12/13	12/14-12/31	1/1-4/5	4/6-5/4
11/10-12/7	12/8-12/31		1/1-1/7	1/8-1/31	2/1-2/24
9/4-9/27	1/1-1/2	1/3-1/27	1/28-2/20	2/21-3/16	3/17-4/9
	9/28-10/21	10/22-11/15	11/16-12/10	12/11-12/31	
10/19-11/11	11/12-12/5	12/6-12/29	12/30-12/31	1/1-1/5	1/6-2/1

VENUS SIGN 1910–1975

	Aries	Taurus	Gemini	Cancer	Leo	Virgo
1954	3/12-4/4	4/5-4/28	4/29-5/23	5/24-6/17	6/18-7/13	7/14-8/8
1955	4/25-5/19	5/20-6/13	6/14-7/7	7/8-8/1	8/2-8/25	8/26-9/18
1956	2/12-3/7	3/8-4/4	4/5-5/7 6/24-8/4	5/8-6/23 8/5-9/8	9/9-10/5	10/6-10/31
1957	3-26/4-19	4/20-5/13	5/14-6/6	6/7-7/1	7/2-7/26	7/27-8/19
1958	5/6-5/31	6/1-6/26	6/27-7/22	7/23-8/15	8/16-9/9	9/10-10/3
1959	2-25/3-20	3/21-4/14	4/15-5/10	5/11-6/6	6/7-7/8 9/21-9/24	7/9-9/20 9/25-11/9
1960	4-10/5-3	5/4-5/28	5/29-6/21	6/22-7/15	7/16-8/9	8/10-9/2
1961	2-3/6-5	6/6-7/7	7/8-8/3	8/4-8/29	8/30-9/23	9/24-10/17
1962	3/11-4/3	4/4-4/28	4/29-5/22	5/23-6/17	6/18-7/12	7/13-8/8
1963	4/24-5/18	5/19-6/12	6/13-7/7	7/8-7/31	8/1-8/25	8/26-9/18
1964	2/11-3/7	3/8-4/4	4/5-5/9 6/18-8/5	5/10-6/17 8/6-9/8	9/9-10/5	10/6-10/31
1965	3/26-4/18	4/19-5/12	5/13-6/6	6/7-6/30	7/1-7/25	7/26-8/19
1966	5/6-6/31	6/1-6/26	6/27-7/21	7/22-8/15	8/16-9/8	9/9-10/2
1967	2/24-3/20	3/21-4/14	4/15-5/10	5/11-6/6	6/7-7/8 9/10-10/1	7/9-9/9 10/2-11/9
1968	4/9-5/3	5/4-5/27	5/28-6/20	6/21-7/15	7/16-8/8	8/9-9/2
1969	2/3-6/6	6/7-7/6	7/7-8/3	8/4-8/28	8/29-9/22	9/23-10/17
1970	3/11-4/3	4/4-4/27	4/28-5/22	5/23-6/16	6/17-7/12	7/13-8/8
1971	4/24-5/18	5/19-6/12	6/13-7/6	7/7-7/31	8/1-8/24	8/25-9/17
1972	2/11-3/7	3/8-4/3	4/4-5/10 6/12-8/6	5/11-6/11 8/7-9/8	9/9-10/5	10/6-10/30
1973	3/25-4/18	4/18-5/12	5/13-6/5	6/6-6/29	7/1-7/25	7/26-8/19
1974	5/5-5/31	6/1-6/25	6/26-7/21	7/22-8/14	8/15-9/8	9/9-10/2
1975	2/24-3/20	3/21-4/13	4/14-5/9	5/10-6/6	6/7-7/9 9/3-10/4	7/10-9/2 10/5-11/9

VENUS SIGN 1910–1975

Libra	Scorpio	Sagittarius	Capricorn	Aquarius	Pisces
8/9-9/6	9/7-10/22	10/23-10/27	1/1-1/22	1/23-2/15	2/16-3/11
	10/28-12/31				
9/19-10/13	1/1-1/6	1/7-2/5	2/6-3/4	3/5-3/30	3/31-4/24
	10/14-11/5	11/6-11/30	12/1-12/24	12/25-12/31	
11/1-11/25	11/26-12/19	12/20-12/31		1/1-1/17	1/18-2/11
8/20-9/14	9/15-10/9	1/1-1/12	1/13-2/5	2/6-3/1	3/2-3/25
		10/10-11/5	11/6-12/16	12/7-12/31	
10/4-10/27	10/28-11/20	11/21-12/14	12/15-12/31	1/1-4/6	4/7-5/5
11/10-12/7	12/8-12/31		1/1-1/7	1/8-1/31	2/1-2/24
9/3-9/26	1/1-1/2	1/3-1/27	1/28-2/20	2/21-3/15	3/16-4/9
	9/27-10/21	10/22-11/15	11/16-12/10	12/11-12/31	
10/18-11/11	11/12-12/4	12/5-12/28	12/29-12/31	1/1-1/5	1/6-2/2
8/9-9/6	9/7-12/31		1/1-1/21	1/22-2/14	2/15-3/10
9/19-10/12	1/1-1/6	1/7-2/5	2/6-3/4	3/5-3/29	3/30-4/23
	10/13-11/5	11/6-11/29	11/30-12/23	12/24-12/31	
11/1-11/24	11/25-12/19	12/20-12/31		1/1-1/16	1/17-2/10
8/20-9/13	9/14-10/9	1/1-1/12	1/13-2/5	2/6-3/1	3/2-3/25
		10/10-11/5	11/6-12/7	12/8-12/31	
10/3-10/26	10/27-11/19	11/20-12/13	2/7-2/25	1/1-2/6	4/7-5/5
			12/14-12/31	2/26-4/6	
11/10-12/7	12/8-12/23		1/1-1/6	1/7-1/30	1/31-2/23
9/3-9/26	1/1	1/2-1/26	1/27-2/20	2/21-3/15	3/16-4/8
	9/27-10/21	10/22-11/14	11/15-12/9	12/10-12/31	
10/18-11/10	11/11-12/4	12/5-12/28	12/29-12/31	1/1-1/4	1/5-2/2
8/9-9/7	9/8-12/31		1/1-1/21	1/22-2/14	2/15-3/10
9/18-10/11	1/1-1/7	1/8-2/5	2/6-3/4	3/5-3/29	3/30-4/23
	10/12-11/5	11/6-11/29	11/30-12/23	12/24-12/31	
	11/25-12/18	12/19-12/31		1/1-1/16	1/17-2/10
10/31-11/24					
8/20-9/13		1/1-1/12	1/13-2/4	2/5-2/28	3/1-3/24
		10/9-11/5	11/6-12/7	12/8-12/31	
			1/30-2/28	1/1-1/29	
10/3-10/26	10/27-11/19	11/20-12/13	12/14-12/31	3/1-4/6	4/7-5/4
			1/1-1/6	1/7-1/30	1/31-2/23
11/10-12/7	12/8-12/31				

MARS SIGN 1910–1975

	Jan.	Feb.	Mar.	Apr.	May	June	July	Aug.	Sept.	Oct.	Nov.	Dec.
1910	AR	TA	GE	GE	CA	CA	LE	VI	VI	LI	SC	SC
1911	SA	CP	AQ	AQ	PI	AR	TA	TA	GE	GE	GE	TA
1912	TA	GE	GE	CA	CA	LE	LE	VI	LI	LI	SC	SA
1913	CP	CP	AQ	CA	AR	AR	TA	GE	CA	CA	CA	CA
1914	CA	CA	CA	PI	LE	LE	VI	LI	LI	SC	SA	SA
1915	CP	AQ	PI	PI	AR	TA	GE	GE	CA	LE	LE	LE
1916	LE	LE	LE	LE	LE	TA	VI	LI	SC	SC	SA	CP
1917	AQ	AQ	PI	AR	AR	VI	GE	CA	LE	LE	SA	VI
1918	LI	LI	VI	VI	VI	VI	LI	LI	SC	VI	VI	CP
1919	AQ	PI	AR	TA	GE	CA	LI	LE	VI	SA	CP	LI
1920	LI	SC	SC	SC	LI	LI	SC	SC	SA	VI	LI	AQ
1921	PI	AR	AR	TA	GE	GE	CA	LE	LE	CP	AQ	AQ
1922	SC	SC	SA	SA	SA	SA	SA	SA	CP	VI	LI	LI
1923	PI	AR	AR	TA	GE	AQ	CA	LE	VI	VI	PI	SC
1924	SC	SA	CP	CP	AQ	AQ	PI	PI	AQ	AQ	SC	PI
1925	AR	TA	TA	GE	CA	AR	LE	VI	VI	LI	SC	SC
1926	SA	CP	CP	AQ	PI	LE	AR	TA	TA	TA	TA	TA
1927	TA	TA	GE	GE	CA	LE	LE	VI	LI	LI	SC	SA
1928	SA	SA	AQ	PI	PI	AR	TA	GE	GE	CA	CA	CA

76

MARS SIGN 1910–1975

	Jan.	Feb.	Mar.	Apr.	May	June	July	Aug.	Sept.	Oct.	Nov.	Dec.
1929	GE	GE	CA	CA	LE	LE	VI	VI	LI	SC	SC	SA
1930	CP	AQ	AQ	PI	AR	TA	GE	GE	CA	CA	LE	LE
1931	LE	LE	CA	LE	LE	VI	VI	LI	LI	SC	SA	CP
1932	CP	AQ	PI	AR	TA	TA	GE	CA	CA	LE	VI	VI
1933	VI	VI	VI	VI	VI	VI	GE	LI	LI	SA	SA	CP
1934	AQ	PI	AR	AR	TA	GE	GE	CA	SC	SA	CP	LI
1935	LI	LI	LI	LI	LI	LI	LI	SC	LE	LE	LI	AQ
1936	PI	PI	AR	TA	GE	GE	CA	SC	SC	SA	AQ	LI
1937	SC	SC	SA	SA	SC	SC	SC	LE	LE	SA	LI	AQ
1938	PI	AR	TA	TA	GE	CA	AQ	LE	SA	VI	AQ	SC
1939	SC	SA	SA	CP	CP	AQ	AQ	CP	VI	VI	LI	PI
1940	AR	AR	TA	GE	GE	CA	LE	LE	CP	AQ	AQ	SC
1941	SA	SA	CP	AQ	AQ	PI	AR	AR	VI	VI	LI	AR
1942	TA	TA	GE	GE	CA	LE	LE	VI	AR	LI	AR	SC
1943	SA	CP	CP	GE	CA	AR	TA	TA	VI	GE	SC	SC
1944	GE	GE	AQ	AQ	CA	LE	TA	TA	LI	SC	GE	GE
1945	CP	AQ	AQ	PI	AR	TA	TA	VI	LI	CA	SC	SA
1946	CA	CA	CA	CA	LE	LE	VI	LI	LI	SC	SA	LE
1947	CP	AQ	PI	AR	AR	TA	GE	CA	CA	LE	LE	VI

MARS SIGN 1910–1975

	Jan.	Feb.	Mar.	Apr.	May	June	July	Aug.	Sept.	Oct.	Nov.	Dec.
1948	VI	LE	LE	LE	LE	VI	VI	LI	SC	SC	SA	CP
1949	AQ	PI	PI	AR	TA	GE	GE	CA	LE	LE	VI	VI
1950	LI	LI	LI	VI	VI	LI	LI	SC	SC.	SA	CP	CP
1951	AQ	PI	AR	TA	TA	GE	CA	CA	LE	VI	VI	LI
1952	LI	SC	SC	SC	SC	SC	SC	SC	SA	CP	CP	AQ
1953	AR	AR	AR	TA	GE	GE	CA	LE	SA	VI	LI	LI
1954	SC	SA	SA	CP	CP	CP	SA	SA	SA	SA	AQ	PI
1955	PI	AR	TA	GE	GE	CA	LE	LE	VI	LI	LI	SC
1956	SA	SA	CP	AQ	AQ	PI	PI	PI	PI	PI	SC	AR
1957	AR	TA	TA	GE	CA	CA	LE	VI	VI	LI	SC	SC
1958	SA	CP	CP	CP	PI	AR	AR	TA	TA	GE	TA	TA
1959	TA	GE	GE	CA	LE	LE	LE	VI	LI	LI	SC	SA
1960	CP	CP	AQ	AQ	CA	AR	TA	VI	GE	CA	CA	CA
1961	CA	CA	CA	CA	CA	LE	VI	VI	LI	SC	SA	SA
1962	CP	AQ	PI	PI	AR	TA	GE	GE	CA	LE	LE	LE
1963	LE	LE	LE	LE	LE	TA	TA	LI	SC	SC	SA	CP
1964	AQ	AQ	PI	AR	TA	TA	VI	CA	LE	LE	SA	VI
1965	VI	VI	VI	VI	VI	VI	VI	LI	SC	SA	VI	CP
1966	AQ	PI	AR	AR	TA	GE	CA	CA	LE	VI	VI	LI

78

MARS SIGN 1910-1975

	Jan.	Feb.	Mar.	Apr.	May	June	July	Aug.	Sept.	Oct.	Nov.	Dec.
1967	LI	SC	SC	LI	LI	LI	LI	SC	SA	SA	CP	AQ
1968	PI	PI	AR	TA	GE	GE	CA	LE	LE	VI	LI	LI
1969	SC	SC	SA	SA	SA	SA	SA	SA	SA	CP	AQ	PI
1970	PI	AR	TA	TA	GE	CA	CA	LE	VI	VI	LI	SC
1971	SC	SA	CP	CP	AQ	AQ	AQ	AQ	AQ	AQ	PI	PI
1972	AR	TA	TA	GE	CA	CA	LE	LE	VI	LI	SC	SC
1973	SA	CP	CP	AQ	PI	PI	AR	LE	VI	TA	AR	AR
1974	TA	TA	GE	GE	CA	LE	LE	VI	LI	LI	SC	SA
1975	SA	CP	AQ	PI	PI	AR	TA	GE	GE	GE	CA	GE

AR—Aries
TA—Taurus
GE—Gemini
CA—Cancer

LE—Leo
VI—Virgo
LI—Libra
SC—Scorpio

SA—Sagittarius
CP—Capricorn
AQ—Aquarius
PI—Pisces

9

The Planets As "Stars"

The Astrological Cast of Characters in Order of Their Appearance

As you learned in the chapter "Defining Terms," the planets are the *sine qua non* of astrology—the factor without which there would be no such study. It is the placement of the planets in the signs of the zodiac that give those signs meaning in human terms, and the placement of the planets in an individual horoscope that "spell out" that individual's character/personality. As for forecasting, it is the movement (transits) of the planets throughout our lifetime that activate one part of our chart or another and bring out certain life conditions.

Those planets are moving bodies and not "stars" in the astrological sense, though they are sometimes referred to with that word. In Shakespeare's play, *Julius Caesar*, Cassius, one of the conspirators, states, "The fault, dear Brutus, is not in our stars but in ourselves that we are underlings." Shakespeare (Cassius) actually knew what he was talking about because astrology was part and parcel of daily life in Elizabethan times when the play was written, as well as in Caesar's ancient Rome. However, Shakespeare seems to have preferred "stars" as a more poetic word than "planets." He also was right about another thing: The "stars" (planets) don't push people around unless you let them. The key is to understand the role each planet plays in your basic astrological makeup through your natal chart and to get to know yourself via this ancient and pragmatic science. Then you will better understand how the transits of the different planets are most likely to affect you.

Though the planets are not stars by astronomical definition (except for the sun), they do play the starring roles in the great cosmic drama that is acted out every day of our lives, and has been since the beginning of life on earth. There are other heavenly bodies—like the asteroids—that play supporting roles, but most astrologers take the Big Ten into consideration when they do a chart or a personal forecast: the sun, the moon, Mercury, Venus, Mars, Jupiter, Saturn, Uranus, Neptune, and Pluto. (Some of these planets, like the Moon, Venus, and Mars, are touched on in other parts of this book, and you may want to read those sections to get a better understanding of their characteristics.)

Each planet rules one or more signs of the zodiac—i.e., is very closely associated with that sign or signs. The one that rules your sun sign is your own personal planet, so to speak, and its description will fill in more of the background of your sign.

The following is a rundown of the planetary cast of characters, presented in their order of appearance, their actual position in our solar system As you know, the sun is the center of our solar system, and the orbits of the planets form rings around it. Looking at the planets this way underscores the fact that the *closer* planets influence us much more strongly as individuals. Planets farther out in the solar system are not only farther away, they also move much more slowly. While a transit of the moon lasts two days, for instance, a transit of Uranus (which takes eighty-four years to circle the zodiac) may influence your life for many months. However, even with these distant planets, their position in a specific *house* of your own horoscope will greatly influence your astrological makeup.

The Sun

Vital Statistics: 864,000 miles in diameter; average distance from earth, 93 million miles; gaseous nature. Appears to circle the zodiac in 365 days.

Rules: The sign of Leo
Fourth period of life: ages 23 to 41
Role: The true "star" ... the male lead ... the doer ... the activator.

Facts and Foibles: The position of the sun in anyone's horoscope is the central fact about that person, astrologically speaking. Your sun sign is your core—your individuality. It is your ego in the best sense of the word, the part of you that moves you in a certain life direction. No matter what your sun sign is, true self-development means developing the highest potential of that sign. People really grow into their sun signs as they mature, and the sun symbolically governs that stage of life (23 to 41) at which we are (or should be) mature individuals who are concerned with creating something in our own right. The sun is considered a masculine planet, because it is the fiery, animating force of life. We are meant to *express* our sun sign; those who do not can literally have a lifeless quality about them.

Those born under the sign of Leo have been said to be favored because of their rulership by the most important "planet" of them all. In ancient times, the sun was often the chief deity and was worshipped for its extraordinary power. It was recognized that without the sun, life on earth could not exist, and the dimming of its light via an eclipse was a terrifying experience for early civilizations that recognized their dependence upon its warmth and vitalizing nature. Whether or not Leo is a special sign is debatable, but there is no doubt that there is a tendency in some Leo sun sign people to become overly self-centered. Perhaps even unconsciously, they sense that it is a heady destiny to be ruled by the sun, but they are unable to handle its tremendous energies properly.

The Moon

Vital Statistics: 238,857 miles from the earth; 2,160 miles in diameter (one-fourth earth's size). Revolves around the earth (circles the zodiac) in about 27 ½ days
Rules: The sign of cancer
The first four years of human life

Role: The leading lady ... the "feeler" ... the mother ... the reactor.

Facts and Foibles: The moon is not exactly a planet, either; it is a satellite of our own planet, earth. However, it is the largest satellite with respect to its parent planet anywhere in the solar system that we know of. It has a tremendous gravitational pull, which is demonstrated on earth by the changing of the tides and other natural phenomena.

The moon has no light of its own, and we can see it shining only because it reflects the sun. Therefore, the moon is considered a *receptive* or "feminine" planet, rather than an active one like the sun. The moon in mythology has always been a woman—often the "Great Mother" to ancient peoples who saw the sun as the "Great Father." Accordingly, the moon rules the first four years of human life, when we are totally dependent on our mothers, and the motherly sign of Cancer, which is closely associated with nurturing and growth. In an individual horoscope, the position of the moon indicates our ability to feel and to respond emotionally. It is our impressionability and sensitivity, i.e., our subjective rather than our objective sign. The moon reacts to experience and remembers it. All our memories are stored in our subconscious, which is the part of the human psyche the moon signifies. In a sense, as the moon rules the night, it rules our dark or hidden side. As it takes some time for us to develop or grow into our sun sign, the moon sign manifests itself much more strongly in young children than the sun sign does. The moon represents the instinctual nature connected with infantile responses; our moon sign acts from habit, often without thinking.

Mercury

Vital Statistics: 36 million miles away from the sun; 2,900 miles in diameter; orbits sun at 108,000 miles per hour; goes through zodiac in 88 days.

Rules: The signs of Gemini and Virgo
Age of curiosity: 4 through 14

Role: The young male lead ... the observer ... the messenger ... the communicator.

Facts and Foibles: Mercury is the hottest, quickest, and smallest of the planets, and is closest to the sun. It is so closely associated with the sun in an astronomical sense, that Mercury is very often in the same sign as the sun in a natal chart. In any horoscope, it is never more than two signs away from your sun sign.

In ancient times Mercury was regarded as the sun's messenger, and the gods with whom it was associated always had some kind of communicating function. In Egypt, Mercury was Thoth—scribe to the gods, keeper of the divine books. The Greeks called him Hermes, the messenger; the Romans renamed him Mercury, but assigned similar functions. Hermes/Mercury always had a golden tongue, and was regarded as the great persuader. Quickness and deftness also associate Mercury with all kinds of human skills requiring manual and mental dexterity.

Mercury has a double role to play as ruler of the signs of Gemini and Virgo. In a sense, Mercury is two-faced; the communicative side in Gemini, his precise specialist side in Virgo. No matter what your sun sign is, in your horoscope Mercury symbolizes your style of thinking and communicating—not so much how intelligent you are as how you tend to put things together mentally.

Mercury is a very human planet, and has a very human foible; occasionally he gets things all mixed up and causes a lot of trouble. About three times a year, for about three weeks at a time, Mercury seems to be going *backwards*. (That appearance is caused by the varying rates of speed of various planets—like two trains traveling in the same direction that can seem as if they are traveling in two different directions.) During these periods Mercury is said to be *retrograde*, it is known to cause problems in all kinds of human interactions. People get the wrong message, or don't get it at all. People who are supposed to meet on a street corner never find each other. Trains and planes are missed, luggage is lost, orders simply never get transmitted or seem to vanish in thin air. There has been quite a bit of research on Mercury retrograde, and it all proves out. Even if people don't know *why* retrograde Mercury

makes things go wrong, they sure know it does. In 1986 Mercury will be retrograde during these periods:
March 7 through March 30.
July 9 through August 3.
November 2 through November 22.

Venus

Vital Statistics: 67.2 million miles from the sun; 26 million to 160 million miles from earth; approximately the same size and volume as earth. Goes through all twelve signs of the zodiac in about 225 days.
Rules: The signs of Taurus and Libra
Period of developing sexuality: ages 14 to 21
Role: The young, nubile female lead ... the love interest ... the artist.
Facts and Foibles: Like Mercury, Venus follows the sun very closely, so in anyone's horoscope it is never very far away from your sun sign. Symbolically, Venus represents your capacity to love and relate, and the capacity to appreciate beauty. In ancient myth, Venus was seen as the daughter of the moon, a feminine planet associated with many of the earthly things traditionally associated with women: the providing of food and shelter, the beautifying of the home, the harmonizing of opposites and settler of strife. Venus is a peaceful planet in every sense of the word. Aphrodite to the Greeks, Venus to the Romans, this goddess/planet was seen as the bounteous giver of life's gifts and pleasures—the personification of beauty. She is supposed to inspire us with the desire for both material and spiritual growth.

Like Mercury, Venus has two faces, but, strangely, one rules a feminine sign, Taurus, and one rules a masculine sign, Libra. In Taurus, Venus shows her earthier side, more concerned with creature comforts, sex, and material prosperity. In Libra, a more refined Venus shines forth as the graceful "hostess," the one who beautifies things and relates to others.

Though most Libra males are quite virile, their rulership by the planet Venus often manifests itself in extremely good looks and a great appreciation of beauty. The virile male hairdresser or interior decorator is the personification of this side of Venus. Because Venus seeks peace rather than war, harmony rather than discord, she rules lawyers, mediators, and arbitrators.

Since Venus rules one feminine earth sign and one masculine air sign, she is sometimes seen as a symbol for the fact that all things in the universe can be made to work in harmony—even the incompatible elements of air (Libra) and earth (Taurus) and the often antagonistic principles of male and female—in real life as in astrology. Divorce courts come under the rulership of Venus.

Mars

Vital Statistics: 14 million miles from the sun; 35 million miles from earth; 10 percent of earth's size; circles the zodiac in about 687 days.
Rules: The sign of Aries
Ages 42 to 56
Role: The virile male antagonist ... the lover ... the warrior.
Facts and foibles: Mars is a rather small planet and has sometimes been called "Earth's little brother." However, since ancient times Mars has been attributed with great powers—possibly because of its fiery red color. Even the earliest peoples associated Mars with strife and sex and a warriorlike attitude. In fact, Mars has had a rather bad reputation in astrology and was sometimes known as the "lesser malefic." But some groups assigned Mars another role and gave him a different dimension. The Egyptians called Mars Artes, and connected him with personal creative expression; to the Hebrews he played a similar role. When you think about it, sex, strife, and creative expression are only a few steps away from each other. Certainly, the act of procreation is a creative one, as it gives new life. War and strife are divisive, but often a new order comes out of them as well.

Mars is pure masculine energy—sometimes a bit rough, but always determined. In a personal horoscope, the sign position of Mars tells how you tend to assert yourself, how aggressive you are likely to be when going after what you want, even how much you will want it. Mars is our desire nature. (See the chapter on Venus and Mars to find out more about Mars in your own horoscope.) As the god of war, Mars is associated with courage and bravery, traits that are available to the Aries sun sign person if he/she cares to develop them. Mars is moral courage too, and the Mars-ruled Aries sun sign person at his/her best will never desert a cause or a person—no matter how rough the going gets.

About once every two years Mars returns to the same place it occupied on the day of your birth; to astrologers this is known as the "Mars return." It is a period of time during which one can make great strides, because Mars is stimulating that area of the natal chart connected with taking on the world. People often feel a great surge of energy during their Mars return, but if that energy is not directed in a productive channel, it can cause a lot of problems in relationships. You are far better taking out your Mars return aggressiveness on another job or another creative project rather than another person.

Jupiter

Vital Statistics: Largest planet in the solar system, 318 times larger than earth; 365 million to 600 million miles from earth; gaseous nature; circles the zodiac in about 12 years.

Rules: The sign of Sagittarius
    Ages 57 to 68

Role: The hero ... the "father confessor" ... the one who saves the day.

Facts and Foibles: From earliest times, Jupiter was assigned a role in the "cosmic drama" almost as important as that of the sun. Huge and luminous, Jupiter was easily visible to the naked eye eons before the age of the telescope. The sun may have been god in the all-encompassing sense, but Jupiter was *the* god who could make things happen, even interfere in human affairs if he was needed. And he has always been a "good guy." The Hindus, whose roots lie in antiquity, call him Vishnu, the preserver. To the Greeks, he was Zeus, the god who reigned supreme on Mount Olympus; he became Jupiter under the Romans. The important thing about this masculine god-planet is that it has always been very godly but very human at the same time. Zeus frequently came down from Mount Olympus to bestow his favors on people—particularly women who caught his fancy (causing his wife Hera to become jealous). Jupiter-Zeus is the god who keeps one foot in heaven and one foot firmly planted on the earth. Since the planet itself is large and impressive-looking, it has always been associated with benevolence and expansiveness. Our English word "jovial" has its roots in the name Jove, by which name Jupiter was sometimes called.

Joviality is one of the characteristics that is available to people born under the sign of Sagittarius, which Jupiter rules. Some Sagittarians are jovial, they spend all their money and all their energy on making life one long party.

But Jupiter has a serious side, too. Jupiter is associated with the divine law, and the ability to make that law known to men on earth. The higher Sagittarian, ruled by Jupiter, has a sense of this mission, and often takes the real-life role of priest-missionary or teacher of higher studies. While Venus and Libra, the sign Venus rules, are associated with the *practice* of law, Jupiter and Sagittarius are connected with the *making* and *interpretation* of laws.

Saturn

Vital Statistics: 75,000 miles in diameter, 95 times as big as earth; 886 million miles from the sun; takes 29 years to circle the zodiac.
Rules: The sign of Capricorn
Ages 68 on
Role: The "older man" ... the taskmaster ... the disciplining father.
Facts and Foibles: Like Jupiter, Saturn is so large it can be seen with the naked eye from earth and was watched carefully by early peoples. It was quickly observed that certain transits of Saturn brought trials and troubles on earth and so the planet earned itself the name of the

"greater malefic" by the time astrologers had begun to record their findings. Is Saturn really a "bad guy" as so many astrology books will tell you? There is no question that Saturn represents the principle of limitation; when you go too far out on a limb or get over expansive, Saturn is always there to teach you that there are rules and restrictions. However, as Saturn also represents the principle of contraction, this planet can and does bring periods of time in which we can consolidate our forces and make a secure place for ourselves in this world.

Saturn is also sometimes called the "lord of Karma." Translated into human terms, that means that Saturn represents our inevitable responsibilities, our "fated" duties in this world. Once again, there is a positive side. When Saturn is strongly placed in an individual's chart, that individual is exceptionally able to handle responsibility and achieve worldly success. As ruler of the sign of Capricorn, Saturn brings to that sign an extraordinary talent for working long and hard as well as reaping the material rewards that come with dedication to a task.

Kronos (or Chronos) was the ancient Greek god who is generally regarded as the prototype for Saturn's particular personality or role, and his story sheds a lot of light on the perceptions of this planet. Kronos was born to the very highest ancient god, Ouranos, and to the original earth mother, Ge. Kronos got a little carried away with this position and overthrew his father (castrating him) to take over the throne. When Kronos was told one of his own children would do the same to him, he swallowed them all—except Zeus, who was miraculously saved and became the "avenger." Later on, Zeus banished Kronos into exile. We know Kronos as Father Time—that shadowy old man who reminds us that it's later than we think. Kronos/Saturn also cautions against runaway ambitions, which is often punished by a downfall like his.

One of the most fascinating aspects of Saturn is that it is an uncannily accurate cosmic clock. Taking about 29 years to make a full circle of the zodiac, Saturn returns to the same place it occupied in your horoscope at your birth when you are about 29 years old. The "Saturn return" is regarded by astrologers as the true end of childhood (astrology is kind to us weak mortals by giving us more time to "grow up" than conventional earthly wisdom does). When Saturn begins to creep up on us in our late twenties, we generally begin to feel that it's time to settle down and do something big in the way of taking on earthly responsibility. Many people go through a "life crisis" at this time, because they feel the push that Saturn is giving them, but have trouble knowing what to do about it. Many, many people resolve the dilemma by getting married, buying a home, having a child, or getting divorced. The point is that it is time to *do something decisive* and to take responsibility for our own lives and actions. There are an incredible number of "Saturn return babies" because having a child is probably the most joyful as well as the biggest responsibility a person can assume.

On its second return—at about the human age of 58—people are generally ready to start relaxing their responsibilities and enjoying the fruits of their labors. It is a wise precaution to make ready for the second Saturn return, because just as Saturn tells us we have to *work*, he also tells us when it is time to *stop* working. But remain a productive human being, with real interests and the wherewithal to pursue them.

Uranus

Vital Statistics: 1.7 billion miles from earth; 29,300 miles in diameter, 15 times larger than earth; takes 84 years to circle the zodiac; has an erratic orbit.

Rules: The sign of Aquarius
Teenagers

Role: The rebel ... the home-wrecker ... the visionary.

Facts and Foibles: Uranus is the first of the "modern" planets, i.e., those unknown to the ancients, and only discovered via the telescope. Uranus, the first planet to be discovered in this manner, was thus a shock to both astronomers and astrologers. Both groups believed the orbit of Saturn defined the limits of our solar system, and both had to revise their thinking at this discovery. Astrologers took things in their stride by calling Uranus a "planet of the higher octave" and interpreting it as a breakthrough from the realm of purely earthly influences (with Saturn as the dividing line) to the "cosmic" or "higher" order of things. They decided that Uranus—an unconventional planet in many respects—must be the ruler of the quirky sign of Aquarius (which had been formerly ruled by Saturn). In a way it is uncanny that the sudden discovery of Uranus in 1781 heralded all the breakthrough discoveries of the 19th and 20th centuries. In a sense, Uranus ushered in the modern world; it also rules our current Age of Aquarius. As that age (approximately 2000 years long) will continue to shock us with discovery after discovery, it hopefully will also bring us the sense of brotherhood of humanity that is the hallmark of the sign of Aquarius.

As Uranus takes 84 years to circle the zodiac, it stays in each sign about seven years. (It is currently about two-thirds of the way through the sign of Sagittarius.) Whatever Uranus touches as it transits a person's natal chart gets a real jolt. Sometimes very suddenly. Uranus hates the status quo and almost always shakes it up. That means that a lot of changes take place when Uranus comes along, but for most people those changes are eventually positive ones. Uranus gets you out of whatever rut you happen to be in and does it quite forcefully. However, those who resist the changes Uranus "suggests" can cause themselves a lot of trouble. If you aren't willing to bend, Uranus can really "break you up."

Uranus is appropriately associated with the teen years, during which young people are often in a state of rebellion. However, here too, it is a *necessary* fact of life that people must eventually rebel against the strictures of childhood in order to become separate individual human beings. Uranus is associated not only with teenagers, but also with many of the things that represent their rebellion, like rock music, blaring radios, and all that goes with them. In essence, Uranus is the symbol of the electronic modern world.

Neptune

Vital Statistics: 2.6 billion miles from earth; 2.7 billion miles from the sun; takes about 165 years to circle the zodiac.
Rules: The sign of Pisces
No specific age.
Role: The fascinating stranger ... the poet ... the one who confuses the issue... the dreamer of great dreams.
Facts and Foibles: As it is difficult to get a handle on people heavily influenced by Neptune (like Pisceans), it took astronomers a while to figure out what Neptune really was. At first they observed nothing but some rather weird abberations in the orbit of Uranus as they began to plot that planet's orbit. In the early 1840s, some of them proved mathematically that there *must* be another planet out there, although it couldn't be seen. Finally, using all the data at hand, a German astronomer spotted Neptune in 1846.

There is a rather "sneaky" character to Neptune, but what this nebulous planet really symbolizes is the love that passes all understanding, the all-encompassing universal love that is virtually impossible for mortals to feel and give. Venus represents two-way love, the sharing kind. Neptune's love goes only in one direction. Neptune gives in a sense of self-sacrifice, and takes nothing in return.

There is evidence that even though no one really *saw* Neptune until 1846, the ancients knew all about its principles, and embodied them in the mythical figure of Poseidon (later called Neptune), the lord of the seas, master of the deep. When you think that more than three-quarters of the earth's surface is covered by water, you realize that Neptune was pretty important in the overall scheme of things. In fact, according to the Greeks, when the universe was created, it was divided among Zeus-Jupiter, who took the heavens, Hades-Pluto who took the underworld, and Poseidon-Neptune who took the oceans.

Just as water is difficult to contain, it is difficult for many people to get in touch with Neptune's higher qualities in their own charts. Water is soul and spirit, metaphysically speaking, so Neptune should make us aspire to much higher things. Not only universal love, but poetry, music and art in its purest forms. However, what Neptune touches in most people's natal charts often turns into an area of confusion rather than creativity. Neptune rules liquid in all its forms and, unfortunately, some people react to Neptune's confusing vibes by turning to alcohol or drugs. For many drug and alcohol abusers, however, the real goal of their vice is to attain a kind of "cosmic consciousness" which is the real realm of Neptune.

Since Neptune takes 165 years to circle the zodiac, it stays in one sign for 13 years or more. Therefore, it is the zodiacal *sign* Neptune makes to the "personal planets" in your chart that really count. People positively influenced by Neptune make the true artists and poets of this world—as well as the visionaries who interpret its meaning in more philosophical and metaphysical terms.

Pluto

Vital Statistics: 3,666 billion miles from the sun; takes about 242 years to circle the zodiac.
Rules: The sign of Scorpio
Prenatal
Role: The "heavy" ... the transformer ... the tragic hero.

Facts and Foibles: As you will note, Pluto is a little light on vital statistics. That's because this immensely distant planet, only discovered in 1930, has yet to reveal some of its secrets to astronomers. Like Neptune, it was discovered only because of the erratic nature of the orbit of Uranus. But, even when Pluto was conclusively sighted in 1930, its small size relative to its extremely strong gravitational pull didn't make sense to astronomers. Either Pluto is much larger than we now think or it is so dense that it exerts a force much greater than its size should account for.

Either way, there's no doubt that Pluto represents *power*. In fact, many astrologers connect the discovery of Pluto with the discovery by man of the extraordinary power in matter itself—the power of the atom. As with Neptune, Pluto's "realm" had been staked out in myth and astrology long before its actual discovery. Pluto is Hades, lord of the underworld—the place of darkness that all men fear. However, since most older religions regard life and death as a cycle, Pluto represents rebirth as well. We die only to be reborn. One of the symbols for Pluto is the Phoenix that rises triumphantly from its own ashes. Pluto—and the sign of Scorpio that it rules—hold onto their secrets, but have an incredible power to endure and triumph over life's circumstances. The extremes of life and death that Pluto/Scorpio is associated with connect neatly with the extremism of this astrological sign. "Plutonic" Scorpios often regard the world as totally black and white, with very few grays in between. They can also be the "best" of people, like reformers and religious leaders, or the "worst" of people, like criminals and those who manipulate others for their own purposes.

10

Astrotrivia

How Do You Rate in the Best Game in Town?

The ancient art of astrology is loaded with bits and pieces of miscellaneous information—all of it fascinating, and some of it more useful than you may think. For instance, did you know that every zodiac sign has a special day of the week and certain colors assigned to it? And, how good are you at guessing sun signs of celebrities—those larger-than-life models of sun signs in the flesh? The Astrotrivia that follows is partly in quiz form, partly in short-take astrological facts. In the first part, you can test your own astrological perceptivity; in the second, you can add a lot to your fund of astrological information—and maybe even learn a few things, you can use in your daily life.

Astrotrivia Part I
Sun Signs of the Rich and Famous

Try to answer the following questions yourself; if you're stumped you'll find the answers on page 103–104.

1. What famous stripper and the famous actress who played her mother in a Broadway show have the sign of Capricorn in common?

2. What two show biz buddies—who run in the same pack—are both Sagittarians?

3. What do these people have in common: Joseph Stalin, Richard Nixon, Herman Goering, Al Capone, and Mao Tse Tung?

4. What two handsome male movie stars, both known for their progressive ideas, have the same sun sign? And, what is it?

5. What highly Scorpionic actor had an on-again, off-again lifetime romance with a glamourous Pisces actress?

6. What two female tennis pros are both athletic Sagittarians?

7. What U.S. president had a "show-me-I'm-from-Missouri" personality, and what was his sun sign?

8. What two famous "lonely hearts" columnists get their soft Cancerian shoulders cried on all the time?

9. What two "greats" of American popular music were both thoroughly American, and both born on the Fourth of July?

10. Under what sign were these warrior peacemakers all born: Dwight D. Eisenhower, David Ben Gurion, Jimmy Carter, Mohandus Ghandi, and Eleanor Roosevelt?

11. What anti-American villainess of World War II was born on the Fourth of July?

12. What sun sign do these people have in common: Oscar Wilde, Truman Capote, and Gore Vidal?

13. What two famous rock stars—one early, one late— were born not only under the same sign, but on the same day?

14. Which of the following is/was not a Scorpio?

Charles Manson	Robert Kennedy
Bo Derek	Pablo Picasso
Katherine Hepburn	Indira Ghandi
Princess Grace	Johnny Carson
Henry Kissinger	Billy Graham

15. All of the following were born under the two most musical signs of the zodiac. What are they?

Judy Collins	Michael Jackson
Barbra Steisand	George Gershwin
Stevie Wonder	Luciano Pavarotti
Fred Astaire	Paul Simon
Irving Berlin	Julie Andrews
Bing Crosby	Anthony Newly
Beverly Sills	John Lennon
Bobby Darin	Guiseppe Verdi

16. All the following ladies of the stage and screen are masters of their craft. Which craftsman-like sun sign were they all born under?

Lauren Bacall	Celeste Holm
Anne Bancroft	Greer Garson
Ingrid Bergman	Twiggy
Greta Garbo	Jo Ann Worley
Sophia Loren	Claudette Colbert
Lilly Tomlin	Raquel Welch

17. What sun sign do the following famous rebels and rule-breakers have in common: Marlon Brando, Warren Beatty, Eddie Murphy, Charlie Chaplin, Hugh Hefner?

18. What sun sign do these medical and research geniuses have in common: Madame Curie, Jonas Salk, Christian Bernard?

19. What present-day famous Leo "princess" lived in Camelot with her Gemini "prince"?

20. What two great ballet stars were both born in the same country, and share the graceful sun sign, Pisces?

Answers on p. 103–104

Astrotrivia Part II
More Celebrity Sun Sign Lore

Just a handful of the many, many stage/screen-struck Leos:

Robert DeNiro	Julia Child
Mike Jagger	Arlene Dahl
Lucille Ball	Alfred Hitchcock
Dustin Hoffman	Mae West
Cecil B. Demille	George Bernard Shaw
John Derek	Dino D. Laurentis
Mike Douglas	Robert Mitchum
Robert Redford	Peter O'Toole
Jason Robards Jr.	Roman Polanski
Esther Williams	Jill St. John
Stanley Kubrick	Robert Taylor
Shelly Winters	Keenan Wynn

And here are some Leos who make/made the international scene their stage:

Fidel Castro	Henry Ford
Jackie Onassis	Alex Haley
Coco Chanel	Lawrence of Arabia
Benito Mussolini	Mata Hari
Rasputin	Napoleon
Neil Armstrong	Andy Warhol
Mike Conners	

Librans are often lovely, like Catherine Deneuve and Brigitte Bardot. Barbara Walters is the ultimate "cool" Libra.

Cancer is the second fame sign, because Cancer rules the public. Cancers who have made it somehow or other are:

Bill Cosby	Ringo Starr
Jimmy Cagney	John Glenn
Ernest Hemingway	Arthur Ashe
Gerald Ford	The Mayo brothers (of the Mayo clinic)

Some outspoken, inventive Aquarians whose opinions have not always been popular, but were always ahead of their time:

Norman Mailer   Ralph Nader
Charles Darwin   Thomas Edison
Jules Verne   Betty Friedan
Ayn Rand   Vanessa Redgrave
Galileo   Franklin D. Roosevelt

Astrotrivia Part III
Fascinating Facts About the Signs

Here are the colors that, by tradition, match each of the signs of the zodiac:

1. Aries: bright red, scarlet, magenta

2. Taurus: pastels in most shades, especially pink and turquoise

3. Gemini: beiges and light gray

4. Cancer: shimmery and irridescent shades of gray and silver; anything luminous

5. Leo: bright golds and yellows

6. Virgo: dark navy, brown, gray

7. Libra: cloudy pales, especially blue-green

8. Scorpio: murky colors, especially blood red and black

9. Sagittarius: rich blues, purples, greens

10. Capricorn: black, "no-color" colors

11. Aquarius: checks, stripes, patterns, electric blue

12. Pisces: deep lilac, mauve, sea green

Each Sign/Planet owns a day of the week:

Sunday = Sun/Leo

Monday = Moon/Cancer

Tuesday = Mars/Aries, Mars/Scorpio

Wednesday = Mercury/Gemini, Mercury/Virgo

Thursday = Jupiter/Sagittarius, Neptune/Pisces

Friday = Venus/Taurus, Venus/Libra

Saturday = Saturn/Capricorn, Saturn/Aquarius

(Since there are only seven days and twelve signs, some of the signs double up. Also, since the ancients only knew seven planets, there are only enough days to match seven of the ten planets we now recognize.)

Astrotrivia Part IV
Where Do You Belong?

Each sign is said to have certain places where it belongs. Long ago, the world was divided up according to astrological tradition, so there are certain countries, cities, and areas that have the vibrations of certain signs. Tradition divides up other kinds of spaces, too, as you will see.

- *Aries places:* In the world: Birmingham, Oldman, Leicester, and Blackburn, *England* ... Florence, Naples, Verona and Padua *Italy* ... Marseilles and Burgundy *France* ... *Denmark, Germany, Palestine, Syria, Japan.*

    Anywhere: sheepfolds, forges, tool houses, fireplaces, on sandy soil, kilns, ceilings, fire houses, emergency rooms.

- *Taurus places:* In the world: Dublin, *Ireland* ... Mantua, Parma, Palermo, *Italy* ... St. Louis, *U.S.A.* ... *The Greek Islands, Asia Minor, the Caucasus.*

    Anywhere: banks, dairies, pastures, shady places, corn fields, middle rooms of houses, altars, maypoles.

- *Gemini places:* In the world: San Francisco, *U.S.A.* ... London and Plymouth, *England* ... Bruges, *Belgium* ... Versailles and Louvaine, *France* ... Nurenburg, *Germany* ... *Lower Egypt, Armenia, Wales.*

    Anywhere: buildings with pillars, bookcases, hills and mountains, upper back rooms, graineries.

- *Cancer places:* In the world; St. Andrews, *Scotland* ... Amsterdam, *Holland* ... New York City, *U.S.A.* ... Stockholm, *Sweden* ... Genoa, Venice, Milan, *Italy* ... *Paraguay, North and West Africa.*

Anywhere: lakes and brooks, salt marshes, pubs, kitchens, cellars, corner houses facing north.
- *Sagittarius places:* In the world: Avignon, *France* ... Stuttgart, Cologne, *Germany* ... Nottingham, Sheffield, Bradford, *England* ... Provence, *France* ... *Hungary, Arabia, Tuscany.*

    Anywhere: highest place around, topmost room in house, stables for racing horses, obelisks, places near fire, where incense is burned.
- *Capricorn places:* In the world: Brussels, *Belgium* ... Port Said, *Egypt* ... *India, Afghanistan, Mexico, Lithuania, Orkney Islands, Macedonia.*

    Anywhere: vaults, convents, thick forests, gates and hinges, old trees, jails, cattle barns, door knockers, game preserves.
- *Aquarius places:* In the world: Brighton and Trent, *England* ... Salzburg, *Austria* ... Hamburg, *Germany* ... the Piedmont, *Italy* ... *Prussia, Red Russia, Westphalia.*

    Anywhere: buses, bridges, ladders, garages, airplanes, power transmitters, fountains, springs and streams, sleds, ice caps.
- *Pisces places:* In the world; Alexandria, *Egypt* ... Seville, *Spain* ... Southport, Lancaster, Bournemouth, Tiverton, *England* ... *Portugal, Calabria, Normandy, Sahara.*

    Anywhere: fish ponds, oceans, oil fields, submarines, séances, flooded areas, bars, aquariums, boat yards, swimming pools, hospitals.
- *Leo Places:* In the world: Rome, Ravenna, *Italy* ... Bath, Bristol, Portsmouth, Blackpool, *England* ... Philadelphia, Chicago, *U.S.A.* ... *Bohemia, Sicily, the Alps, Damascus.*

    Anywhere: wild animal preserves, deserts and forests, castles, furnaces, gold mines, porches, forts.
- *Virgo places:* In the world: Paris, Lyons, Toulouse, *France* ... Boston, Los Angeles, *U.S.A.* ... Heidelberg, *Germany* ... *Turkey, West Indies, Brazil, Silesia, Switzerland.*

    Anywhere: pantries, restaurants, refrigerators, medicine cabinets, desks, malt houses.

- *Libra places:* In the world: Dover, Liverpool, Newcastle, *England* ... Messina, *Italy* ... Halifax, *Nova Scotia* ... *China, Norway, The Transvaal, the Barbary coast.*

   Anywhere: windmills, wood sheds, harbors, tops of mountains, garrets and lofts, guest rooms, tops of dressers, domed buildings.
- *Scorpio places:* In the world: Copenhagen, *Denmark* ... Leeds, Nottingham, *England* ... Johannesburg, *South Africa* ... Burma, *India* ... *Tibet, North China, Argentina.*

   Anywhere: junk yards, meat markets, laboratories, low gardens and streams, vineyards, deepest part of ocean.

Astrotrivia Part V
Which Animal Best Suits You?

Each sign is said to have an affinity with certain kinds of pets. Here's the rundown.

Aries: No animal that needs a lot of taking care of; but if Aries has one pet, he/she will usually have two, so the animals can take care of each other.

Taurus: Almost any kind of soft, warm creature. Taurus is a great nature lover, so even a skunk would be welcome.

Gemini: Anything with fascinating habits, like bees or ants, or anything that talks, like a parrot or a minah bird.

Cancer: Anything in need of a mother is welcome in Cancer's house, no matter how sloppy or in need of care.

Leo: Cats, of course, preferably with good breeding. Peacocks or anything with bright colors or plumage are fine too.

Virgo: Cats are preferable, because they are clean animals, but any animal in distress brings out Virgo's warmth.

Libra: This sign would just as soon do without, but if a pet is preferred, it's the perfectly groomed poodle or other refined breed of dog or cat.

Scorpio: This sign goes for rather dangerous pets, such as snakes, or anything with a sting. Basically, animals are creatures to be observed, not coddled.

Sagittarius: Horses—at home or at the race track. Any very large dog in the city, almost anything of immense size in the country.

Capricorn: Capricorns *need* pets to help pull them out of their frequent depressions. The friendliest kind of animals are the best bet, like sheepdogs.

Aquarius: This sign needs a very smart animal, so is picky about the breed of dog or cat. Actually, birds are preferable to this cool sign.

Pisces: Many people born under this sign will take in any stray that strays into their path, no matter how scraggly or ugly. They often put animals before humans in their scheme of things.

Astrotrivia Part I answers

1. Gypsy Rose Lee and Ethel Merman (who played Gypsy's mother in *Gypsy*).
2. Frank Sinatra and Sammie Davis, Jr.
3. They were all born under the calculating sign of Capricorn.
4. Paul Newman and Alan Alda were both born under the sign of Aquarius.
5. Richard Burton was the Scorpio; Liz Taylor the Pisces.
6. Billie Jean King and Chris Evert.
7. Harry S. Truman, a Taurus.
8. Abigail Van Buren ("Dear Abby") and Ann Landers.

9. George M. Cohan ("Yankee Doodle Dandy") and Louis "Satchmo" Armstrong.
10. Libra.
11. Tokyo Rose.
12. Libra.
13. Elvis Presley and David Bowie (January 5—Capricorn).
14. Henry Kissinger. He's a wily Gemini, but he could easily fool you, because his moon sign is Scorpio.
15. The column on the left are Taureans; those on the right are Librans.
16. Virgo.
17. Aries.
18. Scorpio.
19. Jackie Kennedy Onassis is a Leo; John F. Kennedy was a Gemini.
20. Rudolph Nureyev and Vaslav Nijinsky.

11

Sun Sign Changes. 1920–1975

If you were born "on the cusp" (very near the end or the beginning of a sign) you can find out what your sign really is by using the chart that follows. Many people do not realize that the sun does not "change signs" on the same day every year—or, for that matter, at the same time. For this reason the chart of sun sign changes is calculated to the minute.

How to Use the Chart

Locate your year of birth, then the month in which you were born. Let's say you were born in April of 1942. In the box for that month and year you will see

20–Tau
12:30 P.M.

That means if you are born *after* 12:30 p.m. on April 20 in 1942, you are a Taurus. If you were born before that date and time, your sun sign is the preceding one, Aries.

In this chart (as well as in the rising-sign chart) the signs are abbreviated as follows:

Ar = Aries
Tau = Taurus
Gem = Gemini
Can = Cancer
Leo = Leo
Vir = Virgo
Lib = Libra
Sc = Scorpio

Sag = Sagittarius
Cap = Capricorn
Aq = Aquarius
Pis = Pisces

NOTE: All times given in the sun sign changes chart are Eastern Standard. You must correct for daylight savings time (subtract one hour) and for time zone. For Central Standard Time subtract one hour; for Mountain Standard Time subtract two hours; for Pacific Standard Time subtract three hours.

	1920	1921	1922	1923	1924	1925	1926	1927	1928	1929
Jan	21–Aq 4:05 am	20–Aq 8:55 am	20–Aq 2:48 pm	20–Aq 8:35 pm	21–Aq 2:29 am	20–Aq 8:20 am	20–Aq 2:13 pm	20–Aq 8:12 pm	21–Aq 1:57 am	20–Aq 7:42 am
Feb	19–Pis 5:29 pm	18–Pis 11:21 pm	19–Pis 5:16 am	19–Pis 11:00 am	19–Pis 4:51 pm	18–Pis 11:43 pm	18–Pis 4:35 am	19–Pis 10:35 am	19–Pis 4:20 pm	18–Pis 10:07 pm
Mar	20–Ar 5:00 pm	20–Ar 10:51 pm	21–Ar 4:49 am	21–Ar 10:29 am	20–Ar 4:20 pm	20–Ar 11:13 pm	21–Ar 4:01 am	21–Ar 11:59 am	20–Ar 3:44 pm	20–Ar 9:35 pm
Apr	20–Tau 4:39 am	20–Tau 10:32 am	20–Tau 4:29 pm	20–Tau 10:06 pm	20–Tau 3:59 am	20–Tau 10:51 am	20–Tau 3:36 pm	20–Tau 9:32 pm	20–Tau 3:17 am	20–Tau 9:11 am
May	21–Gem 4:22 am	21–Gem 10:17 am	21–Gem 9:11 pm	22–Gem 9:45 pm	21–Gem 3:41 am	21–Gem 10:33 pm	21–Gem 3:15 pm	21–Gem 9:08 pm	21–Gem 2:53 am	21–Gem 8:48 am
June	21–Can 12:40 pm	21–Can 6:36 pm	22–Can 12:27 am	22–Can 6:03 am	21–Can 12:noon	21–Can 5:50 pm	21–Can 5:21 pm	22–Can 11:30 pm	21–Can 11:07 pm	21–Can 5:01 pm
July	22–Leo 11:40 pm	23–Leo 5:31 am	23–Leo 11:20 am	23–Leo 5:01 pm	22–Leo 11:58 pm	23–Leo 4:45 am	23–Leo 10:25 am	23–Leo 4:17 am	22–Leo 11:02 pm	23–Leo 3:54 am
Aug	23–Vir 6:22 am	23–Vir 12:15 pm	23–Vir 6:04 pm	23–Vir 11:52 pm	23–Vir 5:48 am	23–Vir 11:33 am	23–Vir 5:14 pm	23–Vir 11:06 pm	23–Vir 4:53 am	23–Vir 10:41 am
Sept	23–Lib 3:25 am	23–Lib 11:20 am	23–Lib 5:10 am	23–Lib 9:04 pm	23–Lib 2:58 am	23–Lib 8:43 am	23–Lib 2:25 pm	23–Lib 8:17 pm	23–Lib 2:36 am	23–Lib 7:52 am
Oct	23–Sc 12:31 pm	23–Sc 6:03 pm	23–Sc 11:53 pm	24–Sc 5:51 am	23–Sc 11:44 am	23–Sc 5:31 pm	23–Sc 11:18 pm	24–Sc 5:07 am	23–Sc 10:55 am	23–Sc 4:41 pm
Nov	22–Sag 9:15 am	22–Sag 3:21 pm	22–Sag 8:55 pm	23–Sag 2:54 am	22–Sag 8:46 am	22–Sag 2:36 pm	22–Sag 8:28 pm	23–Sag 2:14 am	22–Sag 8:00 am	22–Sag 1:48 pm
Dec	21–Cap 10:17 pm	22–Cap 4:08 am	22–Cap 9:57 pm	22–Cap 3:53 pm	21–Cap 10:45 pm	22–Cap 3:37 am	22–Cap 9:34 am	22–cap 3:18 pm	21–Cap 9:04 pm	22–Cap 2:53 am

	1930	1931	1932	1933	1934	1935	1936	1937	1938	1939
Jan	20–Aq 1:33 pm	21–Aq 7:18 pm	20–Aq 1:07 am	20–Aq 6:53 am	20–Aq 10:37 am	20–Aq 6:29 pm	21–Aq 12:12am	20–Aq 6:01 am	20–Aq 11:59 am	20–Aq 5:51 pm
Feb	19–Pis 4:00 am	19–Pis 9:06 am	19–Pis 3:29 pm	19–Pis 9:16 pm	19–Pis 3:02 am	19–Pis 8:52 am	19–Pis 2:33 pm	18–Pis 3:21 pm	19–Pis 2:20 am	19–Pis 8:10 pm
Mar	21–Ar 3:30 am	21–Ar 9:40 am	20–Ar 2:54 pm	21–Ar 8:43 pm	21–Ar 2:28 am	21–Ar 8:19 am	20–Ar 1:58 pm	20–Ar 7:45 pm	21–Ar 1:43 am	21–Ar 7:29 am
Apr	20–Tau 3:06 pm	20–Tau 8:40 pm	20–Tau 2:28 am	20–Tau 8:19 am	20–Tau 2:00 pm	20–Tau 7:50 pm	20–Tau 1:31 am	20–Tau 7:20 am	20–Tau 1:15 pm	20–Tau 6:55 pm
May	21–Gem 2:42 pm	21–Gem 8:15 pm	21–Gem 2:07 am	21–Gem 7:57 am	21–Gem 1:35 pm	21–Gem 7:25 pm	21–Gem 1:08 am	21–Gem 6:57 am	21–Gem 12:51 pm	21–Gem 6:27 pm
June	21–Can 11:53 pm	23–Can 4:28 am	21–Can 10:23 am	21–Can 4:12 pm	21–Can 9:48 pm	22–Can 3:32 am	21–Can 9:22 am	21–Can 3:12 pm	21–Can 9:04 pm	22–Can 2:40 am
July	23–Leo 10:42 am	23–Leo 3:21 pm	22–Leo 9:18 pm	23–Leo 3:06 am	23–Leo 8:42 am	23–Leo 2:33 pm	22–Leo 8:18 pm	23–Leo 2:07 am	23–Leo 7:57 am	23–Leo 1:37 pm
Aug	23–Vir 4:27 pm	23–Vir 10:10 pm	23–Vir 4:06 am	23–Vir 9:53 am	23–Vir 3:32 pm	23–Vir 9:24 pm	23–Vir 3:11 am	23–Vir 8:58 am	23–Vir 2:46 pm	23–Vir 8:31 pm
Sept	23–Lib 1:35 pm	23–Lib 7:23 pm	23–Lib 1:16 am	23–Lib 7:01 am	23–Lib 10:45 am	23–Lib 6:38 pm	23–Lib 12:26 pm	23–Lib 6:13 am	23–Lib 12:noon	23–Lib 5:50 pm
Oct	23–Sc 11:25 pm	24–Sc 4:15 am	23–Sc 10:04 am	23–Sc 3:48 pm	23–Sc 9:35 pm	24–Sc 3:29 am	23–Sc 10:18 am	23–Sc 3:06 pm	23–Sc 8:54 pm	24–Sc 2:46 am
Nov	22–Sag 7:34 pm	23–Sag 1:25 am	22–Sag 7:10 am	22–Sag 10:53 am	22–Sag 6:44 pm	23–Sag 12:35 am	22–Sag 6:25 pm	22–Sag 12:17 pm	22–Sag 6:06 pm	22–Sag 11:59 pm
Dec	22–Cap 8:40 am	22–Cap 2:30 pm	21–Cap 8:14 pm	22–Cap 1:58 am	22–Cap 5:49 pm	22–Cap 1:37 pm	21–Cap 7:27 pm	22–Cap 1:22 am	22–Cap 7:13 am	22–Cap 1:05 pm

	1940	1941	1942	1943	1944	1945	1946	1947	1948
Jan	20—Aq 11:44 pm	20—Aq 5:34 am	20—Aq 11:16 am	20—Aq 5:20 pm	20—Aq 11:09 pm	20—Aq 4:55 am	20—Aq 10:44 am	20—Aq 4:23 pm	20—Aq 10:18 pm
Feb	19—Pis 2:04 pm	18—Pis 7:59 pm	19—Pis 1:39 am	19—Pis 7:41 am	19—Pis 1:28 pm	18—Pis 7:15 pm	19—Pis 1:10 am	19—Pis 6:53 am	19—Pis 12:37 pm
Mar	20—Ar 1:24 pm	20—Ar 7:21 pm	21—Ar 1:03 am	21—Ar 7:03 am	21—Ar 12:49 pm	20—Ar 6:38 pm	21—Ar 12:34 am	21—Ar 6:13 am	20—Ar 11:57 am
Apr	20—Tau 12:51 am	20—Tau 6:51 am	20—Tau 12:30 pm	20—Tau 6:32 pm	20—Tau 12:18 am	20—Tau 6:08 am	20—Tau 12:03 pm	20—Tau 5:40 pm	19—Tau 11:25 pm
May	21—Gem 12:23 am	21—Gem 6:23 am	21—Gem 12:01 pm	21—Gem 6:03 pm	20—Gem 11:51 pm	22—Gem 5:41 am	21—Gem 1:34 am	21—Gem 5:04 pm	20—Gem 10:58 pm
June	21—Can 8:37 am	21—Can 2:33 pm	21—Can 8:08 pm	22—Can 2:13 am	21—Can 9:03 am	21—Can 1:52 pm	21—Can 7:45 pm	22—Can 1:19 am	21—Can 7:11 am
July	22—Leo 7:34 pm	23—Leo 1:26 am	23—Leo 6:59 am	23—Leo 1:05 pm	22—Leo 6:55 pm	23—Leo 12:48 am	23—Leo 6:37 am	23—Leo 12:12 pm	22—Leo 6:06 pm
Aug	23—Vir 2:21 am	23—Vir 8:30 am	23—Vir 1:50 pm	23—Vir 7:55 pm	23—Vir 1:47 am	23—Vir 7:36 am	23—Vir 1:23 pm	23—Vir 7:09 pm	23—Vir 1:03 am
Sept	22—Lib 11:46 pm	23—Lib 5:33 am	23—Lib 11:10 am	23—Lib 5:12 pm	22—Lib 11:02 pm	23—Lib 4:50 am	23—Lib 10:41 am	23—Lib 4:29 pm	22—Lib 10:22 pm
Oct	23—Sc 8:39 am	23—Sc 2:22 pm	22—Sc 8:01 pm	24—Sc 2:09 am	23—Sc 7:57 am	20—Sc 1:45 pm	23—Sc 7:37 pm	24—Sc 1:27 am	23—Sc 7:19 am
Nov	22—Sag 5:49 am	22—Sag 11:36 am	22—Sag 5:23 pm	22—Sag 11:22 pm	22—Sag 5:09 am	22—Sag 10:56 am	22—Sag 4:47 pm	22—Sag 10:38 pm	22—Sag 4:29 am
Dec	21—Cap 6:55 pm	22—Cap 12:44 am	22—Cap 6:31 am	22—Cap 12:30 pm	21—Cap 6:15 pm	22—Cap 12:04 am	22—Cap 5:54 am	22—Cap 11:44 am	21—Cap 5:23 pm

	1949	1950	1951	1952	1953	1954	1955	1956	1957
Jan	20–Aq 4:11 am	20–Aq 10:00 am	20–Aq 3:53 pm	20–Aq 9:38 pm	20–Aq 3:22 am	20–Aq 9:14 am	20–Aq 3:03 pm	20–Aq 8:49 pm	20–Aq 2:43 am
Feb	18–Pis 6:27 pm	19–Pis 12:16 am	19–Pis 6:10 am	19–Pis 11:57 am	18–Pis 5:41 pm	19–Pis 11:33 pm	19–Pis 5:19 am	19–Pis 11:05 am	18–Pis 5:01 pm
Mar	20–Ar 5:49 pm	20–Ar 11:30 pm	21–Ar 5:26 am	20–Ar 11:14 am	20–Ar 5:01 pm	20–Ar 10:54 pm	21–Ar 4:36 am	20–Ar 10:21 am	20–Ar 4:17 pm
Apr	20–Tau 5:18 am	20–Tau 11:00 am	20–Tau 4:49 pm	20–Tau 10:37 pm	19–Tau 4:26 am	20–Tau 10:20 am	20–Tau 3:58 pm	19–Tau 9:44 pm	20–Tau 3:45 am
May	21–Gem 4:51 am	21–Gem 10:27 am	21–Gem 4:15 pm	20–Gem 10:04 pm	21–Gem 3:53 am	21–Gem 9:48 am	21–Gem 3:25 pm	20–Gem 9:13 pm	21–Gem 3:09 am
June	21–Can 1:03 pm	21–Can 6:37 pm	22–Can 12:25 am	21–Can 6:13 am	21–Can 12:noon	21–Can 5:55 pm	21–Can 11:32 pm	21–Can 5:24 am	21–Can 11:21 am
July	22–Leo 1:58 am	23–Leo 5:30 am	23–Leo 11:29 am	22–Leo 5:05 pm	22–Leo 10:53 pm	23–Leo 4:45 am	23–Leo 10:25 am	22–Leo 4:20 pm	22–Leo 10:13 pm
Aug	23–Vir 6:49 pm	23–Vir 12:24 pm	23–Vir 6:22 pm	23–Vir 12:03 am	23–Vir 5:46 am	23–Vir 11:37 am	23–Vir 5:19 pm	22–Vir 11:15 pm	23–Vir 5:07 am
Sept	23–Lib 4:05 am	23–Lib 9:44 am	23–Lib 3:38 pm	22–Lib 9:24 pm	23–Lib 3:07 am	23–Lib 8:56 am	23–Lib 2:42 pm	22–Lib 8:30 pm	23–Lib 2:27 am
Oct	23–Sc 1:04 pm	23–Sc 6:48 pm	23–Sc 12:37 am	23–Sc 6:22 am	23–Sc 12:07 pm	23–Sc 5:58 pm	22–Sc 11:44 pm	23–Sc 5:35 am	23–Sc 11:33 am
Nov	22–Sag 10:17 am	22–Sag 4:03 pm	22–Sag 9:52 pm	22–Sag 3:36 am	22–Sag 9:23 am	22–Sag 3:14 pm	22–Sag 9:02 pm	22–Sag 2:51 am	22–Sag 8:45 am
Dec	21–Cap 11:24 am	22–Cap 5:14 am	22–Cap 11:01 am	21–Cap 4:44 pm	21–Cap 10:22 pm	22–Cap 4:25 am	22–Cap 10:12 am	21–Cap 4:00 pm	21–Cap 9:49 pm

	1958	1959	1960	1961	1962	1963	1964	1965	1966
Jan	20—Aq 2:20 am	20—Aq 2:20 pm	20—Aq 8:11 pm	20—Aq 2:02 am	20—Aq 7:49 am	20—Aq 1:55 pm	19—Aq 7:43 pm	20—Aq 1:30 am	20—Aq 8:21 am
Feb	18—Pis 10:49 pm	19—Pis 4:38 pm	19—Pis 10:26 am	18—Pis 6:27 pm	18—Pis 10:16 pm	19—Pis 4:09 am	19—Pis 10:25 am	18—Pis 3:49 pm	18—Pis 9:39 pm
Mar	20—Ar 10:06 pm	21—Ar 3:55 am	20—Ar 9:43 am	20—Ar 5:27 am	20—Ar 9:30 pm	21—Ar 3:20 am	20—Ar 9:43 am	20—Ar 3:05 pm	20—Ar 8:53 pm
Apr	20—Tau 9:28 am	20—Tau 3:17 pm	20—Tau 10:06 pm	20—Tau 2:33 am	20—Tau 8:51 am	20—Tau 2:37 pm	19—Tau 9:00 pm	20—Tau 2:27 am	20—Tau 8:12 am
May	21—Gem 8:52 am	21—Gem 2:38 pm	20—Gem 8:33 pm	21—Gem 1:51 am	21—Gem 8:17 am	21—Gem 1:59 pm	20—Gem 8:33 pm	21—Gem 1:27 am	21—Gem 7:33 am
June	21—Can 4:57 pm	21—Can 10:50 pm	21—Can 4:43 am	21—Can 10:12 am	21—Can 4:24 pm	21—Can 11:04 pm	21—Can 4:43 am	21—Can 9:56 am	21—Can 3:33 pm
July	23—Leo 3:51 am	23—Leo 9:45 am	22—Leo 5:38 pm	22—Leo 9:12 pm	23—Leo 3:19 am	23—Leo 9:00 am	22—Leo 3:38 pm	22—Leo 8:49 pm	23—Leo 2:24 am
Aug	23—Vir 10:47 am	23—Vir 4:44 pm	22—Vir 10:35 pm	23—Vir 3:46 am	23—Vir 10:13 am	23—Vir 3:58 pm	22—Vir 10:35 pm	23—Vir 3:43 am	23—Vir 9:18 am
Sept	23—Lib 5:10 am	23—Lib 2:09 pm	22—Lib 8:00 pm	23—Lib 1:26 am	23—Lib 7:35 am	23—Lib 1:24 pm	22—Lib 8:00 pm	23—Lib 1:06 am	23—Lib 6:43 am
Oct	23—Sc 5:12 am	23—Sc 11:12 pm	23—Sc 5:03 am	23—Sc 10:46 am	23—Sc 4:41 pm	23—Sc 11:30 pm	23—Sc 5:03 am	23—Sc 10:11 am	23—Sc 3:52 pm
Nov	22—Sag 2:30 pm	22—Sag 8:23 am	22—Sag 2:19 am	22—Sag 8:10 am	22—Sag 2:02 pm	22—Sag 7:50 pm	22—Sag 2:19 am	22—Sag 7:30 am	22—Sag 1:15 pm
Dec	22—Cap 3:40 am	22—Cap 9:35 am	21—Cap 5:27 pm	21—Cap 9:25 pm	22—Cap 3:15 am	22—Cap 9:02 am	21—Cap 3:27 pm	21—Cap 8:41 pm	22—Cap 2:29 pm

	1967	1968	1969	1970	1971	1972	1973	1974	1975
Jan	20–Aq 1:05 pm	20–Aq 6:54 pm	20–Aq 12:30 am	20–Aq 6:25 pm	20–Aq 12:14 pm	20–Aq 6:00 pm	19–Aq 11:49 pm	20–Aq 5:47 am	20–Aq 11:37 am
Feb	19–Pis 3:25 am	19–Pis 9:11 am	18–Pis 2:47 pm	18–Pis 8:43 pm	19–Pis 2:28 am	19–Pis 8:12am	18–Pis 2:02 pm	18–Pis 8:00 pm	19–Pis 1:51 am
Mar	21–Ar 2:37 am	20–Ar 8:22 am	20–Ar 2:08 pm	20–Ar 7:59 pm	21–Ar 1:28 am	20–Ar 7:22 am	20–Ar 1:13 pm	20–Ar 7:08 pm	21–Ar 12:58 am
Apr	20–Tau 1:56 am	19–Tau 7:42 am	20–Tau 1:18 am	20–Tau 5:16 am	20–Tau 1:28 am	19–Tau 6:38 pm	20–Tau 12:31 am	20–Tau 5:19 am	20–Tau 12:08 pm
May	21–Gem 1:19 pm	20–Gem 7:07 pm	21–Gem 12:41 am	21–Gem 6:32 am	21–Gem 12:16 pm	20–Gem 6:00 pm	20–Gem 11:54 pm	21–Gem 5:37 am	21–Gem 1:25 pm
June	21–Can 4:23 pm	21–Can 1:13 am	21–Can 6:55 am	21–Can 2:43 pm	21–Can 8:21 pm	21–Can 2:07 am	21–Can 8:01 am	21–Can 1:38 pm	21–Can 7:27 pm
July	23–Leo 8:16 am	22–Leo 2:13 pm	22–Leo 8:05 pm	23–Leo 1:38 am	23–Leo 7:15 am	22–Leo 1:03 pm	22–Leo 6:56 pm	23–Leo 12:30 am	23–Leo 7:23 am
Aug	23–Vir 3:13 pm	22–Vir 9:52 pm	23–Vir 2:35 am	23–Vir 6:35 am	23–Vir 2:16 pm	22–Vir 8:04 pm	23–Vir 1:55 am	23–Vir 7:29 am	23–Vir 1:24 pm
Sept	23–Lib 12:38 pm	22–Lib 6:26 pm	23–Lib 12:07 am	23–Lib 5:59 am	23–Lib 11:47 am	22–Lib 5:34 pm	23–Lib 11:22 pm	23–Lib 4:59 am	23–Lib 10:56 am
Oct	23–Sc 9:44 pm	23–Sc 1:30 am	23–Sc 9:03 am	23–Sc 3:05 pm	22–Sc 8:53 pm	23–Sc 2:42 am	23–Sc 8:31 am	23–Sc 2:12 pm	23–Sc 8:07 pm
Nov	22–Sag 7:05 pm	22–Sag 12:59 pm	22–Sag 6:23 am	22–Sag 12:25 pm	22–Sag 6:15 pm	22–Sag 12:04 am	22–Sag 5:55 am	22–Sag 11:39 am	22–Sag 5:32 pm
Dec	22–Cap 8:17 am	21–Cap 2:00 pm	21–Cap 7:44 pm	22–Cap 1:36 am	22–Cap 5:26 am	21–Cap 1:14 pm	21–Cap 7:09 pm	22–Cap 12:57 am	22–Cap 7:47 am

12

Capricorn: The Big Picture

Because the twelve signs of the zodiac represent twelve ways of being in the world, you will know more about yourself and why you tend toward certain types of behavior and attitudes by knowing more about Capricorn. If you read about the elements and qualities in "Defining Terms," for instance, you'll find out that you are one of the practical, stable *earth signs*, and, as one of the *cardinal signs*, you are the type who can get things and people moving. You can "meet yourself" in the Capricorn prototype described in "Twelve Places At The Table," and your serious, demanding planetary ruler, Saturn, provides some excellent clues about the Capricorn style.

However, even with these broad brush strokes, your Capricorn portrait is still a bit abstract; to "see yourself" in totality, you need more of the background filled in. That means going back to some very important basics: your tenth place position in the zodiac, your picture-symbol, the mountain or sea goat, and the shorthand figure or glyph that astrologers use to indicate Capricorn when they draw up a horoscope. In Capricorn, as in every astrological sign, these three factors link together, forming a strong chain of meaning that holds together everything that is Capricorn.

On or about December 22, the sun reaches zero degrees Capricorn, and appears to stop, if only momentarily. This is the winter solstice, when the earth reaches its maximum tilt away from the sun, and the days on earth are their shortest. After this the earth will reverse its direction, and we know that spring will definitely come again. To the ancients, the winter solstice was a time of feasting and celebration, because, although the long winter nights were still ahead, there was no doubt that the earth would be reborn in the spring. As the first winter sign, Capricorn represents that period of human life where man ceases his endless exploration and expansion represented by Sagittarius, the preceding sign, and turns inward to stabilize his forces, digging in to become a useful and responsible member of society. Like the winter season itself, the sign Capricorn has an outer serenity, but underneath it is constantly planning ahead and thinking about next spring. The symbolism of the Christ Child, born at the winter solstice, is one of man in his infancy and the constant renewal of life. Capricorn is associated not with infancy, but with old age and wisdom—the Father Time with a sickle that is associated with the turning of the new year. During the winter season, mankind must "get by," sometimes existing on the scant rations of the fall harvest. Capricorns exhibit a remarkable ability to endure, and to use their resources sparingly in anticipation of future gain. Capricorn may be penny-foolish, but he/she is always pound-wise.

Capricorn's picture-symbol takes two forms—the more common one is the mountain goat. This creature survives on surefootedness and an ability to climb slowly rather than leap ahead impulsively. Capricorns too are generally careful people, calculating each move precisely to make sure it puts them in a better position to reach the top of the mountain. It is useful to think of the mountain goat in terms of its ultimate goal: the juicy leaves and plants that grow only at the peak. The mountain goat, and the Capricorn, are capable of sacrificing immediate gratification for the sake of future rewards.

The other picture-symbol associated with Capricorn is the sea goat, a divine creature who already possesses the riches of the sea (symbolized by its fishy tail), and now seeks to climb onto the land (with the goat part of its body) in order to make its riches useful to all of mankind. While the mountain goat only wants to satisfy its own hunger and improve its own position, the sea goat represents a higher order and wants to serve and be useful to others. Capricorns too come in several varieties, and can be the most mercenary, earth-bound people, or the most truly spiritual and giving human beings.

The Capricorn goat has many roots in antiquity and was often associated with divinity, sometimes with "God the father." In the natural zodiac, Capricorn is at the zenith or highest point of the wheel—a very privileged position. It is as if Capricorn has always been associated with both power (the father) and the responsibilities that go with it. In the best of Capricorns, this patriarchal attitude comes through as a sincere willingness to help and support others. In virtually all Capricorns, the sense of responsibility is very strong.

The shorthand symbol or glyph astrologers use to indicate Capricorn (see illustration) is sometimes interpreted as an abstract of the sea goat—the top part representing the horns and head of this mythological creature, and the curvy lower half the fish's tail.

A more pertinent interpretation of the symbol is as the knee joints of the human body (one of the parts "ruled" by Capricorn). Without flexible knee joints, man is virtually immobilized; it is the ability to bend the knees that allows us to climb upward—like the typical Capricorn. In a more spiritual connotation, men bend their knees in kneeling, when they demonstrate humility in front of a higher power. The more evolved Capricorn has both great worldly ambition and a sense that there is a higher power to be thanked for it.

13

Capricorn: Objectives and Obstacles

A Game Plan for Being the Most Successful Capricorn Under the Sun

Every astrological sign is a set of possibilities; being born under a particular sign does not guarantee you *are* or *will be* all those things that sign is capable of being. Nor would you want to. There are positive characteristics to be cultivated, as well as negative ones you can avoid or overcome. Living "à la carte"—selecting what you want from all the options available—is open to you, within the overall context of your sign.

You can, of course, order the "prix fixe" dinner by living your life as it comes without attempting to direct it. The choice is yours, which is one good reason it is incorrect to regard your astrological destiny as preordained. You are responsible for how you embody our sign and what results from that embodiment.

Astrologically speaking, your life as a sign is a journey with a starting point, the raw or "primitive" end of the sign, and a destination, the evolved or "ideal" realization of that sign. Once again, you don't have to take the full trip; there are plenty of exits if you choose to use them, and few people are ever totally "finished." But if you at least know where you are going and what potential booby traps lie along the way, you will be way ahead of the game.

Regard the following as a map and use it in charting

your course. The most successful way to be the best of your astrological sign is to work with it, in full knowledge of its up side and its down side. The happiest people of any astrological sign are those who aim high, and are not afraid to stretch their understanding of themselves in order to reach their goal.

Where Capricorn Starts

The common stereotype of the Capricorn as an ambitious, unfeeling, sometimes uscrupulous person is unfortunately an accurate picture of many unevolved Capricorns. All Capricorns must wrestle with their urgent need to be somebody, and some of them lose the battle. Either they take the wrong road up the mountain or get stalled somewhere along the way. When that happens, a Capricorn can become a very bitter person, and an unattractive one as well. A Capricorn who has not made it—at least by his/her own high standards—can bring down upon him-/herself the worst Capricorn demon, loneliness. It is a pity that this earth sign, who has the potential to be warm and supportive, can become so cold and aloof if the world does not live up to his/her expectations.

In some Capricorns, their naturally warm earth sign nature is lived out simply as a desire for material goods rather than an impulse to build. Amassing more and more things for their own sake, this kind of Capricorn can become insufferably materialistic and power-hungry. The unevolved type wants power over others as well, rather than the responsibility for taking care of them. The unevolved Capricorn's way of exhibiting this kind of power can take some unpleasant forms—from relatively mild meddling to out-and-out emotional manipulation, with money often used as the weapon. Capricorns are also very concerned with their image, and can spend an inordinate amount of time and money on looking good and creating a facade of status. Such people are often not only dull, but also snobbishly intolerant of anyone they do not consider worth knowing.

Here are some buzz words by which you can recognize the primitive or unevolved Capricorn type:

Controlling	Pessimistic
Compulsive	Overly conventional
Narrow minded	Stingy
Unsympathetic	Self-centered
Inhibited	Tricky/secretive

Where Capricorn Can Go

What many people misunderstand about Capricorn is that it is a sign destined to work toward a position of responsibility. Capricorn's symbolic meaning in the zodiac is the individual who is a pillar of society—with his internal character totally dedicated to and wedded with his position of responsibility in the world. Metaphysically speaking, a person enters the world in this sign because one is ready to learn about the responsibility of power. The ultimate goal of the evolving Capricorn is *total integrity*. What you see should be what you get, and it should be very sound. The evolved Capricorn does not need to manipulate others; what he/she gets, he/she deserves, because it is earned through hard work and dedication. The real destiny of the Capricorn is to serve in some kind of public office or position where he/she can use his/her talents to better life for everyone.

An evolved Capricorn is a master of one job, one profession, one role in life. He/she is the individual who can *do*, and is totally trustworthy to do what is necessary without supervision. Capricorn *is* the supervisor. The evolved Capricorn is also able to exist without constant patting on the back; he/she approves of him/herself, and does not need worldly approval as desperately as so many primitive Capricorns—and people in general—often do. True self-esteem, without self-aggrandizement, is available to the Capricorn more than to many other signs.

Here are some buzz words by which you can recognize the evolved or "ideal" Capricorn person:

Calmly successful	Reliable
Good problem-solver	Determined
Loyal	Humorous
Structured but not rigid	Prudent but giving
Capable of great concentration	Warmly supportive

How Capricorn Can Get There

It is uncanny how many Capricorns experience a feeling of loneliness, even in the center of a crowd. However, it is really a sense of aloneness that arises from this sign's awareness of the need to become self-sufficient. The wise Capricorn will use that feeling of inner solitude to get to know and like him-/herself and to figure out what his/her goals *really* are. Whatever they are, Capricorn has great resources with which to achieve them. Patience and self-discipline are an inherent part of the Capricorn makeup, and they should be cultivated. One of Capricorn's most powerful success skills is the ability to wait until the moment is right. The correct timing is a critical component of any life victory—which is why Capricorn can so often win the day.

Capricorn is also famous for looking at the practical side of things, which is why this sign is so often in the position of deciding whether or not something will work. Most Capricorns would do well to develop their fantasy lives a bit more, but they should never undervalue their incredible ability to tell a workable idea from a pure flight of someone's fancy. Coupled with Capricorn's iron will and unrelenting logic, this talent should take Capricorn anywhere he/she wants to go.

Potential Pitfalls

The extreme sense of responsibility most Capricorns feel from a very early age can be either a blessing or a terrible burden. It is important for Capricorns to achieve some kind of balance between their necessity to perform useful work and their very human desire for play. The trick for Capricorn is to learn how to relax *without guilt*. It can be as simple as scheduling leisure time as rigidly as many Capricorns schedule their work time.

Along with a sense of responsibility, another dubious Capricorn attribute is the ability to exercise great self-control. What could possibly be wrong with that? Plenty, because some Capricorns self-control themselves right into emotional oblivion. There are Capricorns who literally train themselves not to feel—though that may not be their intention. Even the Capricorn who retains the capacity to feel may have a lot of difficulty expressing those feelings—and strike others as just plain *cold*. The most fortunate Capricorns are those who team up with the right life partner, one who is able to see through that surface reserve and get to the warm, caring person who is really there underneath it all.

14

Pairing Off with Capricorn

Your Compatibility with Other Signs of the Zodiac

Since there are only twelve signs of the zodiac, it would be unusual to go through life without having to interact with each of them at one time or another. Obviously, your astrological makeup is more complex than your Capricorn sun sign, but there are some basic truths about how you tend to react when face to face with someone of another sun sign. If you read "The Geometry of Relationships," you already know that being an earth sign means Capricorn relates more easily to certain elements than to others. Now, getting more specific, you will see what the odds are on your matchups with each of the other signs, including your own.

When people talk about "relationships," they are usually referring to the romantic kind, and there is no doubt that since time immemorial love has been observed to have a great deal to do with keeping the earth revolving in its orbit. However, we also have a lot of other personal interactions, from important ones, like boss-employee and parent-child, to more casual ones, like waitress-patron, cabdriver-rider, and buddy-buddy. The general "rules" that follow apply in all cases; just change the language a little and do a bit of interpretation. You will find that there is more truth than poetry in the matter of astrological compatibility.

Capricorn with Aries Aries's wonderful spontaneity will either drive you to distraction or loosen you up. In most cases, it will probably be the latter. At least you don't feel you have to tell self-starting Aries to get moving; he/she wouldn't let you anyway. Aries' warm heart pours out the pragmatic kind of love you like, not the sloppy kind. You will be good companions for each other, and—if you manage to polish up Aries' rough edges—you will have a life partner that suits you in many ways.

Capricorn with Taurus This is a relationship that may vibrate at a fairly low frequency, but it should work rather well. Since you are both earth signs, your approach to life is essentially practical. You both want the finer things, too, but Taurus will show you how to really enjoy them. Some people may consider the two of you a rather sedate pair, but they don't know what you've really got together. Taurus will awake your slumbering sexuality.

Capricorn with Gemini Gemini's "cool" will appeal to you, because you won't feel as if someone is trying to crawl into your heart. This may start on a purely conversational level, but could go a lot farther rather nicely. However, it's just possible that Gemini may leave you thinking, "there must be more to life than this." If that is the case with you, then you should try one of the zodiac's more intensely emotional types.

Capricorn with Cancer If the Cancer in question is typical, it is doubtful that you will be attracted—even though this sexy sign will appear rather glamorous to you at the outset. Cancer demands much too much of a partner's emotional system for you to be totally comfortable. Also, Cancer's clinging behavior could prove an annoying distraction from your important work in this world. Make it a great sexual affair, and leave it at that.

Capricorn with Leo Leo is not likely to start psychoanalyzing you and telling you to relax. He/she will simply show you how to have a wonderful time. Leo's brand of warmth is also just your cup of tea, and you share a love of what is rich and beautiful. Though Leo will demand your complete loyalty, he/she won't make excessive demands on your time. Mainly because Leo also usually has something very important to do. This could be a marvelous match for you.

Capricorn with Virgo Like you, Virgo is a realist, but the compatibility will probably end there. You've got enough to worry about and won't want to deal with Virgo's hangups and inhibitions; and you could drive each other into a combination of a nervous breakdown and a serious case of melancholia. As business associates you would be fabulous, because you've got the drive and Virgo's got the detail ability to back you up.

Capricorn with Libra This could be the proverbial marriage made in heaven. Libra desperately needs a strong person to lean on and will make few overly emotional demands in return. Libra's also got the light touch that you lack, and is generally as devoted to the luxury life as you are. The only danger here is that you will not be as verbally demonstrative as romantic Libra would like, but it's worth it to try.

Capricorn with Scorpio You've both got wills of iron and incredible powers of self-discipline; therefore, this could be the Mexican stand-off of all time. If you do let yourselves go and get involved, it could mean a whole new life for both of you. You would learn what it's really like to be possessed; Scorpio would find out there is someone who matches his/her strengths. Not the easiest of relationships, but surely an interesting one.

Capricorn with Sagittarius Occasionally "flaky" Sagittarius does not seem to have enough "cement" holding him/her together, though the sign's charming ways and amusing ideas will temporarily capture your fancy. After that, it's all downhill. In business, however, this could be the winning combination of all time. Sagittarius's ideas fly high and your practicality pulls them back down to earth, where they really work.

Capricorn with Capricorn Capricorn may show you a few things about yourself—and you may not like them. Unless you have both matured and done some soul-searching, you are likely to leave each other cold. In spite of the fact that you instinctively understand what makes each other tick, a lasting relationship might just be too serious for both of you. Take Capricorn on for chess.

Capricorn with Aquarius You are likely to feel great admiration for Aquarius, and the feeling is likely to be mutual. Aquarius is a fairly self-contained type like you, so you won't frighten each other off with excessive emotional demands. Your reason appeals to logical Aquarius, and vice versa. As permanent partners, you could build a solid and sensible relationship—and eventually engage each others' deep-lying emotions. Give this relationship a lot of time to develop.

Capricorn with Pisces Unless you are a rather unusual Capricorn, you will eventually be turned off by Pisces' inability to get his/her act together. Pisces may need you desperately and appeal to your protective instincts, but in the long run you would both be miserable. You would expect more stability than Pisces is able to give; Pisces would constantly wonder why you aren't more giving. A no-win situation all the way around.

15

The Capricorn Sex Role Dilemma

One of the most important ways in which the twelve signs of the zodiac are divided is into "masculine" signs and "feminine" signs, and there are six of each. The reason is simple: As one sign follows the other in the zodiac, they alternate energies, much like the Yin/Yang principle of eastern philosophy. The universe is made up of opposites that complement each other: light, and dark, hot and cold, black and white, hard and soft. One is not better than the other; rather, each is essential to the existence of its opposite. In other words, you can't have one without the other.

The six fire and air signs are "masculine," since fire and air are connected with *active, assertive, outgoing* energy.

Aries	Gemini
Leo	Libra
Sagittarius	Aquarius

The six water and earth signs are "feminine," because water and earth represent *reactive, inner-directed, receptive* energy.

Taurus	Cancer
Virgo	Scorpio
Capricorn	Pisces

To put it simply, *the masculine fire and air signs are positive, while the earth and water signs are negative.* To remain neutral and avoid placing a higher value on one or the other kind of energy (or sign) it is useful to think of a battery with positive and negative poles. Without both, it simply doesn't work.

Though the masculine-feminine division of the signs has nothing whatever to do with human physical sexuality or sexual preference, it has very important implications for human behavior. Bluntly put, women born into male signs can be more "masculine"/achieving/competitive than men born into female signs. On the other hand, men born in female signs can be more "feminine"/nurturing/cooperative than women born into male signs. Both men and women born into signs that match their own sex may overemphasize the behavior and attitudes connected with that gender. The "ideal" person, psychologically and metaphysically speaking, has a healthy mix of both "masculine" and "feminine" attitudes. Without at least some of both, we cannot be whole people able to encompass and understand the total range of human emotions, desires, drives, and goals. Since none of us is perfect, just about everyone could stand a bit more "gender blending." Your astrological sign offers some excellent clues about how you can accomplish that.

Since Capricorn is one of the earth signs, the women born under it should find womanliness a natural role. However, the builder-material provider aspect of the feminine principle is so strong in Capricorn, that Capricorn women often have difficulty experiencing an easy flow of emotions and the merging of those emotions with others. The Capricorn woman's power drive is very strong, and the Capricorn mechanism of self-control in order to achieve power sometimes puts a clamp on her emotional life.

The Capricorn male, born into a female sign, should theoretically have a leg up when it comes to achieving a balance between his masculine assertiveness and his feminine receptivity. However, he's got a problem too. The Capricorn male is so determined to be successful that he will use all the weapons at his command to do so. One of his "weapons" is often the ability to manipulate others through his built-in understanding of the emotions that make them tick. The Capricorn male often uses his capacity to understand feeling to *understand the feelings of others* and bend them to his will accordingly. With his own emotional life, however, he sometimes experiences a total blank.

The Capricorn sex role dilemma boils down to this: The women have got to learn to ease up and be the natural women they are. The men must attempt to understand the difference between "using" feelings and really experiencing them. Keep these points in mind as you read the portraits of the Capricorn female and male that follow.

16

The Capricorn Female

A Woman of Substance

There are some Capricorn women, particularly those with lighter rising signs, who appear to be all grace and fluttery charm, carefree and relaxed in whatever environment they inhabit. However, under the surface of even this type lies a strong heart with a steady beat, and a firm conviction that life is a serious business. Early on, the Capricorn female observed that a strong woman is able to both control the ship and keep it on a steady course. Her role model was probably her mother, who dominated the scene, at least in the eyes of the young Capricorn. But even if her childhood scenario was not the classic one of strong mother and passive father, the Capricorn girl was raised in an atmosphere where duty and responsibility had the highest priority and were considered necessary virtues, regardless of one's sex.

Many a Capricorn woman has a hard-won leadership medal hidden away among her souvenirs, and whatever other honors she may gain in her lifetime, they are likely to be treasured. The Capricorn female is born with a built-in desire to win, and it is generally well-fed by her early environment. As she goes on through life, the Capricorn woman may gain in self-confidence, but she will rarely, if ever, say, "now I've made it." There is always a higher mountain to climb, another goal to be reached—and more reason for her to continue driving herself, and sometimes the other people in her life. Self-control comes naturally to her, and she expects it from everyone else. As a result, she is all too often less than satisfied—with herself and the world around her.

As a child, the Capricorn girl is often what is called a "plain Jane." Even if she possesses all the basic features that will eventually confer female beauty and sex appeal, her stable manner and desire to be useful can effectively hide her gentler charms. Capricorn girls desperately desire approval for themselves from both of their parents. By docile behavior and application to responsibilities they may earn some of it, but approval simply for "being a girl" can be frustratingly elusive, particularly from Dad. One of the early lessons she learns very well is to keep a tight lid on her emotions; Whatever signals she receives, they convey the message to her that her own emotions serve very little purpose. And, that everything in life must "work."

As a young woman, the Capricorn female may leave the nest fairly early to try her well-trained wings. However, for all her strengths, she may not realize at first how much she has going for her, and can let lack of self-confidence make her aim rather low. Almost before she's been on the job a week, however, a Capricorn woman's boss will have discovered he/she has got a gem. As the rewards start to come, the Capricorn woman releases the brakes on her power drive, and then there's no stopping her.

No matter what her childhood economic circumstances, most Capricorn women believe that the best things in life come with the highest price tags. Quality and value are likely to be their watchwords in everything. As the money begins to roll in from her own efforts and enables her to "feed her habits," she reaches a point of no return and often adopts an attitude of entitlement. For many a Capricorn woman, the next scenario is a marriage to someone who shares her goals of substance and status, and there's a happily-ever-after ending to her story. However, many Capricorn women—with or without a history of success under their own belts—marry the "wrong man," i.e., one whose drive and dollar sense does not match their own. If the Capricorn woman attempts to change such a man, she can easily destroy the marriage. If she attempts to suffer in silence, she could fall into one of the states of deep melancholy that often plague this sign. Are all Capricorn women mercenary? Certainly not, and money and power alone are not their *real* goals. A strong desire for security and dedication to duty are, however, and in many cases the Capricorn woman finds these things sadly lacking in the man she chooses.

As a mate, the Capricorn woman is capable of great sacrifices for the sake of her husband and family; it is in the role of staunch partner that she really proves her mettle. If she has chosen wisely, she's got a mate who wants it all as much as she does—and she is willing to wait. Patience, too, is one of the greater Capricorn virtues. However, even if circumstances are strict, she will make the best of everything; there is rarely anything slipshod about the Capricorn wife's household or the way she runs it. When happily partnered, the Capricorn woman often begins to let her natural warmth flow freely, and grows comfortable enough with her own emotions to be the natural woman she really is. Any sexual inhibitions she may have had were merely self-protective devices, and she has no need for them anymore. Even if the Capricorn woman does not work outside the home, she will usually seek a leadership position in community work, local politics, or some other group. The need to be useful and the desire to lead don't vanish into thin air with the marriage contract and/or economic security.

As a mother, the Capricorn woman must make an effort to become self-aware, and not to pass some of her more negative attitudes on to her children. She may regard those attitudes as positive—self-discipline, a serious attitude toward life, and the ambition to be "the best"—and, in moderation, they are. However, her children are unique human beings, and her wisest course is to let them develop their own perceptions of the world and make their own mistakes. Capricorn women like everything neat and tidy, and that goes for children too. The Capricorn mother is likely to have the cleanest children on the block, and that is all to her credit. However, as a woman born into an earth sign, she should try to remember that getting dirty is a natural part of childhood.

17

The Capricorn Male

The Strong Silent Type

The Capricorn male often senses the fact that he has a mission in life. Because he is an earth sign, and the most powerful (cardinal) one at that, his "mission" is usually to build something of consequence in the material world. While males of the previous sign—fiery Sagittarius—keep their eyes on the farthest stars, men born under the sign of Capricorn rarely let their steady gaze stray from the objects of their earthly ambitions. The result is that many a Capricorn male can be accused of a lack of imagination and the "creative" sense of humor that usually goes with it. It's sad but true that many men born under this sign can be a bit too serious for comfort. However, equally many have a dry wit and are great at poking fun at the foibles of others.

Reflecting the somberness of their demanding planetary ruler, Saturn, Capricorn men often appear very mature at a very young age—at least in their attitudes. (The paradox is that men of this sign keep their youthful looks a lot longer than most.) However, no matter how grown a Capricorn male may seem in his willingness to accept responsibility, he usually has a rather underdeveloped sense of self, and the lack of self-confidence that goes with it. Underneath his stolid exterior, many a Capricorn man is as jittery as a teenager on his first date when he approaches any life situation where he's got to put himself on the line.

As a child, the Capricorn male begins to exhibit his maturity quite early—often to the astonishment of his parents. Who is this little man who doesn't have to be told to put his toys away? On the other hand, his quiet determination and stubbornness can prove difficult to deal with, even more difficult than the temper tantrums his self-control makes him able to avoid. Many Capricorn boys get quite close to their mothers, developing an admiration for their strength and ability to control things. Though in most cases the Capricorn male sees his father as a man of accomplishment, he also sees his mother as the real power behind the throne. By observing her, he often develops some subtle strategies for dealing with the world.

As a young man, the typical Capricorn male starts out on a power trip that will last his whole lifetime. Perhaps because patience is built in to the Capricorn personality, many Capricorns are late bloomers—particularly the males. They are not so much interested in instant success as in building a firm base from which to step carefully to the next plateau. Though they often perform brilliantly, they do it rather quietly; there is a shyness in the Capricorn male that most people never realize. Yes, they want money and power, but they would just as soon avoid the limelight of glory that sometimes goes along with material success. Contrary to popular belief, when a Capricorn gets money, he rarely splashes it around in the showy way that, for instance, a Leo may. Money means security (a lot of it), comfort, and a freedom to indulge his taste for the best the world has to offer. In most cases, the only person Capricorn is really trying to impress is himself, that inner "task master" who wants tangible proof of hard work and dedication to duty.

In his emotional life, the young Capricorn male is a lot less rational than he appears to be in his professional life. Though he isn't usually prone to hot pursuits and head-over-heels involvements, he is very serious about tracking down the perfect life partner and he sets some pretty high standards. Aside from all the obvious criteria the love of his life must meet—like physical attractiveness, a brain, at least a modicum of breeding—the Capricorn male is also looking for that understanding female who will be able to penetrate his rather stony exterior and get to the real person underneath. Since the typical Capricorn male puts up a rather thick wall between himself and others, it takes a mighty determined female to stick with it long enough to find out how caring he can really be. Ironically, the Capricorn male is pretty good at manipulating women via their emotions; one common ploy is for him to push the "you're-the-only-one-who-understands-me" button and evoke a sense of guilt in the woman who may want to call it quits.

As a mate, the Capricorn man is pretty close to ideal—at least for a certain kind of woman. Once he's let someone into his life, the Capricorn male is generally faithful to her and so appreciative of her love that he will lavish her with the best there is, or whatever he can afford within his particular circumstances. Even the most successful of Capricorn men never forget that the more money you leave in the bank, the more interest you draw. But, since he's usually chosen a woman who shares his ambitions and goals, she is as dedicated to growth as he is, and is willing to take life one reward at a time. The Capricorn male is rarely what you would call "Mr. Excitement," and he may have to extend himself a bit to keep a more restless mate happy. Since you can depend on the fact that he will always do "the right thing," the typical Capricorn man will carefully figure out just what is in order to fix the situation—and order it for his wife.

As a father, the Capricorn man runs the risk of being the stereotypical authority figure who raises children strictly; severe punishment awaits those who violate his rules of discipline. Few ever really approach this extreme, but most Capricorn fathers have to work on being warm, nonthreatening fathers. Since many were such well-disciplined children themselves, they find it hard to forgive the normal antics of more active children. Capricorn men are better with their children after those children have reached the age of reason and can understand that what their father really wants is for them to be happy adults—at least in his own terms.

18

Capricorn Help Wanted

Selecting a Career/Your On-the-Job Style

A vitally important aspect of a successful Capricorn game plan is making sure you land in the right job or career—i.e., the one that best suits your native talents and tendencies. It is more than a truism that people perform better doing what comes naturally. There are some natural careers for Capricorn, and they have several common denominators. One is the setting of limits, as in any kind of regulatory job or career in the public or the private sector. The other is "numbers"—in any form, from statistics to accounting to banking and finance. It is not possible to list all the specific jobs a Capricorn should do well at, but there are some Capricorn images that provide useful guidelines. Though you may not literally end up *doing* any of these things, if you try to conjure up an idea of what it takes to do the following jobs, you'll have a better handle on what kind of inner resources Capricorn people have available to them for career success.

Real estate speculator	Dentist/dental hygienist
Public education administrator	Sculptor/stoneworker
Math professor	Science teacher
Labor leader/lobbyest	Geriatric counselor

Mortgage administrator/loan officer
Sanitation engineer
Tax accountant
Insurance actuary

Equally important to getting in the best job slot for you is understanding how your Capricorn sun sign affects your modus operandi on the job and your potential for moving up. Every sun sign has certain "success skills" that can smooth and widen the career path, as well as "blind spots" that can cause roadblocks. The more you know about both, the better off you will be.

Capricorn has an unusually long and important list of attributes which should spell success for almost anyone born under this sign. As the Cardinal earth sign, Capricorn should have both the drive and the ability to really make things happen. Anyone who has even a modicum of the self-discipline and sense of responsibility that belong to this sun sign should be way ahead of most of the competition.

With Capricorn, it is more important to focus on the potential negatives than all the positives you should have right at your fingertips. The biggest roadblock to Capricorn success can be the inability to see things as they *might* be rather than as they are. It is important for people born under this sign to train themselves to envision the future and not get bogged down in the present. The natural optimism of the fire signs Aries, Leo and Sagittarius is not among the Capricorn givens, so it is difficult for Capricorns to "take things on faith." While it is good to be realistic, it is also often necessary to imagine other possibilities than the ones that seem to exist. It is also important for Capricorn to learn to cooperate with others in their imaginative efforts; the role of the Capricorn in the brainstorming session should not be simply to shoot ideas down, but also to support them with realistic suggestions.

The real moral problem for many Capricorns intent on success is how to achieve that success without harming anyone else in the process. Many Capricorns are very manipulative, but that style comes to them so unconsciously, that they often are not aware of the consequences of their "innocent" actions. Whenever a competitive situation arises, the Capricorns should figure out how to make him-/herself look good without making someone else look unnecessarily bad. Capricorns who try to outsmart their bosses often get their comeuppance in rather unpleasant forms; never forget your natural respect for authority figures, because it is one of your strong points. By the same token, the Capricorn *boss* must consciously refrain from "stealing thunder" from his/her subordinates. It is important to develop enough self-confidence that you can rely on your merits alone without having to feel threatened by others.

Perhaps the most difficult thing for the typical Capricorn person to realize is that a light touch is the right touch in many job situations. The serious individual who rarely (if ever) lifts his/her head from the work at hand is not necessarily always the one who reaps the biggest rewards. Those who know when to smile and when to make others do so often make a more positive impression. Though Capricorns are not always the "personality kids" of the zodiac, there is no reason why they cannot develop a warm, receptive attitude toward others in the workplace, eventually feel safe enough with their co-workers to let down the barriers and reveal themselves as real human beings, with just as many faults as everyone else.

19

How "Pure" a Capricorn Are You?

No one is a "pure Capricorn"—or pure anything, for that matter—when it comes to astrological signs. As you will learn when you read "Defining Terms," there are many other factors in a horoscope that add up to the total person that is you. Yes, there are twelve basic personality types according to the zodiac, but within those broad groups there are almost infinite variations.

Though you are a Capricorn at the core, and can count on the portrait of your sun sign to define you in essence, the two other horoscope factors that count most are in your personality profile: your moon sign and your rising sign. Many people know their moon sign; anyone can quickly determine it via an ephemeris. If you know your birth time at least within one hour, you can use the table in this book to find out what your rising sign is.

The Moon—Your "Dark Side"

Almost more than your sun sign, your moon sign indicates what makes you run. Most of the time, you do not know it yourself, because the moon is your subconscious—your "dark side" not because it is bad, but because it is hidden. When the meaning of your moon sign is added to your Capricorn sun sign, it is a fuller picture and a better indicator of your probable personality. Here's how a Capricorn sun sign mixes with each of the moon signs.

Capricorn sun sign/Aries moon sign It is possible that your determination to be better than everyone else is a bit much. However, you are a more independent-minded and less conventional Capricorn than most, and you will be able to hear that different drummer. You are a keen critic, and can really take things apart; just be more gentle with people than you are with ideas.

Capricorn sun sign/Taurus moon sign You are blessed with both a great deal of persistence and a warm attitude toward your fellow human beings. What you want you go after with skill and determination, and it comes to you fairly easily because you are ultimately practical in your methods. You will probably have a great deal of success—and no one will begrudge it to you, because you are such a caring person.

Capricorn sun sign/Gemini moon sign Your active mentality is firmly harnessed to a steady will, and it is a great combination. This is the kind of Capricorn who is readily able to come up with new ideas and more willing to consider the flights of fancy of others. You could be an excellent public speaker because your way with words is as good as your ability to follow through. Just don't get involved in more things than you can competently handle.

Capricorn sun sign/Cancer moon sign You are one of those rare Capricorns whose emotional life is an open book—at least to you. In fact, it is possible that you could let your sensitivity to slights hamper your progress. You really want to feel "comfortable" in every sense of the word, and will probably accomplish it. Just don't become a success worshipper.

Capricorn sun sign/Leo moon sign It's easy for you to be the boss—or simply try to boss everyone else around. However, you've got a lot of kindness in your heart, and a real warmth that shines through your stern facade. As much of an idealist as you are, you love to display your special talents, and the results of your success. But your "show" is quite harmless.

Capricorn sun sign/Virgo moon sign   Your thinking processes are generally clear as a bell, and your orderly mind can tackle almost anything. However, you may not like to be in the driver's seat as much as the typical Capricorn does. By the same token, you are more willing to cooperate with others. Just lighten up a little and look at life a bit less seriously. Most important, stop *worrying!*

Capricorn sun sign/Libra moon sign   You could be a real sweetheart of a Capricorn, with a genuine desire to please those around you. You also could be a bit less of a workaholic; in fact, you may find it difficult to get yourself going sometimes. Home and partner are more important to you than anything else in the world and you would do anything for them. All in all, a nice balance.

Capricorn sun sign/Scorpio moon sign   This is a rather intractable combination, and you may be rather deaf to the needs and opinions of others. You are so influential in your circle that you may get carried away with your own sense of importance. Your planning ability is excellent; just don't try to make everyone else's plans for them.

Capricorn sun sign/Sagittarius moon sign   This is a super combination for success in every aspect of life. You are determined about what you want, but willing to bend when it is necessary. Your thinking is a lot more broad-based than the typical Capricorn's as well. A built-in sense of fairness will prevent you from taking advantage of others—which you easily could do.

Capricorn sun sign/Capricorn moon sign   You've got all the Capricorn characteristics in depth, and some of them may overwhelm you. The real problem could be a tendency to despondency; Saturn weighs rather heavily on your spirits. It is important—even essential—that you open up and share your feelings with others. You have a tendency to "live in your head," too, and that can be rather lonely.

Capricorn sun sign/Aquarius moon sign   You are extremely perceptive, and able to put your talent to good use. It is easy for you to figure out what works, but you may have a tendency to disregard people you do not consider helpful in your overall scheme of things. Develop your natural warmth and generosity—and some of your rather ingenious ideas.

Capricorn sun sign/Pisces moon sign   Sadly, you may not believe in your own very good powers and abilities. Try to get up the energy and self-confidence that will propel you into the world, where you can do a really great job. Lucky for you, however, that the very things that make you shy and retiring make you very beloved by others. Don't let anxieties overtake you, but learn to trust yourself, as well as the world.

Your Rising Sign—Know Your Cover

The third of the "big three" astrological factors is your rising sign, which you can think of as an *overlay* to your sun sign. Although it does not carry the psychological weight your moon sign does, your rising sign is also "unconscious" because it is a mode of external behavior that comes so naturally to you that you may not be aware of it. In a sense, your rising sign is your cover. It can never totally obscure the real you of your sun sign, but it can temporarily mask that sign, especially when people first meet you. Here's what happens to Capricorn when you lay a rising sign over "typical" Capricorn behavior:

Capricorn with Aries Rising   You appear a lot more open and outgoing than you really are; people are surprised when you don't follow through on your initial enthusiasm.

Capricorn with Taurus rising You may seem a little slow, but you eventually make people feel very comfortable in your presence. Good for you!

Capricorn with Gemini rising There's a sharp edge to your apparent interest in others. Try to *really* listen when people give you answers.

Capricorn with Cancer rising This can be a heavy combination, although there is a certain sex appeal about you. Practice a big, wide grin.

Capricorn with Leo rising You could be a rather showy show-off, and a bit too aware of how you appear to others. Relax!

Capricorn with Virgo rising Unless there are some lighter elements in your chart, you could seem a bit austere; try to be more approachable.

Capricorn with Libra rising People with this combination are often real knockouts; follow through on your graceful ways.

Capricorn with Scorpio rising Your penetrating gaze can positively sweep people off their feet; don't be surprised when they follow you around.

Capricorn with Sagittarius rising You could seem like the most affable person in the world; it's a good cover-up for your basically shy nature.

Capricorn with Capricorn rising You appear to be the ultimate authority figure; take care not to scare off people who are as basically warm as you are.

Capricorn with Pisces rising You could be a really charming person. Underneath it all, you are really together. Good going!

20

Find Your Rising Sign

It is easier than many people think to find out your rising sign. One reason is that it is based on "universal" or "sidereal" time—the measure used in space travel. To ascertain your rising sign, look through the following chart and locate the birthdate nearest your birth date; look across and locate the time nearest your birth time. Remember that if daylight saving time was in effect at your birth, you must subtract one hour from the time stated on your birth certificate. In the section for your date and time, you will find an abbreviation for the sign that was rising when you were born. For instance, if your birthdate is June 12 at 9:30 a.m., your rising sign is Leo; if you were born on the same date at 9:30 p.m., your rising sign is Capricorn.

You will notice that the *year* you were born does not affect your rising sign. However, the geographical latitude does. These tables are calculated for the middle latitudes of the United States. If you were born far to the south, it is wise to look at the sign that *follows* your rising sign as well. If you were born far to the north, check out the *previous* sign.

Rising Signs—A.M. Births

	1 AM	2 AM	3 AM	4 AM	5 AM	6 AM	7 AM	8 AM	9 AM	10 AM	11 AM	12 NOON
Jan 1	Lib	Sc	Sc	Sc	Sag	Sag	Cap	Cap	Aq	Aq	Pis	Ar
Jan 9	Lib	Sc	Sc	Sag	Sag	Sag	Cap	Cap	Aq	Pis	Ar	Tau
Jan 17	Sc	Sc	Sc	Sag	Sag	Cap	Cap	Aq	Aq	Pis	Ar	Tau
Jan 25	Sc	Sc	Sag	Sag	Sag	Cap	Cap	Aq	Pis	Ar	Tau	Tau
Feb 2	Sc	Sc	Sag	Sag	Cap	Cap	Aq	Pis	Pis	Ar	Tau	Gem
Feb 10	Sc	Sag	Sag	Sag	Cap	Cap	Aq	Pis	Ar	Tau	Tau	Gem
Feb 18	Sc	Sag	Sag	Cap	Cap	Aq	Pis	Pis	Ar	Tau	Gem	Gem
Feb 26	Sag	Sag	Sag	Cap	Cap	Aq	Aq	Pis	Ar	Tau	Tau	Gem	Gem
Mar 6	Sag	Sag	Cap	Cap	Aq	Pis	Pis	Ar	Tau	Tau	Gem	Can
Mar 14	Sag	Cap	Cap	Aq	Aq	Pis	Ar	Tau	Tau	Gem	Gem	Can
Mar 22	Sag	Cap	Cap	Aq	Pis	Ar	Ar	Tau	Gem	Gem	Can	Can
Mar 30	Cap	Cap	Aq	Pis	Pis	Ar	Tau	Tau	Gem	Can	Can	Can
Apr 7	Cap	Cap	Aq	Pis	Ar	Ar	Tau	Gem	Gem	Can	Can	Leo
Apr 14	Cap	Aq	Aq	Pis	Ar	Tau	Tau	Gem	Gem	Can	Can	Leo
Apr 22	Cap	Aq	Pis	Ar	Ar	Tau	Gem	Gem	Gem	Can	Leo	Leo
Apr 30	Aq	Aq	Pis	Ar	Tau	Tau	Gem	Can	Can	Can	Leo	Leo
May 8	Aq	Pis	Ar	Ar	Tau	Gem	Gem	Can	Can	Leo	Leo	Leo
May 16	Aq	Pis	Ar	Tau	Gem	Gem	Can	Can	Leo	Leo	Leo	Vir
May 24	Pis	Ar	Ar	Tau	Gem	Gem	Can	Can	Leo	Leo	Leo	Vir
June 1	Pis	Ar	Tau	Gem	Gem	Can	Can	Can	Leo	Leo	Vir	Vir
June 9	Ar	Ar	Tau	Gem	Gem	Can	Can	Leo	Leo	Leo	Vir	Vir
June 17	Ar	Tau	Gem	Gem	Can	Can	Can	Leo	Leo	Vir	Vir	Vir
June 25	Tau	Tau	Gem	Gem	Can	Can	Leo	Leo	Leo	Vir	Vir	Lib
July 3	Tau	Gem	Gem	Can	Can	Can	Leo	Leo	Vir	Vir	Vir	Lib
July 11	Tau	Gem	Gem	Can	Can	Leo	Leo	Leo	Vir	Vir	Lib	Lib
July 18	Gem	Gem	Can	Can	Can	Leo	Leo	Vir	Vir	Vir	Lib	Lib
July 26	Gem	Gem	Can	Can	Leo	Leo	Leo	Vir	Vir	Lib	Lib	Lib
Aug 3	Gem	Can	Can	Can	Leo	Leo	Vir	Vir	Vir	Lib	Lib	Sc
Aug 11	Gem	Can	Can	Leo	Leo	Leo	Vir	Vir	Lib	Lib	Lib	Sc
Aug 18	Can	Can	Can	Leo	Leo	Vir	Vir	Vir	Lib	Lib	Sc	Sc
Aug 27	Can	Can	Leo	Leo	Leo	Vir	Vir	Lib	Lib	Lib	Sc	Sc
Sept 4	Can	Can	Leo	Leo	Leo	Vir	Vir	Vir	Lib	Lib	Sc	Sc
Sept 12	Can	Leo	Leo	Leo	Vir	Vir	Lib	Lib	Lib	Sc	Sc	Sag
Sept 20	Leo	Leo	Leo	Leo	Vir	Vir	Vir	Lib	Lib	Lib	Sc	Sag
Sept 28	Leo	Leo	Leo	Vir	Vir	Lib	Lib	Lib	Sc	Sc	Sag	Sag
Oct 6	Leo	Leo	Vir	Vir	Vir	Lib	Lib	Sc	Sc	Sc	Sag	Sag
Oct 14	Leo	Vir	Vir	Vir	Lib	Lib	Lib	Sc	Sc	Sag	Sag	Cap
Oct 22	Leo	Vir	Vir	Lib	Lib	Lib	Sc	Sc	Sc	Sag	Sag	Cap
Oct 30	Vir	Vir	Vir	Lib	Lib	Sc	Sc	Sc	Sag	Sag	Cap	Cap
Nov 7	Vir	Vir	Lib	Lib	Lib	Sc	Sc	Sc	Sag	Sag	Cap	Cap
Nov 15	Vir	Vir	Lib	Lib	Sc	Sc	Sc	Sag	Sag	Cap	Cap	Aq
Nov 23	Vir	Lib	Lib	Lib	Sc	Sc	Sag	Sag	Sag	Cap	Cap	Aq
Dec 1	Vir	Lib	Lib	Sc	Sc	Sc	Sag	Sag	Cap	Cap	Aq	Aq
Dec 9	Lib	Lib	Lib	Sc	Sc	Sag	Sag	Sag	Cap	Cap	Aq	Pis
Dec 18	Lib	Lib	Sc	Sc	Sc	Sag	Sag	Cap	Cap	Aq	Aq	Pis
Dec 28	Lib	Lib	Sc	Sc	Sag	Sag	Sag	Cap	Aq	Aq	Pis	Ar

Rising Signs—P.M. Births

	1 PM	2 PM	3 PM	4 PM	5 PM	6 PM	7 PM	8 PM	9 PM	10 PM	11 PM	12 MIDNIGHT
Jan 1	Tau	Gem	Gem	Can	Can	Can	Leo	Leo	Vir	Vir	Vir	Lib
Jan 9	Tau	Gem	Gem	Can	Can	Leo	Leo	Leo	Vir	Vir	Vir	Lib
Jan 17	Gem	Gem	Can	Can	Can	Leo	Leo	Vir	Vir	Vir	Lib	Lib
Jan 25	Gem	Gem	Can	Can	Leo	Leo	Leo	Vir	Vir	Lib	Lib	Lib
Feb 2	Gem	Can	Can	Can	Leo	Leo	Vir	Vir	Vir	Lib	Lib	Sc
Feb 10	Gem	Can	Can	Leo	Leo	Leo	Vir	Vir	Lib	Lib	Lib	Sc
Feb 18	Can	Can	Can	Leo	Leo	Vir	Vir	Vir	Lib	Lib	Sc	Sc
Feb 26	Can	Can	Leo	Leo	Leo	Vir	Vir	Lib	Lib	Lib	Sc	Sc
Mar 6	Can	Leo	Leo	Leo	Vir	Vir	Vir	Lib	Lib	Sc	Sc	Sc
Mar 14	Can	Leo	Leo	Vir	Vir	Vir	Lib	Lib	Lib	Sc	Sc	Sag
Mar 22	Leo	Leo	Leo	Vir	Vir	Lib	Lib	Lib	Sc	Sc	Sc	Sag
Mar 30	Leo	Leo	Vir	Vir	Vir	Lib	Lib	Sc	Sc	Sc	Sag	Sag
Apr 7	Leo	Leo	Vir	Vir	Lib	Lib	Lib	Sc	Sc	Sc	Sag	Sag
Apr 14	Leo	Vir	Vir	Vir	Lib	Lib	Sc	Sc	Sc	Sag	Sag	Cap
Apr 22	Leo	Vir	Vir	Lib	Lib	Lib	Sc	Sc	Sc	Sag	Sag	Cap
Apr 30	Vir	Vir	Vir	Lib	Lib	Sc	Sc	Sc	Sag	Sag	Cap	Cap
May 8	Vir	Vir	Lib	Lib	Lib	Sc	Sc	Sag	Sag	Sag	Cap	Cap
May 16	Vir	Vir	Lib	Lib	Sc	Sc	Sc	Sag	Sag	Cap	Cap	Aq
May 24	Vir	Lib	Lib	Lib	Sc	Sc	Sag	Sag	Sag	Cap	Cap	Aq
June 1	Vir	Lib	Lib	Sc	Sc	Sc	Sag	Sag	Cap	Cap	Aq	Aq
June 9	Lib	Lib	Lib	Sc	Sc	Sag	Sag	Sag	Cap	Cap	Aq	Pis
June 17	Lib	Lib	Sc	Sc	Sc	Sag	Sag	Cap	Cap	Aq	Aq	Pis
June 25	Lib	Lib	Sc	Sc	Sag	Sag	Sag	Cap	Cap	Aq	Pis	Ar
July 3	Lib	Sc	Sc	Sc	Sag	Sag	Cap	Cap	Aq	Aq	Pis	Ar
July 11	Lib	Sc	Sc	Sag	Sag	Sag	Cap	Cap	Aq	Pis	Ar	Tau
July 18	Sc	Sc	Sc	Sag	Sag	Cap	Cap	Aq	Aq	Pis	Ar	Tau
July 26	Sc	Sc	Sag	Sag	Sag	Cap	Cap	Aq	Pis	Ar	Tau	Tau
Aug 3	Sc	Sc	Sag	Sag	Cap	Cap	Aq	Aq	Pis	Ar	Tau	Gem
Aug 11	Sc	Sag	Sag	Sag	Cap	Cap	Aq	Pis	Ar	Tau	Tau	Gem
Aug 18	Sc	Sag	Sag	Cap	Cap	Aq	Pis	Pis	Ar	Tau	Gem	Gem
Aug 27	Sag	Sag	Sag	Cap	Cap	Aq	Pis	Ar	Tau	Tau	Gem	Gem
Sept 4	Sag	Sag	Cap	Cap	Aq	Pis	Pis	Ar	Tau	Gem	Gem	Can
Sept 12	Sag	Sag	Cap	Aq	Aq	Pis	Ar	Tau	Tau	Gem	Gem	Can
Sept 20	Sag	Cap	Cap	Aq	Pis	Pis	Ar	Tau	Gem	Gem	Can	Can
Sept 28	Cap	Cap	Aq	Aq	Pis	Ar	Tau	Tau	Gem	Gem	Can	Can
Oct 6	Cap	Cap	Aq	Pis	Ar	Ar	Tau	Gem	Gem	Can	Can	Leo
Oct 14	Cap	Aq	Aq	Pis	Ar	Tau	Tau	Gem	Gem	Can	Can	Leo
Oct 22	Cap	Aq	Pis	Ar	Ar	Tau	Gem	Gem	Can	Can	Leo	Leo
Oct 30	Aq	Aq	Pis	Ar	Tau	Tau	Gem	Can	Can	Can	Leo	Leo
Nov 7	Aq	Aq	Pis	Ar	Tau	Tau	Gem	Can	Can	Can	Leo	Leo
Nov 15	Aq	Pis	Ar	Tau	Gem	Gem	Can	Can	Can	Leo	Leo	Vir
Nov 23	Pis	Ar	Ar	Tau	Gem	Gem	Can	Can	Leo	Leo	Leo	Vir
Dec 1	Pis	Ar	Tau	Gem	Gem	Can	Can	Can	Leo	Leo	Vir	Vir
Dec 9	Ar	Tau	Tau	Gem	Gem	Can	Can	Leo	Leo	Leo	Vir	Vir
Dec 18	Ar	Tau	Gem	Gem	Can	Can	Leo	Leo	Leo	Vir	Vir	Vir
Dec 28	Tau	Tau	Gem	Gem	Can	Can	Leo	Leo	Vir	Vir	Vir	Lib

21

Capricorn Astro-Outlook for 1986

Your concept of ambition may undergo a dramatic change in 1986, worldly Capricorn. You may be more attuned to your inner self and more anxious for different kinds of answers and experiences. Since your imagination is likely to be working overtime, you must take care to avoid self-deception, both in your personal and your business life. Though you can excel in creative projects, you may have difficulty seeing reality clearly at times.

In your relationship life, don't make the mistake of putting someone on a pedestal and making impossible demands about the situation. It would be all too easy for you to be in love with love rather than a flesh-and-blood person. However, you will benefit by your less practical and more mystical attitude toward love, no matter what happens.

Capricorns involved in any field where helping others is paramount (like nursing) will find themselves particularly inspired this year. That goes for anything involving communications as well. However, any Capricorn should beware of becoming the martyr this year by letting your compassion outweigh your common sense. You run the risk of feeling unduly sorry for yourself if things do not go as well as you want them to.

January and October will be highly significant months when you can take big strides forward. New directions are best taken in March and December. Travel will take precedence in May and family matters in August. For more specifics, consult the day-by-day forecasts that follow.

22

Fifteen Months of Day-by-Day Predictions

OCTOBER 1985

Tuesday, October 1 (Moon in Taurus) Things are definitely getting warmer in the romantic department; you are becoming much more serious and perhaps ready to make a commitment. If that is not your circumstance, you are contemplating greater responsibilities in a current relationship. Your position is strong; do not hesitate to take the leading role. The lucky number today is 8.

Wednesday, October 2 (Moon in Taurus) This is a day for major moves—in love, if you like, or in the area of personal accomplishment. Those things could blend when a member of the opposite sex helps you transform a dream into reality. Among those you may interact with today are an Aries and a Libra—either one of whom would be competitive with you, but helpful.

Thursday, October 3 (Moon Taurus to Gemini 8:26 a.m.) Today is a day to stamp your individuality on. Your arena could be your place of business or your own home—even a party. Wherever you are, adventure will seek you out, and you should be able to respond in a highly personal way. In a sense, you are your own entertainment. The lucky number today should be 1.

Friday, October 4 (Moon in Gemini) You may experience some mood swings today and your emotional responses may be unreliable. Keep a watchful eye on yourself, and don't overreact. Also, don't eat while you're under pressure; your stomach could be extrasensitive. Someone older could have a very calming influence.

Saturday, October 5 (Moon Gemini to Cancer 8:42 p.m.) You have an excellent opportunity to expand your base of operations now. The key is enthusiasm—both in thought and in word. And don't forget action. Your body image may be uppermost in your mind today, and you should pay a great deal of attention to your grooming. A Sagittarian could be a bit overwhelming. The lucky number today is 3.

Sunday, October 6 (Moon in Cancer) Now's the time to get serious—particularly about matters of marriage and partnership. If you are single, you may have to review some kind of contract or agreement with someone else. Either way, you should be willing to maintain a low profile, have patience, and go slowly. Watch out for a Leo or an Aquarian.

Monday, October 7 (Moon in Cancer) You may get some rather confusing signals from an important person today; try to interpret them without undue emotion. There may be some game-playing going on. Don't force yourself on anyone—especially a mate or partner or associate. Wait for a better time, and things will be better.

Tuesday, October 8 (Moon Cancer to Leo 6:58 a.m.) You may be wondering where you can scrape together the money for something you wish to do that would improve your home surroundings; today, you might be able to find it. Someone who has been rather negative recently probably will change his/her tune—especially if you use tact. Take your cue from a sweet-smiling Libra who may be around you. The lucky number today is 6.

Wednesday, October 9 (Moon in Leo) Some things that seem too good to be true are just that. And that applies to a proposition someone offers you now. In these matters, it is best to put your faith in the experts rather than in friends. It is also wise to get things in writing. At this time, you must make a special attempt to see people as they really are. You may be surrounded by emotional types today—one could be a Pisces.

Thursday, October 10 (Moon Leo to Virgo 1:24 p.m.) An ambitious, steady individual sets a great example for you today; here is someone you can rely on with confidence. Not that you need so much help now—your own position is a very powerful one. Nevertheless, accept the help from some top people who are ready to extend it. The lucky number today could be 8.

Friday, October 11 (Moon in Virgo) A real go-getter gets your attention today. He/she may even compete for your love and affection. However, you should not limit yourself to such interpersonal matters; it is time to start out and make your mark in a large, bold way. You may even have some kind of prophetic insight into the future now. Use it to good advantage.

Saturday, October 12 (Moon Virgo to Libra 2:38 p.m.) Your original ideas are still coming thick and fast today. You may even be responsible for some kind of "first" that gets a lot of recognition. A rather dramatic person wants to make his/her impression felt; it could even lead to romance—if you want it. The lucky number is 1.

Sunday, October 13 (Moon in Libra) Someone needs reassurance, and it could possibly be a parent or a parental figure. Whoever it is, be prepared to give proof of your affection. The warmth of home and family is especially important to you now, though you may be a bit moody. Try not to force any issues now, but rather take a conservative stance.

Monday, October 14 (Moon Libra to Scorpio 2:50 p.m.) You start out the week with an invitation to a social affair; you may not be sure whether or not to accept it. Be willing to be flexible, because it could be the scene of an important contact. At any rate, you will find people with whom you can discuss your views in an intelligent manner. In all respects, you are rather popular now. The lucky number today is 3.

Tuesday, October 15 (Moon in Scorpio) It is important to take one careful step at a time now in order to realize your goals. You must learn to separate the significant from the trivial. Don't be shy in accepting some help from a friend who says he/she will help you get some routine things out of the way; you are lucky to have this kind of backup. An Aquarian may figure very prominently today.

Wednesday, October 16 (Moon Scorpio to Sagittarius 2:25 p.m.) This is a period of time during which your views about love and friendship could undergo a transformation. Today the two may become rather confused when a member of the opposite sex engages you in witty conversation. Try to step back from the details, and ask yourself what is really going on here—especially in your own emotional life. For all of you, a rather sparkling celebration is indicated. The lucky number today could be 5.

Thursday, October 17 (Moon in Sagittarius) Someone close—possibly a family member—could unload a lot of problems on you today. Are you ready for this? You might be better off retiring from the scene and entering your "private world"; however, you may also have to deal with an adjustment in your domestic sphere. Be prepared, and forgive and forget.

Friday, October 18 (Moon Sagittarius to Capricorn 3:37 p.m.) No matter who else needs you, you should take time to be alone with your own thoughts and feelings today. You will learn a lot about yourself—and about others. Your compassion should extend to yourself now. However, don't neglect one person who would be delighted to hear from you. The lucky number is 7.

Saturday, October 19 (Moon in Capricorn) It's your time to shine, as the moon moves into your birth sign of Capricorn. You should be very enterprising and active today, and able to make your influence felt—no matter where you are. With your cycle so high, you can rely on your intuition. Someone who is going places fast wants to take you along. Good luck!

Sunday, October 20 (Moon Capricorn to Aquarius 8:04 p.m.) You are much less hung-up than you used to be about a losing proposition—possibly a relationship. You may be willing to drop it now and dare to love again. No matter what your situation, you complete something important and are able to take a new step in a new direction. Speak to an Aries who does it all the time.

Monday, October 21 (Moon in Aquarius) There are lots of ways to be creative—even a shopping trip could be very self-satisfying today. For one thing, you may figure out some way you can make things do double duty, and save some money. That's almost like finding a new source of income. Listen carefully to some information you get about a new project; you could get in on the ground floor. The lucky number is 1.

Tuesday, October 22 (Moon in Aquarius) It is essential to be conservative in your financial planning. You have great possibilities for turning a profit at this time. However, you are going to have to be a bit hard-nosed and perhaps alienate some people. Keep your eye on your main goals and don't hesitate to do what you must.

Wednesday, October 23 (Moon Aquarius to Pisces 3:35 a.m.) You wake feeling rather optimistic and in the mood for a change. If you can, get out and get around town. There, you will run into some rather wonderful experiences. No matter where you are, however, the day should hold some delightful surprises. Don't take on more than you can handle though; you could get carried away.

Thursday, October 24 (Moon in Pisces) It may take all the patience you have to stick with a routine today; in fact, you may feel as if you were being "tested." Don't give in to the desire to goof off, however, because you may learn some very important things today—particularly from a "solid citizen" who has some definite plans and a very concrete offer. Try to concentrate. The lucky number is 4.

Friday, October 25 (Moon Pisces to Aries 2:09 p.m.) Today, you are much freer and able to move about. You also will get the opportunity to engage in conversation with some lighthearted people who should inspire your own sense of humor. One of them may be a member of the opposite sex who is a very different type than you have encountered before. Learn from it! Creative thinking could save your day.

Saturday, October 26 (Moon in Aries) Some major differences may threaten peace on the home scene; a warm affectionate manner on your part could smooth everything over. Resolve to treat your family members with the same respect that you treat yourself. Try a little tenderness, too. A soft Taurus or a sensitive Libra would be an excellent person to discuss the matter with.

Sunday, October 27 (Moon in Aries) Today, you should enjoy the luxury of being in your own home and contemplating those things that mean the most to you. It is an excellent time for introspection. As you learn to be alone without being lonely, resolve to be realistic in matters that concern the emotions of other people. Make allowances for shifts in mood, and you will be a lot better able to cope.

Monday, October 28 (Moon Aries to Taurus 2:11 a.m.) You start out the week in a rather serious, determined mood; you should be able to make a lot of headway. In fact, team up with someone who shares your interests and together you can make a real power play. For any of you, it is possible that a relationship is deepening; a willingness to take on responsibilities is important now.

Tuesday, October 29 (Moon in Taurus) Wrap up a project and start looking for new fields to conquer. You have all the equipment to do it—plus the proper lunar cycle. Someone who has been a burden suddenly drops out of your life; you should be relieved, and you should start developing a new social circle. The lucky number today could be 9.

Wednesday, October 30 (Moon Taurus to Gemini 2:36 p.m.) You may find yourself at center stage in a rather dramatic scenario; it could involve your own romantic life. Whatever happens try not to act like a martyr. Most of you can expect to make new contacts today, and have the chance to display your individuality. Dressing up a bit could cure "the blues" that threaten to move in.

Thursday, October 31 (Moon in Gemini) You are able to keep your mind on your work today—and to be exceptionally sharp. With your intuition right on target, you could even see a new employment opportunity beyond the position you hold now. The most important thing is to be receptive to new methods and new techniques. If you cling to the past, you could be left back. The family may figure prominently today. The lucky number is 2.

NOVEMBER 1985

Friday, November 1 (Moon in Gemini) Simply refuse to carry a burden that is not your own; if necessary, dig in your heels and say "no." On a more positive note, you should be gaining wider recognition now for your excellent way of handling things. A rather competitive person may "throw down the glove"; are you ready for the challenge?"

Saturday, November 2 (Moon Gemini to Cancer 3:12 a.m.) Today, you may feel as if someone is holding you back; be prepared to examine a partnership or marriage. You may have to make some adjustments or even consider a new lifestyle. For all of you, there may be difficult interactions with others today. However, for some, a member of the opposite sex will let you know how much he/she cares. Either way, it's serious.

Sunday, November 3 (Moon in Cancer) The way to keep the peace is to defer to someone else in an important matter, and to do more listening than talking. Some nostalgic memories of the past may make you feel a bit sad today; they shouldn't. Think of how many wonderful things you remember. It is wise to play a waiting game.

Monday, November 4 (Moon Cancer to Leo 3:12 a.m.) You could be feeling too independent for your own good today, so resolve to take things more slowly than you are usually inclined to. Adventure is on the calendar, and you should be very active. Don't forget to show consideration for someone who has gone out of his/her way for you; don't be accused of being insensitive. And be willing to compromise.

Tuesday, November 5 (Moon in Leo) Practical methods are absolutely necessary today; if you are sloppy, you will pay the consequences. If you are willing to read the fine print, and to ask for further details, you will be able to rebuild things on a more solid foundation. The lucky number is 4.

Wednesday, November 6 (Moon Leo to Virgo 9:34 p.m.) You would do well to put your fate into someone else's hands—possibly a creative member of the opposite sex. There will be a change of plans, and it requires the ability to turn on a dime. You will enjoy it, but you may wish for a slower pace. Things will calm down soon.

Thursday, November 7 (Moon in Virgo) There may be some talk of travel now, but perhaps there are other things that need taking care of. Some may require tact and diplomacy—a family dispute is highly probably. Don't expect an easy time of it; a Taurus, a Libra, or a Leo could be very much in the picture—and give you a run for your money. The lucky number is 6.

Friday, November 8 (Moon in Virgo) No matter what else you have to do, you should try for a break in the everyday routine. It could be as simple as a brief interlude listening to music and/or seeking emotional solace. Your ultra-sensitivity could cause you pain—or it could provide you insight into the fundamental change that is necessary now.

Saturday, November 9 (Moon Virgo to Libra 1:14 a.m.) You should wake feeling refreshed, and stay that way all day long. In fact, you should be ready to plunge into action and enjoy the public position you will have today. Someone who counts lets you know that you are admired for your performance; realize that your responsible attitude has a lot to do with it.

Sunday, November 10 (Moon in Libra) Your "audience" should be increasing now, and you should be getting much more acclaim. It is an excellent time to make new contacts in important places. Perhaps you should get a second opinion of someone who is more aggressive than you, and more alert for opportunity. The lucky number today is 9.

Monday, November 11 (Moon Libra to Scorpio 1:53 a.m.) Don't be afraid to speak up and let your wishes be known now; you will be heard in the right places.

Socially, things are quite good, and you may even be attracting a new social circle. Try to let your innovative side show through so that people will see how interesting you can be when you want to.

Tuesday, November 12 (Moon in Scorpio) Follow through on a hunch—one concerning your real goals. It is possible that a recent contact can do more to further your cause than any amount of hard work; for once, something may come easily! Don't let moodiness get in the way of your dreams—they are very important. The lucky number today is 2.

Wednesday, November 13 (Moon Scorpio to Sagittarius 1:12 a.m.) Something strikes you as totally absurd today, and it stimulates your sense of humor. Appreciate how much laughing can do for a gloomy mood; it is an excellent antidote. No matter how tied down you may feel, get out and mix with other people today. A Sagittarian or a Gemini could be an excellent "playmate."

Thursday, November 14 (Moon in Sagittarius) You must be willing to dig in and probe deeply for the answers you seek; nothing will come easily to you now. If someone gives you surface explanations, demand to know the truth behind the truth. Don't get discouraged when you have to attend to a lot of routine matters. The lucky number is 4.

Friday, November 15 (Moon Sagittarius to Capricorn 1:10 a.m.) Now you are at a peak of energy—and possible accomplishment. A lot depends on you. If you use your intuition, you will zero right in on the right thing to do—and the right people to talk to. In fact, you should make an attempt to open all lines of communication; and don't neglect those of the opposite sex. A Gemini could play an extremely important role.

Saturday, November 16 (Moon in Capricorn) You run the risk of overdoing it in the area of personal pleasures today—particularly those that involve your palate. A sweet tooth that gets out of control could add weight. The more attention you pay to your personal appearance now, the happier you will be about it later on. Show your family particular affection today. The lucky number is 6.

Sunday, November 17 (Moon Capricorn to Aquarius 3:54 a.m.) Take special pains to avoid any kind of confusion about financial details now. It could lead you into some serious trouble. At any rate, it is wise to count your change and to steer clear of secret deals. No one gets something for nothing—not even you. Think more about your real values.

Monday, November 18 (Moon in Aquarius) You may be called upon to help someone with money; whatever commitment you make, be prepared to back it up. This is far from a halfway day, and anything that happens is highly significant. Make the most of everything—including love. The lucky number today should be 8.

Tuesday, November 19 (Moon Aquarius to Pisces 10:04 a.m.) Reach beyond the everyday to universal principles. In fact, try to respond when someone asks you to make a philanthropic gesture. The best thing you could do now is to give wholehearted support to those less fortunate than yourself. Surprisingly, an Aries may be the person to point it out to you.

Wednesday, November 20 (Moon in Pisces) You may be feeling rather "romantic" today—no matter what your situation. The best thing is to focus on your powers of self-expression, and try to find an original outlet for them. It is not as difficult as it sounds. For many, it may be obvious that a member of the opposite sex is interested. Don't hesitate to open up the lines of communication and ask some vital questions. The lucky number is 1.

Thursday, November 21 (Moon Pisces to Aries 8:00 p.m.) Intuitive answers will win over logical thoughts today. Try to be open to certain kinds of "messages." You may do a lot of moving about, but it may be in a rather small circle. An emotional person needs your warmth, and you should be willing to give it. Someone from the past may be back in the picture—and very prominent.

Friday, November 22 (Moon in Aries) Today, you are feeling quite single-minded, and able to zero in on very specific matters. One of them should be your own domestic environment, which may need some attention. Try to be flexible when discussing plans with family members, and be ready to handle a tricky situation with a sense of humor. Intellectual interests should be satisfied today. The lucky number is 3.

Saturday, November 23 (Moon in Aries) You should be ready to confine your activities to rather routine tasks today, because a lot of details need attending to as does some paperwork. However, you will find it easy to cut through a lot of red tape, to overcome obstacles, and to come through with flying colors. Take some time out to listen to a very sensible person with a solid proposition. This could be very important. The lucky number today should be 4.

Sunday, November 24 (Moon Aries to Taurus 8:37 a.m.) Now the lid is off, and you should be ready for some variety in your life. A much brisker pace is set as restrictions are lifted and you are able to go places and do things. You may even find family members encouraging you to enjoy life more. As if you didn't want to! A Gemini could be an excellent companion today.

Monday, November 25 (Moon in Taurus) You may be feeling rather lazy as this work week begins; blame it on the moon in Taurus. All you want is a nice, placid existence, and the companionship of someone warmly affectionate. You could easily get it. Try to plan some kind of get-together that includes music—and possibly dancing. It could be real balm to your soul. Family relationships should be a lot better. The lucky number is 6.

Tuesday, November 26 (Moon Taurus to Gemini 9:02 p.m.) Some mysterious circumstances could cause some misunderstandings today. Try to state things as clearly and openly as possible; at all costs, do not delude yourself. It is not a time to speculate—even if a proposition seems too good to be true. It probably is.

Wednesday, November 27 (Moon in Gemini) You may be feeling like making a deeper commitment to your job now; be sure the right people know it. There are employment opportunities indicated, and you should be ready to take advantage of them. Some of you may be surprised when top people say how much they value you and express extreme admiration; you should know how good you are. The lucky number today should be 8.

Thursday, November 28 (Moon in Gemini) Refuse to get bogged down by petty details today; stand back and look at the big picture. If you will let go of some negative thoughts and stop dwelling on an unhealthy past situation, you can complete a project in record time—and get a lot of compliments for it. Rely on an upbeat Aries who rarely worries about such things. The lucky number is 9.

Friday, November 29 (Moon Gemini to Cancer 8:59 a.m.) Don't push yourself too hard today, and avoid overly strenuous activity. Spend some time thinking about your health and how you can improve it—particularly by improved eating habits and exercise regimes. If you are very clever, you can invent some new techniques at work and be the center of attention. A Leo or an Aquarian could be very helpful.

Saturday, November 30 (Moon in Cancer) Relax, sit back, and let someone else take the lead today. That applies particularly to matters of partnership and marriage. No matter what your situation, you will get a lot more cooperation if you take a deferential position. You might listen to the advice of an older person who has been through this before, and definitely has the answers. He/she is an excellent example of tact and diplomacy. The lucky number is 2.

DECEMBER 1985

Sunday, December 1 (Moon Cancer to Leo 8:04 p.m.) You may have to tone down your independent attitude and be willing to compromise. Share and share alike is the watchword now—and you may even have to go more than 50 percent of the way. The reward is greater harmony, and some warm romantic moments. Admit that you like it this way.

Monday, December 2 (Moon in Leo) There is a lot of physical attraction in the atmosphere now, and it could be the most important factor in a relationship. It is important to listen to the promptings of your intuition and to be aware of the subtle nuances of feeling. If you are a bit confused, talk it over with someone who understands this kind of thing—it could be a Cancer or a Capricorn. The lucky number is 2.

Tuesday, December 3 (Moon in Leo) It would be all too easy for you to be led into an extravagant escapade now; however, it is important to hold down expenses. It is not penny-pinching, it is saving for greater things—like travel and other grand schemes. In another situation, strive to maintain your sense of humor. Take a tip from a Sagittarian or a Gemini.

Wednesday, December 4 (Moon Leo to Virgo 4:38 a.m.) You have been putting off some rather important obligations to keep up with people at a distance; resolve now to give them your careful attention. Some of you may be laying down foundations for a long-range project; realize that what you do now is vital to the eventual payoff. Stick with it, and try your luck with number 1.

Thursday, December 5 *(Moon in Virgo)* A "sentimental journey" may be very much on the agenda; whether it is real or imaginary, it should be extraordinarily enjoyable. The general accent today is on communication and change—plus a new outlook on relationships. Be careful when a fast-talking person has to "sell" you on an idea—isn't it something you could have thought of yourself? However, you should be willing to listen and to be flexible today.

Friday, December 6 *(Moon Virgo to Libra 9:44 a.m.)* Do some much-needed fence-mending today, and you will improve conditions all around you. For people at a distance, you may find it necessary to start sending off cards, packages, and gifts. Don't forget anyone! Now you may be able to make a rather diplomatic move which will eventually ease strained feelings. Don't tangle with a Scorpio or a Taurus who could be rather difficult today.

Saturday, December 7 *(Moon in Libra)* Steer clear of a conflict with an authority figure today, even if your feelings are a bit bruised. Remember—you are not calling the shots. Also, you are ultra-sensitive now and very vulnerable to the opinions of others. Get back your strength, indulge in the beauty of music or nature—it can do wonders. The lucky number today should be 7.

Sunday, December 8 *(Moon Libra to Scorpio 1:05 p.m.)* You are back on the track now and full of ambition. It enables you to take the leading role and give an impressive display of power. Finally you are beginning to realize your potential and learning how to make use of it. Good for you! A rather important person enters your life now; recognize it and be prepared to respond.

Monday, December 9 (Moon in Scorpio) Face it—someone has been wasting your time and has actually contributed very little to your life or your happiness. Now's the time to make a break. You may be surprised and pleased when you are invited to a rather elite gathering; you underestimate your appeal. The lucky number today is 9.

Tuesday, December 10 (Moon Scorpio to Sagittarius 1:11 p.m.) You should be feeling in a very expansive mood today and open to new kinds of experiences. A new kind of freedom is available to you now, if you will recognize it. For one thing, you have a kind of magnetic appeal that makes you exceedingly popular with all kinds of people. Don't underplay it. A warmhearted individual desires your admiration, and may show it. Be prepared to return the favor.

Wednesday, December 11 (Moon in Sagittarius) You may be giving advice today, and getting it as well; be open to suggestion. In fact, you may find that an older person can be extremely helpful in getting to the bottom of something that has been bugging you for some time. That answer is quite simple. In another area, rely on your intuition and your "sixth sense"—it is quite sharp right now. The lucky number is 2.

Thursday, December 12 (Moon Sagittarius to Capricorn 1:03 p.m.) Things can go either way today—that is, you could be extremely happy or extremely gloomy. One way to raise your spirits is by helping others. At this time of the year, it is important to remember those who are confined in some way, and to remember your obligation to spread good cheer. At some point during the day, your spirits begin to pick up and you realize that tomorrow is coming.

Friday, December 13 (Moon in Capricorn) Now you feel revitalized and you should look it as well. However, you should start being diligent in matters of diet and exercise now; realize that it is all too easy to slip during the holidays. In another matter, you can be original without going to extremes. Don't try to impress somebody with how clever you are. The lucky number is 4.

Saturday, December 14 (*Moon Capricorn to Aquarius 1:39 p.m.*) You may have a great urge to be on the move, but you may not be able to indulge it. Let your mind go places instead, and allow yourself a wider latitude in your ways of thinking. Holiday parties may provide some interesting new contacts—which you may feel desperately in need of. For some, this could be a most romantic day of the month. Keep an eye out for a sparkly type—possibly a Gemini.

Sunday, December 15 (*Moon in Aquarius*) You may be especially willing to spend money on luxury items today—particularly if they are for the enjoyment of the whole family. Your instinct for making others happy is very good right now. Someone in your circle is being rather stubborn, but you can turn the tide by getting him/her to share in one of your artistic pursuits. Be willing to spend some time.

Monday, December 16 (*Moon Aquarius to Pisces 6:21 p.m.*) It could be all too easy for you to go overboard with generosity now. It is all well and good to have the holiday spirit, but you should think carefully before you commit yourself to any extra expenses. Sometimes you can be a soft touch—and you cannot afford that right now. People will love you just as much anyway. The lucky number is 7.

Tuesday, December 17 (*Moon in Pisces*) If you have any special requests to make, you should make them today. There is every likelihood of your getting a "yes" answer. It is an excellent time to throw your weight around with confidence and get the desired results. Contact key people now without fear—or reservations. The lucky number now is 8.

Wednesday, December 18 (Moon in Pisces) Don't get caught up in all kinds of small and petty details today; try to see the big picture and make the big gesture. Someone may ask you for help, and you should be willing to respond and do as much as you are able to. Family and friends may be more involved in today's scenario than you would like; try not to let your annoyance show.

Thursday, December 19 (Moon Pisces to Aries 2:55 a.m.) It is time to be original and daring—even bold! New projects are accented, such as a revamp of the home or your own person. Don't be afraid to make some drastic changes—they will turn out quite well at this time. Realize you are building foundations for a secure future. The lucky number today is 1.

Friday, December 20 (Moon in Aries) As the work week ends, you find your thoughts turning to the pleasures of home and family. You are very much in the mood for any kind of recreation. Before you are able to indulge yourself, however, you may have to help someone who needed your attention in the past. Don't hesitate to give it again. If you follow your instincts, you will be able to smooth over some troubled waters with a relative.

Saturday, December 21 (Moon Aries to Taurus 3:09 p.m.) This should be an excellent pre-holiday weekend—with your home the center of celebration and fun. Even if you are not surrounded with that many people, you will enjoy an excellent repartee with a very witty person. It should make you feel quite brilliant! Show your generosity of spirit to one and to all.

Sunday, December 22 (Moon in Taurus) It shouldn't surprise you that young people need a lot of attention at this time of the year. However, you may find that the best thing you can give them is a sense of routine and discipline. It needn't spoil holiday fun. This is one of those times you should not delegate your key duties; you should see to things personally for best results. The lucky number today should be 4.

Monday, December 23 (Moon in Taurus) Today, you are much more able to think about your own needs—and desires. In fact, for some of you a romantic situation may be getting quite exciting. Someone may be ready to make a commitment. For all, change and variety should add to the excitement of a pleasure-filled day. The best part is that you attain a greater understanding of how much some people mean to you.

Tuesday, December 24 (Moon Taurus to Gemini 3:46 a.m.) Peace is the order of the day—and the evening. You are willing to work very hard to promote it. As far as you are concerned, the spirit of service to others prevails. However, you find you are rewarded with lots of love and attention from people who appreciate you. It is a lovely feeling! Now you know all your efforts have not been in vain.

Wednesday, December 25 (Moon in Gemini) You will be especially sensitive to the feelings of others today and could get a bit overemotional. Try to stay on an even keel, and even be willing to work to maintain harmony. Things will be made a lot easier by the general spirit of cooperation around you. For a spiritual lift, talk to a Pisces.

Thursday, December 26 (Moon Gemini to Cancer 3:41 p.m.) It should be a very quiet day in which you do not have to force any issues—for which you are very grateful. You feel like lying low and basking in the good holiday feelings. Take advantage of the quiet time to put some affairs in order—and to do some practical things like paying bills. The lucky number today is 8.

Friday, December 27 (Moon in Cancer) Today, you are ready to move out into the world again—and even to move ahead in a rather large project. Your horizons are definitely expanding, and on top of it, you find you can dump something or someone that has simply become a drag. Enjoy the freedom, but be willing to compromise in a domestic situation.

Saturday, December 28 (Moon in Cancer) You should listen to what others want to do today and not insist on having your own way; be receptive. For some, a permanent relationship—possibly marriage—may be a prominent topic today. Realize that emotions are running deep and that what is expressed today is likely to be the real thing. The lucky number today should be 1.

Sunday, December 29 (Moon Cancer to Leo 1:51 a.m.) You may feel as if you are in limbo today; try to settle down to one activity and concentrate on it. A good one would be how to save rather than to spend. However, realize that it is a touchy subject and that if you are too outspoken, you could provoke an emotional outburst from someone else. There are subtleties here you must be sensitive to. For good, solid advice, go to a Cancer or another Capricorn.

Monday, December 30 (Moon in Leo) A holiday mood is coming upon you, and you may be feeling rather adventurous. Take care that you do not become reckless—that is a real possibility. Whatever temptations come your way today, try to resist them. Be particularly wary of being led astray by some high-spirited people—one could be a Sagittarian or a Gemini. The lucky number today is 3.

Tuesday, December 31 (Moon Leo to Virgo 10:06 a.m.) You end the year on a rather thoughtful note rather than a frivolous one. You should be feeling rather settled and quietly happy tending to the needs of others. However, there is a fair amount of fun on the day's agenda, and you should prepare to participate in it fully. Celebrate—and congratulate yourself on a good year!

JANUARY 1986

Wednesday, January 1 (Moon in Virgo) As the New Year begins, you may be taking steps to release yourself from some past conditions that held you back. You are right to reach beyond your current goals and dreams. A very broad approach is the right one now, and you should even be thinking of travel. And Aries is an excellent person to give you a push.

Thursday, January 2 (Moon Virgo to Libra 3:45 p.m.) Distance makes little difference when love is strong, and that may be your situation now. In some cases, you may be going out of your way to get in touch with someone who has great appeal. Your own personal magnetism is quite high at this point, so it will be highly charged in character. You will definitely be able to get your message across. The lucky number is 1.

Friday, January 3 (Moon in Libra) Some are in for honors and recognition now. Be sure to share the credit with someone who deserves it. As a matter of fact, you should really spread the glory around, and let everyone share in it. Your spirit could be bolstered by a Cancer or another Capricorn who is around you now. The lucky number is 2.

Saturday, January 4 (Moon Libra to Scorpio 7:44 p.m.) This will be a fast-paced day in which you are highly visible. It is important to dress for success now, because you could easily make a valuable contact with somebody who is ready to help you. However, don't permit your hectic schedule to throw you off-center; maintain your good sense of organization.

Sunday, January 5 (Moon in Capricorn) There is no way that wishful thinking will help you today. In order to make your dreams come true, you are going to have to throw yourself into your work. This is hardly a day of rest for most Capricorns. There may be those around you who threaten to be a distracting influence; tell them you will be ready to "play" another day. The lucky number is 4.

Monday, January 6 (Moon Scorpio to Sagittarius 9:47 p.m.) You did something for a friend not too long ago; you will get your reward—a gift is on the way. A member of your family shows he/she is behind you all the way. In fact, this person makes a confession to you which makes you feel much better about yourself.

Tuesday, January 7 (Moon in Sagittarius) Today you may be playing the parental role to someone else. You are good in the role of counselor and should be able to help a great deal. In another instance, you may be able to use psychology to gain access to a vital secret. You will then be in a much better situation to see what adjustment has to be made. It is important to show compassion rather than take a judging attitude now.

Wednesday, January 8 (Moon Sagittarius to Capricorn 10:42 p.m.) Get ready for change, because a change is on the way—as are a travel opportunity and a variety of other experiences. You are probably ready for this, because you have been feeling rather rejected lately. Now you will have more room to move around in and a barrier to your progress is removed.

Thursday, January 9 (Moon in Capricorn) This is the best moon in Capricorn time of the year for you. Because both sun and the moon are in your own sign. That means your judgment will be excellent, and your business sense can easily make you a winner. Start projects that require a lot of initiative because you will have it now. Deep commitment will be required, but that will be no problem for you. Show someone you love that you can definitely be trusted.

Friday, January 10 (Moon in Capricorn) You continue on your winning cycle, and should make the most of every opportunity that comes your way. There should be several. However, if you let self-doubt hold you back, you will do yourself a disservice. Some Capricorns are taking stock of relationships; it may be that someone has been wasting your time. A break with this person may be necessary.

Saturday, January 11 (Moon Capricorn to Aquarius 12:01 a.m.) You can be even more productive in achieving today than yesterday. Pull out all the stops and go full steam ahead. You can even make a power play in a relationship where you have wanted to do so recently. Now you are in the driver's seat and you should take advantage of it.

Sunday, January 12 (Moon in Aquarius) Today you must have a more cautious intuitive approach. Particularly in the financial area. It is wise to take time out to balance the checkbook and to bring things up to date. Many will be thinking about security of home and family; an older person has advice you can count on. You are better off taking a wait and see attitude toward major decisions now.

Monday, January 13 (Moon Aquarius to Pisces 3:39 a.m.) You may be bubbling over with enthusiasm for new ideas now. You also may be much more full of wit, humor and a lighthearted attitude than usual. Take advantage of it, because it could make you extremely popular in your immediate circle right now. A Sagittarian or a Gemini could be excellent foil.

Tuesday, January 14 (Moon in Pisces) It is important to take one logical step at a time today if you are to make significant gains. However, that should not be difficult for you. You will do your best by sticking to routine settled conditions. Also, you will do yourself a big favor by checking over carefully everything you send out. The fine print could reveal an error. The lucky number is 4.

Wednesday, January 15 (Moon Pisces to Aries 11:03 a.m.) Someone rather restless and versatile will capture your imagination today. And possibly your heart as well. Life today could qualify as "life in the fast lane." At the very least you will be mixing with people who are full of wit and information. Don't miss a word!

Thursday, January 16 (Moon in Aries) You could be taking on more than your share of responsibility now, particularly with respect to family. It may be necessary for you to carry an extra burden or play the role of mediator in a family dispute. In other cases, there could be a whole new start in your home life. Possibly even a change of residence. Consult with a Libra or a Taurus who is in the picture. Your lucky number is 6.

Friday, January 17 (Moon Aries to Taurus 10:14 p.m.) For you, there is a tremendous need to "get away from it all." For one thing, you may be a bit disappointed by a relationship that promised to be glamorous, but turned out to be a lot less spectacular than you expected. Enjoy your privacy, and take time out for wishful thinking. Later on there will be time to get in tune with reality. It is important not to be fooled now.

Saturday, January 18 (Moon in Taurus) For many, a romance could be intensifying, and your feelings could be growing a lot more serious. In some cases, you may actually be talking about settling down or adding to a family. As you make a deeper commitment, realize that this is a significant turning point in your life. Another Capricorn or Cancer could be an excellent person to use as a sounding board.

Sunday, January 19 (Moon in Taurus) You could run into a rather aggressive forward-looking person who is ready to champion your cause. If you show that you are willing to look at the big picture rather than just a small portion of it, you will do yourself a lot of good. A broader scope is what you need now, and a break with the past may also be in the cards. A lucky number is 9.

Monday, January 20 (Moon Taurus to Gemini 11:12 a.m.) A family celebration could find you in the middle of an admiring group. Don't hang back, but prove that you can be a fun person. Your personal magnetism should be rather high right now and so should your chances for a dramatic scenario, which might include a love relationship with a deeply affectionate person.

Tuesday, January 21 (Moon in Gemini) You could very easily be focusing in on your appearance now, as well as your health. Some could have been using food for emotional security as a substitute for affection. Now it's time to take your weight and your diet in hand. If you let close family members know you care, they will understand you better. It is possible that you are particularly moody now, and it could cause temporary problems. The lucky number is 2.

Wednesday, January 22 (Moon Gemini to Cancer 11:14 p.m.) As much of a cliché as it may sound, a fascinating stranger could wander upon your scene today. If that is not your particular scenario, you will enjoy a break in routine anyway. It could possibly be a surprise trip in connection with business. Keep on the lookout, because a lot of opportunities are floating around, but nothing will happen if you don't take advantage of it.

Thursday, January 23 (Moon in Cancer) It may be obvious to you that you have to shore up your defenses now, or perhaps maintain a lower profile for the moment. This applies particularly to partnership matters. Some may feel they are carrying more of a load than they should, but in the long run you will be rewarded for it. Get a new perspective from an Aquarian or a Leo.

Friday, January 24 (Moon in Cancer) Get set for a rather deep talk with someone you love—and who loves you too. One of your relationships is about to take an amazing new turn, and it might leave you breathless.

However, it is important not to force any changes now or to try to take the lead; defer to your partner in all matters of major importance. The lucky number is 5.

Saturday, January 25 (Moon Cancer to Leo 8:47 a.m.) Someone with a rather possessive nature and a very distinctive voice could suddenly be the key to a change in your luck—particularly with respect to money. For the most part, you will be seeking peace and quiet artistic surroundings. Because of the full moon, be willing to make some concessions to promote harmony.

Sunday, January 26 (Moon in Leo) You could be particularly sensitive now, and willing to listen to a hard-luck story or some other sad tale of woe. Don't lend any money unless you have all the facts first. Realize that you are not seeing the situation quite clearly. A Pisces or a Virgo could be quite analytical and helpful now.

Monday, January 27 (Moon Leo to Virgo 3:51 p.m.) This is an extremely significant day, and you could find yourself in the driver's seat. Particularly where money or some other transaction is concerned. Some of you will be able to name your price. As you buy or sell, as well as in affairs of the heart, you will find that you have an excellent bargaining position. The lucky number is 8.

Tuesday, January 28 (Moon in Virgo) Travel, long-range plans, and new horizons are very much in the picture. Some of you may have been feeling rather limited lately, but that feeling is now gone as you reach out to new opportunities and complete an important phase of your life. Some Capricorns will be attracting rather ardent, impatient people; are you ready for adventure too?

Wednesday, January 29 (Moon Virgo to Libra 9:10 p.m.) Marriage, or any relationship that is based on love, is accented now. Some are quite ready to change their status, even if it means taking chances. The important thing is to be an individual now. Someone who loves to be the center of attention can act as a teacher as well as a lover. The lucky number today is 1.

Thursday, January 30 (Moon in Libra) An older person could make a deep impression on you and act as advisor in career matters. You will be very able to tune into the needs of others, and to understand what pleases the group at large. Trust your intuition now! A Cancer or another Capricorn could be an excellent buddy today.

Friday, January 31 (Moon in Libra) Now your social status is in the spotlight. You can be versatile and lighthearted, as you engage in a flurry of activity. Spend some time on your personal image, even if it means going out and buying some new clothes. You could vastly improve your position by improving your looks. Someone at the top is well aware of your presence. The lucky number is 3.

FEBRUARY 1986

Saturday, February 1 (Moon Libra to Scorpio 1:19 a.m.) Now you are ready to make a creative new start with an attractive romance, or intensify a current romantic situation. If you are involved with someone, select a rather dramatic setting for today's encounter. Something as simple as a good film or a good meal can greatly help your cause. The lucky number is 1.

Sunday, February 2 (Moon in Scorpio) Someone who has helped you in the past is now back in a surprise reappearance, and could help you fulfill a new dream. Make sure you say "Thanks" for the last time. Follow through on a lucky hunch because your intuition is right on target. Don't shut yourself off from someone you love simply because of hurt feelings or moody attitude.

Monday, February 3 (Moon Scorpio to Sagittarius 4:31 a.m.) Focus on joy and optimism rather than gloom or self-doubt. Also, let loose with that sense of humor that is bubbling beneath the surface. Some who are struggling with heavy burdens will really appreciate your light touch now. For best results, team up with a Sagittarian or a Gemini.

Tuesday, February 4 (Moon in Sagittarius) Admit that you need a solid foundation for an upcoming project, and be willing to work for it. It may mean checking out a lot of details and putting in some extra time while you plan strategy. Also realize this is a testing time for you personally, so it is not wise to delegate too much to someone else. You are the one who must do it. The lucky number is 4.

Wednesday, February 5 (Moon Sagittarius to Capricorn 7:02 a.m.) A fast-talking, clever member of the opposite sex figures prominently in a scenario you get involved in today. Some of it could be a bit sub rosa. None of you should believe anything you hear—and should insist upon getting it in writing from the person who tries to sell you a bill of goods. If something is a matter of public record, you can feel secure. Learn to differentiate between fantasy and reality now.

Thursday, February 6 (Moon in Capricorn) This is the time to start spending some time on yourself; it could be that your overactive sense of responsibility has kept you from doing what you should to gain personal points. Now's an excellent time for self-improvement projects and an expression of your artistic talents. A Taurus or a Libran can help draw you out.

Friday, February 7 (Moon Capricorn to Aquarius 7:15 a.m.) Today you get your reward for something you did in the past. In some cases, it will be simply prestige—but that in itself is very valuable. You should approach a relationship with caution, but realize it could bloom if you show serious intent. Another Capricorn will play a serious role. The lucky number is 8.

Saturday February 8 (Moon Aquarius to Pisces 11:32 a.m.) You are going to run into somebody with a very bright idea today, and you should listen carefully. However, before you jump into anything, take stock of your own assets and reevaluate your future goals. The person is a lot more action oriented than you, and a bit more daring; it could be a good matchup.

Sunday, February 9 (Moon in Pisces) Things could be so busy today they even rattle you, stolid Capricorn. You don't mind a lot of work—but sometimes a lot of nervous activity can bend you out of shape. Try to keep your cool. Someone rather quiet may "sneak up" on you and be surprisingly perceptive about what's bugging you. It's a nice shoulder to lean on.

Monday, February 10 (Moon in Pisces) Someone is going to keep after you until you respond the way he/she wants you to. It may take more than words however. This is time for action. In some cases, the scenario is a romantic one, and the lines of communication are definitely opening up. The lucky number is 1.

Tuesday, February 11 (Moon Pisces to Aries 6:21 p.m.) Trust your intuition today. That means you should listen to that "still small voice" within you rather than people who are trying to put you down. In some cases, there will be a lot of involvement with siblings or other close relatives today. There will be some changes on the home front. Show warmth and affection rather than moodiness no matter what happens.

Wednesday, February 12 (Moon in Aries) There is someone you can get if you want him/her by simply saying the word. Amuse yourself, but realize that this fascinating person could get you in farther than you planned. In many cases, there is a very warm atmosphere around the home—in the good sense of the word. You should be optimistic about some previous problems. The lucky number today is 3.

Thursday, February 13 (Moon in Aries) Someone close to you needs a lot of reassurance that you are responsible and willing to stick with something until it is done. You may resent this, because you know how serious you really are. You may have to reprove yourself, however. Pay some attention to practical matters and needed repairs around home. The lucky number is 4.

Friday, February 14 (Moon Aries to Taurus 5:38 a.m.) The restrictions are off now and you should find time for some real R&R. However, someone may be even more interested in partying than you are now; try not to be a drag. In some cases, unless you maintain a fast-paced schedule, you could easily bore someone and consequently lose him/her.

Saturday, February 15 (Moon in Taurus) You should be in a very mellow mood today and willing to go for that extra mile for people you love. It is unlike you to allow yourself to be taken advantage of, so this should not be a problem. However, you don't have to spend that much to make everyone feel pampered.

Sunday, February 16 (Moon Taurus to Gemini 5:17 p.m.) Caution! You could easily be fooled by someone's actions today. The point is that you are being too idealistic and rather see it the way it looks good to you. Some Capricorns could be dealing their opposite numbers as characters from romantic novels; know that they are not. It is all well and good to make concessions, but draw the line well this side of self-sacrifice.

Monday, February 17 (Moon in Gemini) This could be a highly significant day for your work. Some of you may even see a previously hidden pathway to the top, or be given the opportunity to talk about your ambitions. In some cases, your executive ability will not only be recognized, it will be rewarded. Another Capricorn could be very prominent today. The lucky number is 1.

Tuesday, February 18 (Moon in Gemini) You can do yourself a big favor today—both in your work and from the point of view of your health—by expanding your knowledge and perhaps adopting a new viewpoint. You are not as well informed as you may think. Also, be willing to share your talents with other people, but without making them dependent on you. Sometimes you like the feeling of being "big daddy/big mommy." Someone will show up at a vital moment—it could be an Aries or a Libra. The lucky number is 9.

Wednesday, February 19 (Moon Gemini to Cancer 7:39 a.m.) Now it's time to blow your own horn—wherever it is you are performing work or service today. Some will have an excellent opportunity to display their leadership abilities, and to show just how original and clever they can be. Some of you will have renewed vitality and will be able to keep on going when others have simply dropped by the wayside. Good for you!

Thursday, February 20 (Moon in Cancer) Don't feel you have to make a major decision today; this is one time it's okay to turn over the reins to someone else. In all situations, you are better off doing more listening than talking. For some, marital status will be up for discussion, along with home and family in general. All kinds of ties to the past are possible subjects of high drama today. Don't let it get out of hand. A Cancer or a Capricorn could play an important part.

Friday, February 21 (Moon Cancer to Leo 3:25 p.m.) You probably will be extra conscious of your looks today; some of you will want to look especially good to appeal to a member of the opposite sex. Some could get involved in a lighthearted discussion that really masks a much more serious subject—possibly a permanent partnership. Take care, and don't take promises that are made now too seriously. The lucky number is 3.

Saturday, February 22 (Moon in Leo) Nothing good is going to happen in your money sector unless you see some basic tasks through to their finish. If you skimp on any essentials, you will ruin your chances for later success. No matter what your particular scenario, it would be a good idea to focus on paying bills and keeping your financial records up to date in general.

Sunday, February 23 (Moon Leo to Virgo 11:58 p.m.) Now you are ready for some much more personal satisfaction—and in some cases, the satisfaction of physical desires. Secret wishes are going to come to the fore now, and could lead to exciting changes. Some of you may even have someone lavish affection on you that you didn't expect. Enjoy!

Monday, February 24 (Moon in Virgo) This particular full moon is going to make you focus on "higher thoughts." In some cases, there could be a real transformation of values, and possibly even an interest in spiritualism or religion. All will be acutely aware of the need for movement and change now; however, it could conflict with the wishes of loved ones. At all costs, remain tactful. The lucky number is 6.

Tuesday, February 25 (Moon in Virgo) It would be all too easy for you to "fall for a line" today, or believe something someone wants you to believe. Realize that you are suffering from the "the-grass-is-always-greener" syndrome; if you really knew, you would see the situation as it is. On the other hand, if someone rather glamorous wants to sweep you off your feet, you could enjoy a wonderful fling. A Pisces could be involved.

Wednesday, February 26 (Moon Virgo to Libra 4:07 a.m.) For many of you, an important career opportunity could appear to drop in your lap. Realize that you planted the seeds for this a while back. Others have friends in high places who are really ready to help you; why don't you ask? However, be ready with all the facts and figures about your past history in the employment field. This could be your big break. The lucky number is 8.

Thursday, February 27 (Moon in Libra) If you are willing to put your past behind you, you will be in a much better position to clear the way for your future. Many are having an excellent chance to show their talents now, and should not miss a step. Someone rather competitive, but also dynamic, is fully behind you. Don't get into a match of wits, because this person is very willing to lend you support.

Friday, February 28 (Moon Libra to Scorpio 7:06 a.m.) Once again, you are going to have to be rather daring if you are to make any progress. Don't let shyness or fear hold you back. No matter in what circle you move today, you will find yourself among rather high-level types; make sure your looks and your manner match theirs. The lucky number is 1.

MARCH 1986

Saturday, March 1 (Moon in Scorpio) You will be particularly sensitive to the moods and feelings of others today, and so you should let your intuition be your guide. However, don't let some sensitive feelings of your own make you cling to someone else rather than asserting yourself in a bold manner. Another Capricorn or Cancer could be an excellent role model now.

Sunday, March 2 (Moon Scorpio to Sagittarius, 9:51 a.m.) A festive celebration is on the agenda. In some cases, you could be the center of attraction in a real "triumph" as people gather around you to appreciate your wit. And your incredible fund of knowledge. Some will find that a person who was only an acquaintance could now become a close friend—or more. Just don't spread yourself too thin today. The lucky number is 3.

Monday, March 3 *(Moon in Sagittarius)* Okay, now it's time to settle down to a basic routine. For some, a rather hush-hush project could require a lot of stick-to-itiveness—without much recognition now. In any case, you will have some peace and quiet, and the opportunity to "work on" yourself—and to perfect your techniques. There may be an undercurrent of expectation today; you are right to feel that things will be happening rather fast rather soon.

Tuesday, March 4 *(Moon Sagittarius to Capricorn 12:56 p.m.)* Some Capricorns could be involved in a secret romance now. And there could be some exciting developments in that area. However, don't let a story you hear throw you too far off-base; stick to your own impressions. And come to your own conclusions. A Virgo could play a vital role. The lucky number is 5.

Wednesday, March 5 *(Moon in Capricorn)* Now you really swing into the high of your lunar cycle. In many cases, you will be able now to take the lead in straightening out a situation that had a potential for disaster. You are the one to bring it back into the realm of the possible. You should congratulate yourself for being able to create harmony. Even if you are not comfortable with the situation, you are going to be very much in the spotlight today. So will a Taurus person.

Thursday, March 6 *(Moon Capricorn to Aquarius 4:42 p.m.)* You could be positively psychic today, because your perceptions are right on target. Some will be attracted to things of the mind, possibly even something rather mystical. If you try it, you will find that you can be alone without feeling lonely. As a matter of fact, you will learn to know yourself better. If you must share, Pisces or a Virgo would be an excellent companion. The lucky number is 7.

Friday, March 7 (Moon in Aquarius) The accent today is definitely on your ambitions and your chances for advancement. You are wise to take some advice—particularly in a financial area. You can make smart money if you listen to the right people. For a purchase that you've been considering, be sure to shop around. It is a good time to make a long-term investment.

Saturday, March 8 (Moon Aquarius to Pisces 7:48 p.m.) You could be in a very generous mood, but you should not let someone else take advantage of your good nature. Investigate someone's "hard luck story" before you agree to help. If at all possible, totally retire from the world of competition today and consider where you really want to go. The lucky number is 9.

Sunday, March 9 (Moon in Pisces) Romance could be blooming right in front of your eyes; be sure that you recognize it. Some Capricorns will be getting involved with a new group of people and participating in a joint project. Realize that you are among real friends. One in particular will be very enthusiastic, but could scare you a bit by his/her tendency to overstatement. Try to hear between the words.

Monday, March 10 (Moon in Pisces) You are wise to display your typical Capricorn caution in all communications today. You could be a bit more emotional than usual, and consequently not as buttoned up. Be sure you give your logic as much time as you give your feelings. Someone older and wiser—or at least more experienced—could have some excellent advice. Don't be too proud to listen. The lucky number is 2.

Tuesday, March 11 (Moon Pisces to Aries 5:03 a.m.) You could be feeling especially restless today. Your urge to get out and get around could easily conflict with some duties you cannot avoid. Try reaching out to faraway places through letters—or your own mind. There are things you could investigate now that might prove very lucrative later on. Be willing to laugh at yourself, it may be necessary.

Wednesday, March 12 (Moon in Aries) The accent today is on home, property, and the beginnings of a new project. No matter how much time you have to put in, realize you are building a strong foundation for future efforts. There will be some initial obstacles, but by paying strict attention to duty, you will overcome them. An Aquarian or a Leo could be an excellent co-worker.

Thursday, March 13 (Moon Aries to Taurus 3:04 p.m.) There is a lighter note to this day, and some Capricorns could hear words they have been waiting to hear. In some cases, they will be romantic. In other cases, a question-and-answer period could lead to some very exciting developments. A Virgo or a Gemini could play a prominent role. The lucky number is 5.

Friday, March 14 (Moon in Taurus) You could be feeling rather sentimental today, and consequently reach out to people you haven't seen for a while. Some Capricorns will actually rediscover someone they have not appreciated very much lately. It's an excellent time to entertain at home, and to soothe yourself with music or art. If you can, simply luxuriate.

Saturday, March 15 (Moon in Taurus) Today an escapist attitude could take over, and you may go to great lengths to avoid things that need to be done. Or you may take a totally realistic attitude toward a situation that is not the way you would like it to be. Try not to look at the world through the proverbial rose-colored glasses, or to fall in love with love. A Pisces could easily lead you astray. The lucky number is 7.

Sunday, March 16 (Moon Taurus to Gemini 3:23 a.m.) For many of you, this could be payday when you collect something that is due you for past accomplishment. A relationship with someone you want to impress could become a lot more serious now; your ability to plan and organize is suddenly being noticed—and rewarded. Good for you.

Monday, March 17 *(Moon in Gemini)* Try to shake off some fears and self-doubts you have now, and move ahead optimistically. It is the key to progress now. If you can't really work yourself up to that, try to finish a current project and get ready for something big. It is well within your grasp. The lucky number is 9.

Tuesday, March 18 *(Moon Gemini to Cancer 4:04 p.m.)* Today you may be feeling like pampering yourself and reaching out for "the sweets of life." Realize that this is no way to help your sense of well-being. It is crucial to maintain a balanced attitude toward work and leisure now. Let a Taurus or a Scorpio show you how. The lucky number is 1.

Wednesday, March 19 *(Moon in Cancer)* For many Capricorns, a partnership will call for a diplomatic approach now; in many cases, it will be marriage. Exercise patience, and time your moves; do not force any issues now. Some may have to read the fine print in some kind of contract. Listen to someone older who has the right advice.

Thursday, March 20 *(Moon in Cancer)* Most will have a rather busy social schedule and should be ready to put on a smiling face. No matter how you feel. Your interest may definitely perk up when you run into someone whose background is very different from your own, and quite fascinating. In some cases, you may have to defer to a partner, and not be able to move around as much as you want. The lucky number is 3.

Friday, March 21 *(Moon Cancer to Leo 2:38 a.m.)* Hang on to your money today, no matter how you are tempted to spend it. It is vital that you are practical now, and bring all your records up to date. In some cases, a rather puzzling situation could be unsettling; you can clear it up if you really scratch below the surface.

Saturday, March 22 (Moon in Leo) Some love situations could be becoming too hot to handle. Don't let your's get out of hand. Try tuning in on a more intuitive level with the one you love; sometimes words are not enough. You are able to understand a relationship on a deeper level if you really try.

Sunday, March 23 (Moon Leo to Virgo 9:39 a.m.) Some Capricorns may have discovered that they are taking on more than their share of the financial burdens; now it's time to let others do their share. A lighter scenario includes some purchases that make life easier and more beautiful for everyone. It's a good way to patch up what may be a rather splintered relationship. The lucky number is 6.

Monday, March 24 (Moon in Virgo) Something is going to inspire you today; it could be a piece of news about something that has happened elsewhere that affects your life a great deal. In other cases, you would do well to get away from a trying situation. It is important to take time out to reflect on recent happenings, and to understand the true motives of others.

Tuesday, March 25 (Moon Virgo to Libra 1:22 p.m.) You may be asked to make a big commitment now—or at least a promise. Realize that this is a very serious business, and that the future is involved. Try to look beyond your current situation and to see the long-range consequences. And also realize that you are not limited. You are ready for a big break in your life-style. The lucky number is 8.

Wednesday, March 26 (Moon in Libra) The only way you are going to be able to free yourself up to do what you want to do is to do what you have to do first. Take advantage of an opportunity that comes along to promote yourself, and to get on with your large-scale plans. Some Capricorns will have an opportunity to show how artistic and creative they can be. An Aries or a Libra could be very prominent in today's scenario.

Thursday, March 27 (Moon Libra to Scorpio 3:05 p.m.) A big compliment comes your way now, and should encourage you to strike out in a new direction. In some cases, the subject will be business—in others love and romance. Pleasure is definitely indicated, so you should dress the part. Let others know who you are and what you stand for!

Friday, March 28 (Moon in Scorpio) A rather shy, nonaggressive person could indicate that he/she would like to spend some time with you; consider it seriously. This person is much warmer and more affectionate than you may think. It is important to get beyond surface indications. In many cases, Capricorns should spend some time around home luxuriating in a pleasant atmosphere.

Saturday, March 29 (Moon Scorpio to Sagittarius 4:20 p.m.) A lighthearted atmosphere colors this day; in many cases, there will be group activity. If you have the opportunity to meet new people, take full advantage of it. You will gain a lot by exchanging ideas and opinions. Some may look at their wardrobe and realize that it is definitely time to do some revamping; a shopping spree is indicated—and okay. The lucky number is 3.

Sunday, March 30 (Moon in Sagittarius) Don't start feeling sorry for yourself if you have to take care of business while others are enjoying the day off. If you avoid extremes, and do not pressure yourself, you can get things done quickly—and then have some time for fun. Realize that you are building a foundation for future success. Team up with an Aquarius who could lighten the atmosphere considerably.

Monday, March 31 (Moon Sagittarius to Capricorn 6:25 p.m.) It may become obvious that a member of the opposite sex is definitely interested, even though he/she is not revealing true feelings. There is a lot of secrecy indicated today, and it may be difficult to figure out people's real motives. In some cases, you will suffer from a communications breakdown. Be willing to make the first move to exchange thoughts. The lucky number is 5.

APRIL 1986

Tuesday, April 1 (Moon in Capricorn) It may become painfully obvious that you've got to do something about your personal appearance; in many cases, the subject will be weight loss. However, this is an excellent lunar cycle for you, and you may find yourself in the spotlight. Some Capricorns could actually meet that "fascinating stranger" you hear so much about. Enjoy a light flirtation.

Wednesday, April 2 (Moon Capricorn to Aquarius 10:11 p.m.) You may have to take life a little more seriously today. However, discipline and follow-through will bring you what you want. Someone may try to tempt you to goof off, but realize you will not enjoy the consequences. It is definitely not the day for play. The lucky number is 4.

Thursday, April 3 (Moon in Aquarius) The written word could easily bring you financial gain now, giving you the chance to shine in the eyes of someone who counts. No matter what else happens, be willing to share your ideas and information with someone else. It is one of those times when you are investing in the future, even though you don't know it. This is one of those days you could definitely live by your wits, and get away with it.

Friday, April 4 (Moon in Aquarius) Someone close to you may have rather lavish taste, and it could be showing in your checkbook balance. You are going to have to deal with it head-on. You do not need an additional financial burden. In some cases, home will be the center of a lot of activity, and you may be the center of admiration for your great finesse with entertaining.

Saturday, April 5 (Moon Aquarius to Pisces 4:03 a.m.) Someone could easily fool you now by smooth talk; realize that you've got to see things in a realistic light. Don't promise more than you can give, and don't listen to someone who promises a lot—but probably won't deliver anything. You are exceptionally drawn toward glamour now, and should realize it. The lucky number is 7.

Sunday, April 6 (Moon in Pisces) Some new professional opportunities could fall in your lap—through close associates or relatives. Realize that a simple phone call could be the start of something big, and be ready for action. Many Capricorns are definitely on their way up to more profit and prestige now. The lucky number is 8.

Monday, April 7 (Moon in Aries) Now you are going to have to cut ties with someone who depends on you in an unhealthy way. Be willing to give help where help is needed, but draw the line at becoming a crutch to someone else. You are the one who has to give yourself greater self-expression and broaden your horizons. Team up with a real self-starter.

Tuesday, April 8 (Moon in Aries) If you really try to be your own person today, you will get a great sense of security out of it. Don't follow some outworn guidelines that someone else has given you. Some Capricorns will find that a member of the opposite sex is definitely warming up—and brightening life. Your lucky number is 1.

Wednesday, April 9 (Moon Aries to Taurus 10:36 p.m.) Follow your impressions today, as well as your hunches. However, realize that you have to be diplomatic today and tread lightly where someone else's feelings are concerned. It is no time to give in to moods. Some will feel that there is a fresh start in their home life; it could be a pleasant change. Another Capricorn or a Cancer could easily be involved.

Thursday, April 10 (Moon in Taurus) Those who have been feeling confined will now feel that "school's out" and embark on exciting events. Be open to everyone and everything, because there is much to be learned. Give your curiosity full reign. Be particularly attentive when a Sagittarian or a Gemini speaks. The lucky number is 3.

Friday, April 11 (Moon in Taurus) There is a focus on responsibility today, and it may not be as stimulating as yesterday's activities. Some deadlines are pressing and you are going to have to put your nose to the grindstone if you are going to make them. Throw yourself into it and get the whole thing out of the way.

Saturday, April 12 (Moon Taurus to Gemini 10:51 a.m.) You need to relax today; some worry about your current situation is really pointless since you can't do anything about it now. Let another, more playful type get your mind on something more amusing. Try to be creative in your thinking—particularly with a member of the opposite sex. The lucky number is 5.

Sunday, April 13 (Moon in Gemini) You may run smack into an abrasive encounter today, and it could throw you. Make your comeback by taking a deep breath and willing yourself some new psychic energy. Don't be extravagant with something today, including your emotions. Toss out some unneeded and hindering materials. You are able to settle some relationship differences.

Monday, April 14 (Moon Gemini to Cancer 11:42 p.m.) The past few days' mood of gloom and doom vanishes totally and you feel a lot better—especially when an exciting invitation comes your way. Accept, but make sure you do the necessaries as well. You are a good negotiator, so take the opportunity to wind up some legal matters.

Tuesday, April 15 (Moon in Cancer) Don't push your own ideas today, but let someone else take the lead. Your marital status could be a prime topic of conversation. Others are going to have to make a firm commitment if asked; realize that you've got the bulk of advantage on your side. Including prestige and money. The lucky number is 8.

Wednesday, April 16 (Moon in Cancer) Everyone you have to deal with today proves to be in a highly cooperative mood, and it makes things go smoothly. You learn through a contact that there are some interesting deals available. Be willing to let go of petty fears, doubts, and bickering, and take a broader view of the world and your place in it.

Thursday, April 17 (Moon Cancer to Leo 11:10 a.m.) Your desire to be independent and creative could easily conflict with your need to work as a team now. Be willing to hold back your need to be dominant, and defer to someone else in important matters. In some cases, personal magnetism is bringing love to you; realize how lucky you are. The lucky number is 1.

Friday, April 18 (Moon in Leo) You could be in a rather frugal mood, even stingy. That is sometimes a Capricorn problem. However, it is not your own security that you are concerned about, but that of your family as well. Okay, bring your checkbook up to date and put some money away for a rainy day. You will feel a lot better if you do.

Saturday, April 19 (Moon Leo to Virgo 7:24 p.m.) A flurry of social activity could bring you in contact with an attractive member of the opposite sex; you may almost feel as if you have met this person before. Other Capricorns will be drawn to solving the mysteries of life and could be dramatically transformed in some way. Open up your mind in every possible way now.

Sunday, April 20 (Moon in Virgo) Today you will want to bring your ideas down to earth and put them into practical form. You can. In fact, some will be making a very important breakthrough that could mean real money. Others will have to be more diligent, and follow the rules. Realize that a steady pace is the best. The lucky number is 4.

Monday, April 21 (Moon Virgo to Libra 11:50 p.m.) The week starts out in a real flurry of activity. Most Capricorns will refuse to be tied down by limiting circumstances; variety and change are what you want now. Some will be traveling, and will meet a very interesting person in transit. It could be a Gemini or a Virgo.

Tuesday, April 22 (Moon in Libra) A rather sticky situation will be resolved in your favor now; it puts you in a much better position than you were before. Try to make peace with someone who has been rather stubborn and resistant to your idea; you can create harmony around you. It's an excellent time to shop for a gift that shows your personality. The lucky number is 6.

Wednesday, April 23 (Moon in Libra) Don't deceive yourself with regard to career plans; they could be a bit on the dreamy side. Also draw the line at mixing business with pleasure, or reacting emotionally to someone in your professional sphere. Realize that your feelings could be running away with you.

Thursday, April 24 (Moon Libra to Scorpio 1:15 a.m.) This full moon brings you a power-play day, one in which you should be well able to win friends and influence people. By making a dynamic move. However, there is tension in social situations and in relationships; take care. One way to avoid trouble is to show someone you care about that you are truly serious. The lucky number is 8.

Friday, April 25 (Moon in Scorpio)   Now's the time to evaluate your relationship with someone and possibly rid yourself of a burdensome situation that is a constant drain on you. It is a time to widen your circle of acquaintances and to feel more optimistic about life in general. You can fulfill yourself more than you are doing. An Aries plays a prominent role.

Saturday, April 26 (Moon Scorpio to Sagittarius 1:16 a.m.)   Let your creative juices flow today, no matter what you doing. Do not permit self-doubt to cloud your perspective; realize that good things are on the way. Many can be in touch with their inner selves and tap it for brilliant new ideas. A dramatic member of the opposite sex could easily be in touch with you.

Sunday, April 27 (Moon in Sagittarius)   You may need a lot of reassurance, and should let someone else know about it. It is okay to be dependent and sensitive once in a while. Whatever your situation, try to retreat a bit and get some relaxation. Among the other things that happen, you will learn the story behind the story, and it will help you in the future. The lucky number is 2.

Monday, April 28 (Moon Sagittarius to Capricorn 1:41 a.m.)   You should start out the week in a very positive frame of mind, because of your high lunar cycle. Treat yourself well, and dress to match. Your popularity is virtually assured now; in a sense, you can dance to your own tune. Reach out to others today, and you will be able to touch them very well. Keep your eye on a Sagittarian.

Tuesday, April 29 (Moon in Capricorn)   You have a serious purpose today, so you should not let a frivolous person distract you from what needs doing. Show that you can stick to the job until it's done. It is an excellent day to organize your personal surroundings—at home or at your place of business. Team up with an Aquarian or a Leo for good results.

Wednesday, April 30 (Moon Capricorn to Aquarius 4:06 a.m.) You may get the opportunity to tell someone exactly how you feel; do not hold back, even if you have to be a bit critical of him/her. You should be able to soften it. Some will definitely have romance on their minds, and could attract someone with a similar way of thinking. Realize that the status quo is undergoing some changes now. Be willing to change with it. The lucky number is 5.

MAY 1986

Thursday, May 1 (Moon in Aquarius) You will get the chance to prove how reliable you can be today, probably in a financial matter. In some cases, you will be paying a bill that is overdue and thereby showing good faith. Work at a steady pace and get something out of the way. By evening, you will feel a glow of satisfaction at a job well done. It is a practical day in every respect.

Friday, May 2 (Moon Aquarius to Pisces 9:30 a.m.) You could sell virtually anything, including yourself. Your way with words can easily convince others now. In matters of the heart, expect some changes—positive ones in general. Others can expect some kind of surprise—probably a reversal of opinion on someone else's part. The lucky number is 5.

Saturday, May 3 (Moon in Pisces) You can have a lot of fun if you get involved in a community project now; it could allow you to express your true talents and abilities. People around you may be talking about change—possibly even a move of residence. Do not let it throw you. Let a Libra be a steady influence.

Sunday, May 4 (Moon Pisces to Aries 8:01 p.m.) You can distinguish between dreams and reality and should when you make a promise today. If you allow wishful thinking to enter the picture, you will distort your usual practical view of reality. If you must "escape," read a good romantic novel—or get away from your everyday routine in some other way. The lucky number is 7.

Monday, May 5 (Moon in Aries) Your mind and your interest may be firmly focused on home and property now. In some cases, Capricorns are considering a purchase of real estate. Whatever business deal you are involved in will be concluded with great success. Realize that easy street is not far away. Someone is definitely on your side, and understands your ambitious nature.

Tuesday, May 6 (Moon in Aries) If you keep on hanging on to the past, you will hold yourself back. This is the time to clean up your act as far as family and others you depend on are concerned. Get ready to strike out on your own. Some Capricorns may want to get rid of some old clutter now; realize what you no longer need.

Wednesday, May 7 (Moon Aries to Taurus 4:59 a.m.) Come on, Capricorn, let down your hair and enjoy yourself. If you do, this could be a banner day—particularly in the area of love and romance. Your personal magnetism could easily attract a fun-loving, generous person who could make a big difference in your life. Be daring. The lucky number is 1.

Thursday, May 8 (Moon in Taurus) Don't rush into anything today; now's the time to plan and to listen to your inner voice of intuition. Many will be starting out on a new project, and should contemplate it carefully. In other cases, younger people may demand a lot of time and attention. Be willing to help and provide good counsel.

Friday, May 9 (Moon Taurus to Gemini 5:26 p.m.) Many Geminis will find themselves the center of attention at a social occasion; no matter how much you feel like staying home, resolve to get out. Your sense of humor and intellectual curiosity will make you absolutely sparkle now. Someone you haven't seen in a while could suddenly turn up, and you could have a fascinating discussion. Perk up and get out! The lucky number is 3.

Saturday, May 10 (Moon in Gemini) Today you should not count on too much time for fun and games—unless work is your greatest pleasure. No matter how you try to avoid it, you are not going to be able to get around serving others today. It will require discipline and true grit, but it will pay rewards. No, you can't delegate anything. An Aquarian could be fun—but not much help.

Sunday, May 11 (Moon in Gemini) Now the emphasis is on much more variety, and a lighter atmosphere. Some Capricorns will feel a distinct improvement in their health through an exercise program. Those who haven't started yet should begin to stretch their muscles—both physically and mentally. You may get an opportunity to exchange ideas with someone who is particularly witty and creative. Romance could develop quite spontaneously.

Monday, May 12 (Moon Gemini to Cancer 7:18 a.m.) Realize that you are the one who is going to have to make adjustments to keep the peace. Don't resent having to be the responsible, adaptable one. Your true satisfaction will come from maintaining a low profile and being willing to give more than you take. A Taurus could play a key role. The lucky number is 6.

Tuesday, May 13 (Moon in Cancer) Don't sign anything today or enter into any kind of an agreement without expert advice. You are much too ready to believe a sad story or to expect someone else to be impossibly perfect. If you are a "bleeding heart," you may miss some obvious truths. A Pisces could be in the picture.

Wednesday, May 14 (Moon Cancer to Leo 6:15 p.m.) Someone else is going to get the glory today, but in the long run it will benefit you greatly. Be willing to take a back seat temporarily and to bask in reflected glory. In a work matter, be willing to ask for advice from someone who has a proven track record. Don't be too proud! The lucky number is 8.

Thursday, May 15 (Moon in Leo) You are going to have to force yourself to see some new trends now if you are not to be left behind. Associate with people who are willing to be daring in both thought and deed; you could make a good money move thereby. On the more mundane level, clear up some old debts and unpaid bills. The lucky number is 9.

Friday, May 16 (Moon in Leo) You can advance your own interests now by teaming up with influential people; don't feel like a name-dropper. Someone will admire your spirit and say that he/she wants to get to know you better; realize that this person could be key to launching some important plans you have. However, don't be surprised if you find yourself getting in rather deep.

Saturday, May 17 (Moon Leo to Virgo 3:45 a.m.) This is a day to take a sentimental journey—either mentally or by actually going back to somewhere you've been before. It is an especially dreamy time when feelings are uppermost and a relaxed approach should be taken. Otherwise, you could get very raveled. Family is all important now, and you should take the lead from another Capricorn or a Cancer.

Sunday, May 18 (Moon in Virgo) Your restlessness and need for change could easily color this entire day. Without disrupting anyone else, try to schedule some activity that will get you out and around. In your rather frivolous mood, others may not take you particularly seriously—but you should not care.

Monday, May 19 (Moon Virgo to Libra 9:41 a.m.) Resolve to work with materials at hand to build foundations for a long-range project; you aren't going to get very far asking for more. All Capricorns should make an attempt to be their practical selves now; do not be led on a wild goose chase. There are some rather minor obstacles that do not require major moves. The lucky number is 4.

Tuesday, May 20 (Moon in Libra) If you want something, go right to the top today. A favor could easily be granted. Or changes you want could be made. You are exceptionally able to sell your own interests today, and will be able to do it with a lot of flair. It is a good time for creative thinking of all kinds, and for putting ideas down on paper. A Gemini or a Virgo could be an excellent sparring partner.

Wednesday, May 21 (Moon Libra to Scorpio 12:02 p.m.) Don't try to bulldoze somebody with an argumentative attitude today; tact will get you much farther. Many will find themselves in a position of power, and dealing with powerful people. You are able to be the master diplomat and should be able to bring two sides together. Listen for a distinctive voice; this person will be very important in the future.

Thursday, May 22 (Moon in Scorpio) You may attract a lot of people now, but you can relate only to a very select few. You are in a mood for privacy—and for secrecy. It is important to get at the real truth—particularly in a very personal situation. Talk the subtleties over with a Pisces or a Virgo. The lucky number is 7.

Friday, May 23 (Moon Scorpio to Sagittarius 11:57 a.m.) This full moon will find you having to make a very critical decision—probably with respect to a personal relationship. In some cases, you may have to choose between "the crowd" and someone you love very much on a one-to-one basis. Realize that a deep commitment is required, and a sense of responsibility is mandatory. If you are not willing to give it all, give nothing.

Saturday, May 24 (Moon in Sagittarius) Your conscience could be bothering you today, and it may prompt you to remember someone who is at a disadvantage. In your mood of altruism, you should draw the line at contributing to the continued dependence of someone who can really help him-/herself. Don't feel too lonely today, because you are not really alone at all. The lucky number is 9.

Sunday, May 25 (Moon Sagittarius to Capricorn 11:15 a.m.) Allow yourself free rein as far as creativity is concerned, but maintain your secrecy. It is possible that someone could steal your original ideas. Rumors may be flying today and some of them sound pretty tempting. Your best course is to stick with the way you have been doing things for now. As you go along, you will get a more complete story.

Monday, May 26 (Moon in Capricorn) You could have a highly emotional confrontation today; you are wise to let the past go, and to be willing to take a more creative approach to a relationship. Your cycle is very high, so you will be consulted by others, and should be able to come up with all the right answers. And earn yourself some very important points. No matter what else happens, resolve to be kind today.

Tuesday, May 27 (Moon Capricorn to Aquarius 12 noon) Your spirits should take a swift upward turn, and you should be feeling outgoing. Dress the part, because new and interesting contacts are a distinct possibility today. Trust your first impressions of people because they are bound to be accurate. Others will admire your joy in living. The lucky number is 3.

Wednesday, May 28 (Moon in Aquarius) This is self-improvement day, and you should take stock of yourself and what you have. You will not be the slightest bit put off when someone offers you some constructive criticism; your self-confidence is pretty solid now. An annoying job you've been avoiding is easy to push off. But try to handle routine matters.

Thursday, May 29 (Moon Aquarius to Pisces 3:54 p.m.) You may have to go on a "dig" today and the buried treasure is information you need. Don't be afraid to lean on some people who are key to your search; keep jabbing away until they come up with the answers. You are finally able to put it all together so it all makes sense, and you are satisfied. A quick change in routine may be needed to handle things well.

Friday, May 30 (Moon in Pisces) The world is very much with you today, and you may not like having to spend so much time filling people in. Give up your privacy for the day, and keep a sharp eye on messages that come in. Some may have a hidden clue. Indulge your love of things beautiful today—particularly music and art. The lucky number is 6.

Saturday, May 31 (Moon Pisces to Aries 11:43 p.m.) You could be rather foggy today, so you should avoid making important decisions. Instead, seek out the beauties of nature and try to lose yourself in some pursuit like reading. Or simply fantasizing. Realize that a romantic encounter may not be what you think it was; it's possible that love is "all in your head." Spend more sentimental time with a Pisces or a Virgo.

JUNE 1986

Sunday, June 1 (Moon in Aries) It's always nice to get presents, but one you receive today is particularly welcomed because it benefits everyone in your circle and makes you look like a hero. Take the credit, even though you know it's really a piece of good luck. Romance may be closer than you think. The lucky number is 5.

Monday, June 2 (Moon in Aries) Yesterday's experience makes you realize you really have to work on some intrafamily communications; not everybody knows exactly where you are coming from. Set them straight. Money, real estate, and related affairs are under good aspects.

Tuesday, June 3 (Moon Aries to Taurus 10:45 a.m.) Whether you like it or not, you are in the driver's seat of a project and it all depends on you. If you take your responsibilities seriously, you will raise your standing among some important people. Accept the challenge and go to work. In the privacy of your home, you can solve some puzzling relationship problems and get to know someone else's sentiments more fully.

Wednesday, June 4 (Moon in Taurus) Loved ones—particularly children—are an unexpected source of delight and pleasure today. Sometimes we forget how great it is to play. Enjoy the refreshment the interlude gives you, and enjoy the fact that romance may be in the picture too. Some Capricorns could have a kind of "triumph" today. The lucky number is 8.

Thursday, June 5 (Moon Taurus to Gemini 11:26 p.m.) You will succeed only if you are willing to completely break with the past in terms of people and procedures. It's tough to do, but you must, in order to show your own style—which can be pretty great. A strong creative drive could lead you to reach for new opportunities. And a dynamic Aries could help you a lot in breaking free of limiting circumstances.

Friday, June 6 (Moon in Gemini)   Today you feel far more self-assured—and loved. You know you are terrific because someone special tells you so, and gives you a great deal of support. At work, your original ideas will score a lot of points—particularly with someone who has perceived your romantic side. Don't go overboard in an exercise program.

Saturday, June 7 (Moon in Gemini)   It's OK to be lazy today and not to demand too much of yourself—no matter what anyone else thinks. A slow pace and leisurely attitude toward everything is the way to go now. You might simply enjoy some domestic chores that are pure fun—like cooking a good meal. The lucky number is 2.

Sunday, June 8 (Moon Gemini to Cancer 12:16 p.m.)   The best approach is to sit back and look at the total picture; it's possible you have gotten so close to it that you can't see the forest for the trees. You have plenty of time, so don't panic. Someone you don't trust can't hurt you significantly. You need some adventure, but you will have to content yourself with finding it with some amusing companion—possibly a Gemini or a Sagittarian.

Monday, June 9 (Moon in Cancer)   Others will be demanding a great deal of you today. You will be required to stick to the work at hand, and to overcome a few obstacles—but they will be minor. Take the solid approach, and don't worry. You will come through with flying colors. The lucky number is 4.

Tuesday, June 10 (Moon in Cancer)   The momentum is building again in a partnership or relationship. In a most positive way. However, you are wise to let your romantic partner make the first move, and simply to be receptive. No matter what your situation, be ready for a quick change of plans—or a most telling heart-to-heart talk. A dizzy pace could leave you rather breathless.

Wednesday, June 11 (Moon Cancer to Leo 12:11 a.m.) If you are warm today, in every sense of the word, you will do yourself a big favor. Many are yearning for more love and affection, and by showering attention on someone they can get it. Any kind of money you have to spend in this regard will be well spent. Someone very loyal will back you up, and make you feel a lot more appreciated.

Thursday, June 12 (Moon in Leo) Don't be afraid to delve into the mysteries of life and love; your spiritual side may be coming to the fore. In some cases, Capricorns are able to have "ESP" as far as a loved one is concerned. He/she will be amazed and delighted by your sensitivity. By sharing beliefs, you will gain love and togetherness. The lucky number is 7.

Friday, June 13 (Moon Leo to Virgo 10:18 a.m.) The key to power is pooling resources now. What you can't accomplish alone can be done with someone else—possibly a rather high-level person. Do not be afraid to approach and ask for what you need. Some Capricorns are getting added recognition and prestige now. Let another Capricorn tell you how it feels.

Saturday, June 14 (Moon in Virgo) If you get some necessary things out of the way early in the day, you could be off on the road to "adventure." In some cases, you are breaking through barriers now and successfully going past limiting circumstances. It is important to keep your ideals in mind, and to get your message across. You could express yourself successfully now. The lucky number is 9.

Sunday, June 15 (Moon Virgo to Libra 5:38 p.m.) You should have a "clean slate" feeling now, and it should allow you to put the accent on new ideas and new theories. There could even be something new in the romantic sector; some will meet a person with a very different background, who could prove rather fascinating. Be ready to alter some long-range plans and some cherished beliefs; you may find they are not as substantial as you thought.

Monday, June 16 (Moon in Libra) Expect to be in the right place at the right time to advance yourself. If you follow your own intuition now, but stay aware of the rules and regulations, you can make a lot of progress. Some Capricorns are so favored that someone in a position of authority could overlook your shortcomings. Lucky you! For many, watchful waiting is advised.

Tuesday, June 17 (Moon Libra to Scorpio 9:36 p.m.) Relax and rely on your sense of humor to keep things in perspective today. You may be in some rather high-powered company, and could feel a bit at a disadvantage. You shouldn't. Some should attempt to diversify their interests now, and not to concentrate everything in one area. Let a Sagittarian show you how. The lucky number is 3.

Wednesday, June 18 (Moon in Scorpio) You may have to revise your goals to bring them more in line with reality. Even though you are a Capricorn, you may have forgotten that hard and not wishful thinking is what brings ultimate rewards. The moral of the story is that you should not delegate details to someone less responsible than you; you will regret it if you do. This is your chance to prove that you can follow through.

Thursday, June 19 (Moon Scorpio to Sagittarius 10:36 p.m.) Now the limits on you ease up, and you're able to experience some change and variety. Don't take a light conversation you have with a member of the opposite sex too lightly; it could be extremely revealing. And don't turn down any invitations; you never know what is there to be learned. Or who is there to be met. A wish can come true. The lucky number is 5.

Friday, June 20 (Moon in Sagittarius) The emphasis is much more on family and home now, as well as extra efforts that lead to greater harmony and understanding. Be diplomatic and willing to listen to problems. You probably have some good solutions to offer. An Aries, a Libra, or a Scorpio could be particularly comforting today. As could home life.

Saturday, June 21 (Moon Sagittarius to Capricorn 10:00 p.m.) You could find yourself rather restless today. An aura of glamour and intrigue colors everything. If you attempt to "escape," you could do yourself a lot of harm; do some soul-searching instead. Peace and quiet will help you figure out a puzzling situation involving a relationship. It will get better—promise. The lucky number is 7.

Sunday, June 22 (Moon in Capricorn) This is a very powerful full moon for you—the most powerful of the year. It could find you at the peak of your powers. Don't waste them. For one thing, you should be able to exert great influence over someone who has been rather hesitant and slow to commit. Show that you are responsible and serious, and ready for the most long-reaching kind of involvement. For all Capricorns, a new attitude will bring you significant gains.

Monday, June 23 (Moon Capricorn to Aquarius 9:50 p.m.) You should attack this day full of resolve to complete tasks and start out on a new road to progress. In some cases, your activities will be as mundane as sorting through papers, clothes, and other material that is no longer useful to you. Be brave in discarding links to the past. An Aries could be extremely helpful in this regard.

Tuesday, June 24 (Moon in Aquarius) Ingenuity and invention are your best weapons now. And the keys to greater earning power. Some of you could be overlooking important potentials of gain right under your nose. Keep on the alert! And dress for success.

Show people you believe in yourself, and they will believe in you. The lucky number is 1.

Wednesday, June 25 (Moon in Aquarius) Your security feelings could take over today and cause you to focus on what you have and what more you can save. You are right to have concern for the future. Let someone who has experience play a major role in resolving a situation—particularly with regard to money. Realize that you do not have to worry or pinch pennies too much—the situation is not that bad.

Thursday, June 26 (Moon Aquarius to Pisces 12:12 a.m.) Go ahead and take that step you've been hesitating about. It need not be a very big one, because there are many ways you can expand your horizons now. For instance, someone new has information that can considerably brighten the picture for you—and make life seem a lot more interesting. All should do what they can to stimulate their mental processes now; your biggest enemy is stagnation at this point. The lucky number is 3.

Friday, June 27 (Moon in Pisces) You are going to have to stick with the paperwork today, much as you may resent it. Some of you are going to have to ask for agreements in writing and to read things carefully before they sign on the dotted line. For anyone, paying attention to minor points will now serve you very well; what seems insignificant now will be extremely important later on. An Aquarian could be very much in the picture.

Saturday, June 28 (Moon Pisces to Aries 6:35 a.m.) There could easily be a glitch in one of your relationships now; be willing to change your ways and transform your ideas if you want to restore a good feeling. For others, an exciting change could be on the agenda if you simply open up your mind, and allow something new to come in to your sphere of interest. A

Gemini, a Virgo, or a Sagittarian could be an excellent companion.

Sunday, June 29 (Moon in Aries) To negotiate this day successfully, you are going to have to be especially charming. You might even consider going all out and splurging on a luxury gift—or some lavish entertaining. You may be amazed when a rather stubborn person suddenly switches over to your side and proves to be a tower of strength. Don't hide your natural talents today.

Monday, June 30 (Moon Aries to Taurus 4:54 p.m.) You may put yourself temporarily out of circulation in order to work on something that desperately needs working on. Don't feel sorry for yourself, because this is your chance to find out who the "real you" really is. Some may find themselves caught up in escapist experiences—even a job that seems especially glamorous. You may have to come down to earth later on. The lucky number is 7.

JULY 1986

Tuesday, July 1 (Moon in Taurus) The accent is definitely on pleasure today and possibly self-indulgence. At all costs, watch your calorie intake, because your sweet tooth could be especially sweet now. Enjoy romance or a family celebration instead. Let a Taurus or a Libra show you how. The lucky number is 6.

Wednesday, July 2 (Moon in Taurus) A romantic "thing" that seems too good to be true may be just that. You are much better off playing a waiting game than plunging in without knowing what is really going on. At this point in time, you are not seeing people or situations as they actually are, and run the risk of "falling in love with love." Be more self-protective. The lucky number is 7.

Thursday, July 3 (Moon Taurus to Gemini 5:32 a.m.) No matter what you do today, a responsible attitude is the key to making it work. Some may be asked to accept new responsibilities or even a leadership post; ask yourself if you are really ready to move up the ladder. Any could be in line for more prestige and an increase in income, but you must be able to put it in perspective.

Friday, July 4 (Moon in Gemini) This should be a rather pleasant holiday, but not one during which you can totally goof off. You are the one who is going to be called on to make the day work and to put some new methods and techniques into practice. Many will get a great hand for their innovative ideas. Others will run into someone with big ideas about the future. Listen, but don't "bite."

Saturday, July 5 (Moon Gemini to Cancer 6:19 p.m.) You may feel like plunging feet first into a self-improvement program, but realize that you could overdo things today. It is well to think about your diet and a dramatic change in your appearance, but don't let it carry you past the point of good sense. A Leo or an Aquarian could have some excellent suggestions for you.

Sunday, July 6 (Moon in Cancer) The emphasis is on home, property, security, and closer partnership ties. Be willing to see both sides of the question in any direct confrontation you find yourself involved in. You should be aware of the fact that this is the time for watchful waiting rather than action. Subtlety and diplomacy will work a lot better than direct action.

Monday, July 7 (Moon in Cancer) Your light touch and sense of humor could be your best weapons today. You also should ask more questions than you answer. That is often the technique public relations people use, and you should try it now. Realize that some are judging you by your appearance now, and do something about it. The lucky number is 3.

Tuesday, July 8 (Moon Cancer to Leo 5:56 a.m.)
Someone may say "Let's play" today, but you should realize that it is better to say "Wait until tomorrow." Don't let any kind of details slip by your notice today if you are going to be on solid ground. It is critical to be as well-informed as possible. Some may find that they can find a genuine bargain when they shop.

Wednesday, July 9 (Moon in Leo) Now you can let out all the stops—particularly where love and the physical expression of it are concerned. You can also alter a situation that was going down the wrong track; now you can get it back on the right one. The key is to have a frank, down-to-earth exchange of ideas. It could transform things totally.

Thursday, July 10 (Moon Leo to Virgo 3:50 p.m.)
Today you will benefit through the generosity of someone else. In some cases, an extravagant member of the opposite sex could arrive bearing gifts. If that is not your scenario, then you can expect loyalty and stability from someone who is important in your scheme of things. There could even be a marriage offer. Your lucky number is 6.

Friday, July 11 (Moon in Virgo) You could easily have a mad urge to get away from it all. Possibly because you want to really see if the grass is greener on the other side of the world. It's okay to have a rosy view of the future now, particularly if you share your plans and dreams with someone else. Just make sure that person's sensitive and warmhearted. Take some time out to appreciate art of any kind, and the beautiful things of life.

Saturday, July 12 (Moon Virgo to Libra 11:40 p.m.)
Even though this is a weekend, you should count on the fact that someone in a high place is pulling strings for you. No matter what your particular scenario, things are looking up, and you could be recognized for some efforts you made in the past. Another

Capricorn or Cancer could be extremely prominent today, and worth listening to. The lucky number is 8.

Sunday, July 13 (Moon in Libra) You could get the distinct feeling that someone who is holding you back is about to drop out of your life; you are right. And you do not have to spend any time crying over *this* spilt milk. Instead, put your efforts on projects that will definitely bring you more income—monetary or psychic. Start thinking big, and big things will happen.

Monday, July 14 (Moon in Libra) You could easily charm the birds out of the trees today, and you should use your appeal to your best advantage. Try using your charm and magnetism on someone who has both authority and some rather creative ideas. If you show how independent you can be, you might find yourself in your own business—or at least in the catbird seat. The lucky number is 1.

Tuesday, July 15 (Moon Libra to Scorpio 4:58 a.m.) There is definitely a slower pace to this day, and you should relax and enjoy it. Your attitude will definitely help you to win friends and influence people. If you are subtle and tactful, and do not force issues, there is no limit on what you can accomplish now. Someone who is very security conscious will influence your thinking today. Pay special attention to your hunches or "psychic feelings."

Wednesday, July 16 (Moon in Scorpio) You should find yourself breaking out of a rut and running into fascinating new people in new places. There are a lot of contacts to be made, and you should do everything to cultivate them. However, it is not a time to put all your eggs in one basket; realize that there is more than one route to success. Don't be such a single-minded Capricorn.

Thursday, July 17 (Moon Scorpio to Sagittarius 7:34 a.m.) If you gang up with some other people, you can easily solve what seems to be an overwhelming obstacle. Do your part, but realize that you can't be as effective alone as you can be with others. Some may have to settle for little glory now, but the knowledge that they are doing good things for others. You are wise to avoid those who are merely out for a good time. The lucky number is 4.

Friday, July 18 (Moon in Sagittarius) If you get involved in a confidential conversation today, you will find that you have a lot greater rapport with someone. It could be someone of the opposite sex. It is not the time to count on unspoken words; you need to spell things out if you are to be understood. Some will find that love is blooming after a rather negative atmosphere is transformed.

Saturday, July 19 (Moon Sagittarius to Capricorn 8:10 a.m.) Watch out for a troublemaker today—possibly someone right in your own midst. Listen to some confidences and try to play the role of mediator; realize that it is up to you to promote harmony. However, draw the line at being used—you do not have to be a doormat for others.

Sunday, July 20 (Moon in Capricorn) This is finally your day. However, although others may seek you out, you may prefer to be alone. It is an excellent time for searching inward, and finding new ways to express yourself. The better you get to know yourself, the more you can do for yourself. Many will find you rather glamorous and mysterious now. The lucky number is 7.

Monday, July 21 (Moon Capricorn to Aquarius 8:17 a.m.) This is the best full moon of the year for you. It finds you at the peak of your powers, as nothing occurs halfway. Now's the time to make a power play or gain glory. In love, a relationship could grow a lot more serious and possibly lead to a long-term commitment. Don't waste a minute!

Tuesday, July 22 (Moon in Aquarius) Many could be involved in a rather large money transaction now. In some cases, it will be an investment. Realize that you are ready to use your skills and talents much more widely, and perhaps that is the best thing you can invest. It is important to give up rather limited ideas about income, and assets. Let an Aries or a Libra give you a better perspective on this. The lucky number is 9.

Wednesday, July 23 (Moon Aquarius to Pisces 9:59 a.m.) The way to make solid gains is to have original ideas and fresh concepts. Don't continue to be dependent on someone else, but begin to see how you can earn more money yourself. For many, there will be the chance to get in on the ground floor of a new enterprise. Be confident, and don't hang back. There is no reason to.

Thursday, July 24 (Moon in Pisces) Today your intuition is right on target, and you should play those "lucky hunches." Your ability to sense what someone else is up to could easily save the day. People around you may be particularly anxious to communicate now and teach you what they know. A particularly sensitive individual will play a key role.

Friday, July 25 (Moon Pisces to Aries 3:02 p.m.) You will have your choice of pals and companions today, but you should be rather discriminating. Know who your real friends are. A lot of good fun is indicated, and you could find yourself involved in all kinds of activities. Let yourself go for once! The lucky number is 3.

Saturday, July 26 (Moon in Aries) Routine matters will keep you rather occupied today. In fact, someone will be watching you to see if you will do the things you promised to do. It may be worth it, because you could be well rewarded if you see current projects through. However, you do not have to knuckle under to someone else's dominating attitude. An Aquarian or a Leo could figure prominently.

Sunday, July 27 (Moon in Aries) Don't expect anything to go as you expected it to today. Nothing will be static, but there could be some very exciting developments. In some cases, an impromptu change of plans will find you involved in a very serious conversation. Realize that it can lead to a much greater rapport.

Monday, July 28 (Moon Aries to Taurus 12:11 a.m.) This is a time for sharing. You may be acutely conscious of your responsibilities to others, but you should try to turn them into pleasure rather than "work." There are a lot of ways you can turn routine things into creative activity and amusement now. Others are depending on you. The lucky numbers is 6.

Tuesday, July 29 (Moon in Taurus) A personal relationship is heavy on romantic illusion now, but short on a realistic view of things. If you feel that you are walking on air, realize that you could abruptly find yourself coming down to earth—with a rude shock. Do not continue to deceive yourself. And reject false flattery. A Pisces could clarify things for you considerably.

Wednesday, July 30 (Moon Taurus to Gemini 12:19 p.m.) Don't let yourself be thrown off course by someone who really isn't very significant; try to brush off this minor annoyance. Instead, make your own opportunities—in both love and money. There are gains to be made now, particularly if you are daring. The lucky number is 8.

Thursday, July 31 (Moon in Gemini) Someone may try to drag you into a rather petty argument, but you should do your best to rise above it. However, even though someone is jealous of you, do not allow him/her to take credit for your accomplishments. This is no time for the line of least resistance—you deserve recognition. Start now to get more competitive.

AUGUST 1986

Friday, August 1 (Moon in Gemini) Be absolutely realistic about how valuable certain people are, especially those who assist you. Don't expect anything that is less than what meets your standards. In some cases, Capricorns will be learning the "true story" and could be a bit disappointed. It may become absolutely clear that someone has been pulling the wool over your eyes, and it could hurt a bit. If you can, postpone an important decision.

Saturday, August 2 (Moon Gemini to Cancer 1:04 a.m.) A partnership situation holds great promise for the future. The key is to show how dependable you can be. Some Capricorns will find themselves dealing with "big wheels" and should make every effort to show how responsible they are. It is important to be willing to compromise now. Try your luck with number 8 today.

Sunday, August 3 (Moon in Cancer) Now's the time to get your message across. No matter where you find yourself, it is a good day to focus on self-promotion and self-advertising. If you prove that you can do things on a grand scale, you will show that you can rise above some limiting conditions. Let some other people help you make a good showing—possibly an Aries or a Libra could be particularly important to you now.

Monday, August 4 (Moon Cancer to Leo 12:26 p.m.) For many Capricorns, today could be the start of something big in a relationship. Do not hang back or wait to be asked; this is the time for action. No matter what your scenario, drama, romance, and unique new experiences await you. Get ready! And go out to meet them. The lucky number is 1.

Tuesday, August 5 (Moon in Leo) Today an urge for greater security could overtake you. One thing that may mean is that you are willing to forego extravagances in order to start building a savings account. In some cases, it will cement a relationship that was in danger of falling apart. Others may be contemplating a move to a bigger or better residence. Realize that teamwork is needed to make your dreams come true.

Wednesday, August 6 (Moon Leo to Virgo 9:44 p.m.) Something is rather baffling today, but if you apply your intellectual curiosity to it, you can solve the mystery. Some of you may be rather bored with everyday routine, but if you scatter your energies in too many directions, you will get absolutely nowhere—and possibly even take a few steps backward. Try to stick with it today, even though a Sagittarian may tempt you to run away.

Thursday, August 7 (Moon in Virgo) The emphasis today is on routine and attention to a rebuilding program. For some, a message comes in that will build hopes and expand vistas. If you put your mind to it, you can cut through a lot of red tape and overcome some obstacles. The key is to stick to the job at hand. The lucky number is 4.

Friday, August 8 (Moon Virgo to Libra 5:05 a.m.) Now you should feel a lot less restricted, and ready to move into some new areas. In some cases, a fascinating new contact will arrive on the scene and add some definite sparkle to your life. No matter what happens today, keep your eyes open for some new experiences and possibly a surprising message. However, you could easily miss it if you keep your eyes on the ground instead of on higher things.

Saturday, August 9 (Moon in Libra) Be willing to see both sides of the story—especially in dealing with a parent or other authority figure. The way to get your way is through diplomacy and not through tough tactics. Most of you are on the verge of getting greater recognition, but realize that you could blow your chances for it. In some cases a family reunion is on the agenda. Don't compete with someone who has definite artistic tendencies.

Sunday, August 10 (Moon in Libra) An inspiring message will give you hope today—and some comfort as well. Even with that, you may want to surround yourself with music and other beautiful things to soothe your soul. A glamorous individual could be coming into the picture, and could be the key element in a rather dramatic change of values for you, and a new direction in life. The lucky number is 7.

Monday, August 11 (Moon Libra to Scorpio 10:36 a.m.) If you focus your energies properly today, you can make a really good move on your job. In some cases, it will help you immensely in pursuit of your long-range career goals. You should realize that you have the leadership capabilities to go to the top, and only you are holding you back. A member of the opposite sex may show that he or she really believes in you. The lucky number is 8.

Tuesday, August 12 (Moon in Scorpio) Many Capricorns are going to get a very special invitation around this time; realize that it will greatly add to your social circle. Some of you are being held back at this time by your own limited viewpoint; if you resolve to broaden out and reach out, you have every chance of making your dreams come true. Don't ignore someone who makes a bold approach.

Wednesday, August 13 (Moon Scorpio to Sagittarius 2:17 p.m.) Members of a certain group or circle show that they are willing to back you all the way now. Do not underestimate this valuable help. In some cases, there will be the opportunity to show how pioneering you can be when a rather unique situation lands in your lap. That new direction in life, including a romantic overtone, continues for many.

Thursday, August 14 (Moon in Sagittarius) You are wise to rely on your sixth sense in solving problems now. If you are very subtle, and a bit indirect, you can find out what the real story is. However, no matter how much confidential information falls in your hands today, resolve to guard the secrets of another person. He/she has confided in you. The lucky number is 2.

Friday, August 15 (Moon Sagittarius to Capricorn 4:22 p.m.) You can raise your own morale by helping other people, including someone who is confined to home or hospital. You yourself may be feeling a bit under the weather, and could have a tendency to self-doubt today. If you get out and socialize, you will feel a lot better. The more you spread hope and optimism, the better you will feel yourself. A Sagittarian could play a key role.

Saturday, August 16 (Moon in Capricorn) As the moon moves into Capricorn, you move into the monthly high of your lunar cycle. That means you are in an excellent position for pushing forward some personal projects. Most will have a lot of self-discipline today, and should be able to begin any kind of ambitious program. For some, it will be diet and exercise. Admit that you are a little distressed with the way you have been looking lately.

Sunday, August 17 (Moon Capricorn to Aquarius 5:44 p.m.) Some kind of "romantic adventure" is on the agenda, no matter how much disguise it wears. It is important to be flexible now, especially when you get into a rather stimulating conversation. Whatever you do, do not become dogmatic. Some of you will be the center of all attention and eyes as you move around a lot today. Enjoy your popularity! The lucky number is 5.

Monday, August 18 (Moon in Aquarius) There may be some tension in the atmosphere over someone's spending habits—possibly yours. Don't get into a knockdown and drag-out fight with someone who wants to debate over the things you choose; even if you feel you are in the right, you should be willing to back down. It's wise to explain to someone rather stubborn that you are really willing to compromise.

Tuesday, August 19 (Moon Aquarius to Pisces 7:52 p.m.) This full moon could easily make you feel as if money is burning a hole in your pocket. You may be tempted to take a quick money scheme seriously. It's important not to be fooled by a line someone gives you, and to realize that there is really no such thing as something for nothing. Any Capricorn would be wise to let someone else handle the checkbook today. The lucky number is 7.

Wednesday, August 20 (Moon in Pisces) Today you are in a much better position to make an agreement involving business or money. Some of you will be on a power "high" and confident of future success. You are right to feel that way and should take advantage of this by talking with important people in high places. In a relationship matter, you can reach an understanding now about a long-term commitment.

Thursday, August 21 (Moon in Pisces) Don't let yourself get drawn into someone else's battle today; resolve to overlook some petty gossip—even though it may sound interesting. A lot will be going on in your own backyard now, and you could be feeling a bit fenced in. However, you still should be able to evaluate just where you are headed. Realize that there is a lot more to life than this. Your lucky number is 9 today.

Friday, August 22 (Moon Pisces to Aries 12:27 a.m.) There may be some kind of "drama in everyday life" right around your own home. You and someone else may be at odds about how things should be done. However, you can utilize some very good current vibes that make you rather artistic at the moment. If you want to make your surroundings more distinctive, this is an excellent time to do so.

Saturday, August 23 (Moon in Aries) Follow your hunches today, but don't make any major moves. Instead, take some time out to enjoy your home, your family, and some quiet time. If you must be useful, concern yourself with safety and security. Plus do some reminiscing about the past. Some Capricorns could find that researching family roots could be a pleasant hobby. The lucky number today is 2.

Sunday, August 24 (Moon Aries to Taurus 8:36 a.m.) You will probably be very quick on the uptake today, and find that you can be the life of the party. The party may be right in your own domestic environment. And you should find yourself sharing some common interests with someone very interesting. It could be a Sagittarian, a Gemini, or a Virgo.

Monday, August 25 (Moon in Taurus) Approach something with great care today; you may find that it is necessary to tear it down before you can rebuild it to everyone's satisfaction. Even if it is a bit of a drag, don't skimp on the necessary research and preparation before you begin. For best results, stick with someone who has a very solid reputation.

Tuesday, August 26 (Moon Taurus to Gemini 8:00 p.m.) Many Capricorns could have a romantic experience now that becomes "one for the memory books." All of you should be prepared to throw the status quo out of the window to prepare for a sudden change, new faces, and new places. At the very least, you will be involved in a very stimulating conversation today; once you establish rapport with someone, there is no telling where it may go. The lucky number is 5.

Wednesday, August 27 (Moon in Gemini) For some of you, a recent break with a close relationship is on its way to repair. The way to speed things up is to show that you care—through affectionate words or just plain doing for someone else. It could be as simple as cooking a good meal. Listen to a Libra or a Taurus who has been down this road before.

Thursday, August 28 (Moon in Gemini) You may be especially sensitive to the moods and feelings of others today; you can really help them by listening and offering a shoulder to cry on. For some of you, co-workers may be especially in need of your compassion. Be willing to work behind the scenes and to give someone else the glory now; your time will come.

Friday, August 19 (Moon Gemini to Cancer 8:40 a.m.) Today you should have an enormous amount of ambition, and it will be greatly backed up by somebody at the top who is definitely on your side. No matter what your situation, something will happen that allows you to display your leadership ability. Don't blow it! The lucky number is 8.

Saturday, August 30 (Moon in Cancer) Today you are going to have to sit back and take a rather unselfish position while someone else gets the limelight—and the applause. Try not to be envious, and to pitch in and help someone else's dreams come true. He/she may do the same for you someday. An Aries or a Libra could be an excellent role model today.

Sunday, August 31 (Moon Cancer to Leo 8:08 p.m.) You should be especially able to persuade people today, and draw them over to your point of view. In fact, you may find that a member of the opposite sex is particularly attracted and shares interests openly. Enjoy being center stage, but don't insist on making all the major decisions. Realize that your judgment may be slightly off target now. The lucky number is 1.

SEPTEMBER 1986

Monday, September 1 (Moon in Leo) A relationship with a member of the opposite sex is deepening now, and you can be assured of solid ties for the future. Stability counts more than excitement now, and you should be very aware of that. In fact, you should be more than willing to make firm commitments. For some, joint finances look much brighter. The lucky number is 8.

Tuesday, September 2 (Moon in Leo) Let go of some limiting ideas and petty fears now. Also, resolve to be less selfish in your approach. It is a time to share and to express your humanitarian feelings. In some cases, you will do something like joining a charity drive or getting involved in bettering a financial situation for someone else.

Wednesday, September 3 (Moon Leo to Virgo 5:06 a.m.) A new start in a new direction is definitely indicated. In many cases, you will find yourself in touch with people of a very different background. No matter who you meet, try to be open-minded; you never know when you will be the "foreigner" yourself. For some, a long-distance phone call comes in and dramatically changes the situation. A rather impressive person could come along and impress you a lot.

Thursday, September 4 (Moon in Virgo) The accent is on long-range plans, including education. For some, someone from the past could suddenly reappear and throw a different light on the current situation. Do enjoy nostalgic memories, because an evaluation of your current life direction could come out of it. Don't be afraid to be a bit sentimental. The lucky number is 2.

Friday, September 5 (Moon Virgo to Libra 11:33 a.m.) You may hear someone talking about a career training opportunity that could make you a lot more qualified to move forward in your career; listen carefully. You should be very eager for knowledge now, and intellectual challenge. However, don't scatter your forces or spread yourself too thin. A Sagittarian could play a key role.

Saturday, September 6 (Moon in Libra) Almost without your wanting it, you could find yourself thrust into a leadership role now. Or simply taking a lot more responsibility than you think you are ready for. Realize that this is not the time for a "glamour job"; routine and details are strongly accented now, plus the ability to follow through. Someone who counts is watching you carefully to see whether you are able to "carry the ball."

Sunday, September 7 (Moon Libra to Scorpio 4:12 p.m.) A "summit meeting" may assume great importance today. Your suggestions for key changes will not only be solicited, they will be listened to and respected. Don't be afraid to open your mouth and say what you think. A Gemini could play a major role, and could be an extremely good ally now. The lucky number is 5.

Monday, September 8 (Moon in Scorpio) Someone may be holding a grudge, and you are the key to resolving this rather disturbing situation. A tactful manner is all-important, even though it may be difficult for you to maintain it. For most Capricorns, hopes and wishes now revolve around family and friends. In some cases, those who want to move will find the right place to go to now.

Tuesday, September 9 (Moon Scorpio to Sagittarius 7:40 p.m.) Don't feel sorry for yourself if someone disappoints you. Sometimes your expectations are unrealistic. If you concentrate on listening to somebody else's sad story, you will be able to take a much more positive attitude. Toward your own situation as well. Wishful thinking will get you nowhere now. A Pisces could be in the picture. The lucky number is 7.

Wednesday, September 10 (Moon in Sagittarius) You could easily make a name for yourself now by handling yourself right in a rather high-level conference. In fact, you could easily make a power play. At the very least, you should insist that you are given credit for your ideas—although you may have to wait until the time is right. Another Capricorn or a Cancer could be a really good buddy at this time.

Thursday, September 11 (Moon Sagittarius to Capricorn 10:28 p.m.) Now opportunities for greater self-expression should be easy to find. For some, that will include an opportunity to convey true feelings to someone who is loved—if rather secretly. Do not continue to hide your light under a bushel; you really have a lot of talent, and it can benefit others as well as yourself. The lucky number is 9.

Friday, September 12 (Moon in Capricorn) You should have an abundance of original ideas now, and whatever creative talents you have should be shown. In this high of your lunar cycle, you are at the peak of your powers, and should be ready to assume the spotlight. If you feel rather fainthearted, look around for a rather generous warmhearted person who will provide the aid you need.

Saturday, September 13 (Moon in Capricorn) Today you should allow yourself to relax and pay some attention to your personal well-being. For some, that will mean spending both time and money on appearance. Don't be afraid to do a total make-over. Family members should be especially willing to give you backing now. Also depend on your intuition to take you where you want to go. The lucky number is 2.

Sunday, September 14 (Moon Capricorn to Aquarius 1:07 a.m.) You are going to have to watch your spending habits. For many, there will be a tendency to splurge or to live beyond their means. Realize that you could regret it tomorrow. If you hook up with friends, realize that you do not have to pick up the check for everyone. Nor do you have to scatter your energies in every direction.

Monday, September 15 (Moon in Aquarius) Now it's time to face up to reality and to settle accounts. For some, that literally means paying bills and balancing checkbooks. If you take care of financial details while the timing is right, you will find that you benefit. A practical, down-to-earth mood should help a lot. Let an Aquarian or a Leo provide solace for you today.

Tuesday, September 16 (Moon Aquarius to Pisces 4:27 a.m.) You should be able to sell your ideas with great ease today. If you don't get a chance to talk about them, you should get things in writing; your creative juices should be flowing freely now. Some will find it much easier to communicate with someone of the opposite sex who has been a bit aloof. The lucky number is 5.

Wednesday, September 17 (Moon in Pisces) Try to get in touch with someone who has been at a distance for quite a while; it could be an important member of the family who is greatly missed. Some may find themselves discussing domestic changes, including a possible move. Don't despair if you can't find the ideal thing right away. Simply keep on looking for more information, and put out feelers in every direction.

Thursday, September 18 (Moon Pisces to Aries 9:33 a.m.) Whatever happens, don't agree to anything today that is not absolutely clear. You could be creating a reality of your own rather than looking at things squarely. In some cases, someone may offer you a half-baked proposal. Don't bite! If you must escape, you are far better off reading a good book or watching a good movie.

Friday, September 19 (Moon in Aries) In many cases, a deeper commitment is being asked for—in love or in marriage. It is important for you to let your partner know that you are looking for stability, not simply a fly-by-night romance. No matter what your situation is. Home, property, and greater prestige are important values at this time. The lucky number is 8.

Saturday, September 20 (Moon Aries to Taurus 5:25 p.m.) You could get a grand and glorious feeling today by devoting yourself to some kind of cause. It will help you rise above self-interest and put some money in your "psychic bank." In the course of whatever good things you do today, you will meet people who will be in a position to help you a great deal. You are not wasting time.

Sunday, September 21 (Moon in Taurus) You could easily be feeling rather daring today, and you are right to take an active rather than a passive role. Express yourself in any way possible—even by dressing up in a rather bold bright manner. It should be easy for you to attract both love and attention now. For some, an affair of the heart is getting hotter all the time. A Leo could play a key role.

Monday, September 22 (Moon in Taurus) Many Capricorns will find themselves heavily involved with children now. And it should provide a lot of pleasure. It's an excellent time for some kind of generous gesture—possibly involving the preparing or serving of good food. However, don't force any issues now, or make any major decisions. You are much better off taking a more passive role. Listen to the advice of someone older who steps in to play a "teacher" role.

Tuesday, September 23 (Moon Taurus to Gemini 4:13 a.m.) There should be a lot of opportunities in the air today, possibly one including travel. A lighthearted, positive attitude will earn you most points today. Some will have to deal intelligently with a rather unsettling phone call. A Sagittarian or a Gemini could help you resolve the matter with humor.

Wednesday, September 24 (Moon in Gemini) You should get the opportunity to show how sincere you can be, particularly when it comes to helping someone else overcome obstacles. Though you will have to attend to basic routine, you should be able to make a brilliant revision of plans. Realize that patience and self-discipline are needed in order to get to the finish line. Don't let anyone distract you, particularly in Aquarian.

Thursday, September 25 (Moon Gemini to Cancer 4:44 p.m.) Someone you work with could easily be attracted now, and make no secret of it. If you choose your words carefully today, you can make some constructive changes in your immediate environment. However, you are going to have to make some efforts to break loose of your own inhibitions; dare to be different. The lucky number is 5.

Friday, September 26 (Moon in Cancer) Love, romance, and marriage are very prominent in the picture today. No matter what your situation, if your partner shows that he/she is ready for a fight, be the first to make peace. In some cases, it may be necessary to rearrange your schedule to make yourself available for more "togetherness." It is not the worst thing you could do today. Keep an eye on a Taurus.

Saturday, September 27 (Moon in Cancer) You are going to have to insist on something more substantial than vague promises now; get it in writing. For some Capricorns, legality will become an issue, and it could involve some kind of partnership activity. It is important to take off your rose-colored glasses and to see people, places, and events as they really are.

Sunday, September 28 (Moon Cancer to Leo 5:39 a.m.) Someone will be very generous with you today, and you should be willing to express your thanks in an equally generous manner. It is a day in which you should be lucky—in love, money, or any area of your life. It also could be a day in which responsibility pays off. You will not be sorry that you have proven yourself stable as far as someone else is concerned. The lucky number is 8.

Monday, September 29 (Moon in Leo) For a number of Capricorns, one chapter of life is coming to a close, and another is beginning. At this juncture, you are experiencing a major shift in values and goals. Realize that if you are willing to release your past, your long-term objectives will be much easier to reach. Don't neglect to hear the message of a rather dynamic individual; he/she has an eye on the future.

Tuesday, September 30 (Moon Leo to Virgo 1:57 p.m.) A rather dramatic day is indicated. Some Capricorns will have the chance to turn an intense physical attraction into a permanent relationship. Marriage, children, and all passionate aspects of love are high on the list of issues of the day. Some will be solving a mystery, and it could involve a Leo. The lucky number is 1.

OCTOBER 1986

Wednesday, October 1 (Moon in Virgo) The accent now is on new horizons, including travel to rather fascinating new places. Listen to someone who is both aggressive and future oriented. He/she can show you the way. No matter what your situation, you will be far better off putting aside petty emotions in favor of a bigger viewpoint. Be ready for adventure at any moment!

Thursday, October 2 (Moon Virgo to Libra 8:03 p.m.) Some may meet the proverbial "fascinating stranger" today. Since you should be dynamic and original now, you should have no problem attracting this person. If you are interested, you can get what you want. The key is to be willing to assume the role of decision maker. The lucky number is 1.

Friday, October 3 (Moon in Libra) Listen to that "inner voice," especially with regard to your career path. Some of you may feel pulled in two different directions by the events of the day. This is a time for change, but mainly in tactics, not so much in your actual situation. Do not force any issues now.

Saturday, October 4 (Moon Libra to Scorpio 11:35 p.m.) Get ready for contact with a person or persons who can really make you make a big step forward. However, you are going to have to show how witty and flexible you can really be—and how optimistic an attitude you can have, when you are in the right mood. And you should be today. Dress for the occasion!

Sunday, October 5 (Moon in Scorpio) This is no time for wishful thinking; you are going to have to prove yourself. That means, attend to all those practical, routine matters that form a solid foundation on which you can build your hopes and dreams. In some cases, you may have to say no to any enticing invitation. What you give up you will get back in spades. The lucky number is 4.

Monday, October 6 (Moon in Scorpio) A rather witty, well-informed person may come on the scene and make some sweeping changes in your life. However, you may not realize how important he/she is immediately. If necessary, be ready to take off at a moment's notice; if you do not jump at a chance, it may not come again. Most should wait expectantly for the phone to ring.

Tuesday, October 7 (Moon Scorpio to Sagittarius 1:48 a.m.) Someone may desperately need your help today; be willing to give it in large measure. For you, a rather shocking secret could be revealed. And it could have to do with confidential family matters. Don't let it throw you. The lucky number is 6.

Wednesday, October 8 (Moon in Sagittarius) Don't start feeling sorry for yourself if you feel very alone today; this is your chance to find inspiration from within. Of course, if you choose, you can simply find some "escape." However, you are far better off trying to get in touch with some higher spiritual values. If necessary, get out and commune with nature to uplift your thoughts.

Thursday, October 9 (Moon Sagittarius to Capricorn 3:52 a.m.) Now you should feel as if you are out of the woods, and be able to take a rather aggressive mood. In fact, you could easily increase either your money or love quotient today. You are at a high in your lunar cycle, and your intuition should be right on target. Don't be afraid to step up and ask for what you want. The lucky number is 8.

Friday, October 10 (Moon in Capricorn) Whatever you do today should appeal a lot to others. Don't be afraid to express yourself with abandon. However, if you are really going to get anywhere, you are going to have to let go of some limiting thoughts or influences from the past.

Saturday, October 11 (Moon Capricorn to Aquarius 7:45 a.m.) You should really get the chance to get in on the ground floor of something big now. In many cases, it will be a business enterprise. However, you are still in danger of focusing on the past rather than the present or the future. It is important to break that mold, and to be creative and original. Some may find themselves bowled over by a lavish token of affection by a member of the opposite sex.

Sunday, October 12 (Moon in Aquarius) Your thoughts may turn to your security needs now, and it could make you take a slower pace. In some cases, you will find yourself successfully collecting money long overdue. There are a lot of investment opportunities around you now, and you are wise to take time out to survey them leisurely. The lucky number is 2 today.

Monday, October 13 (Moon Aquarius to Pisces 11:03 a.m.) You are going to have to watch out for a reckless urge to splurge now. You could feel desperately in need of new clothes, or a totally new environment. Take it one step at a time. A whirlwind of social activity could also leave you rather breathless; don't let it. Keep your mind on what you are doing, or you could easily lose something. A Sagittarian could play a key role.

Tuesday, October 14 (Moon in Pisces) Be utterly practical in your thinking today; that could mean paying a lot of attention to the fine print and reading between the lines. Pay attention to every bit of mail you receive, and every phone call. In some cases, it may be necessary to review and revise your thinking. Perhaps it needs to be more concrete and more logical. The lucky number is 4.

Wednesday, October 15 (Moon Pisces to Aries 5:13 p.m.) You could be absolutely dazzled today by someone who expresses him-/herself very eloquently. For some, the result could be a rather exciting romantic involvement. No matter what your relationship, if you open your heart now and let your feelings be known, you will do a lot for your own cause. This is no time for guessing games.

Thursday, October 16 (Moon in Aries) Someone may come to you asking for a shoulder to cry on; do everything you can to provide it. For others, a minor dispute could arise in your closest circle; you can resolve it if you are absolutely tactful and diplomatic. You could also be particularly susceptible to the "sweets of life" today; watch your diet.

Friday, October 17 (Moon in Aries) Don't take anything for granted where property or real estate matters are concerned. The full moon could contribute to tensions in what could already be a shaky situation. If you can, avoid signing any contracts or making any verbal commitments now. You are far better off playing a waiting game. A Pisces or a Virgo could show you how to be evasive. The lucky number is 7.

Saturday, October 18 (Moon Aries to Taurus 1:35 a.m.) This is no time to play games—particularly with a romantic partner. Sincere commitment is called for rather than flirtation or beating around the bush. For some, marriage and children are going to be hot topics of the day. Others can make their own opportunities now to connect with important people.

Sunday, October 19 (Moon in Taurus) There's a lot going on for you now, and you should end this day with a wider circle than you started it. For some, a creative project or a hobby will be the key that opens the new door. It may be difficult to say no to someone who comes at you rather directly; he/she is so aggressive, it really gets you going too. The lucky number is 9.

Monday, October 20 (Moon Taurus to Gemini 12:15 p.m.) Dare to be daring today; this is the time for action. There are any number of ways you can bring original ideas to bear on some long-standing situations. However, you will need a lot of courage and a throw-caution-to-the-winds attitude. It's worth it, however, because you will profit a lot from taking a leading role in your current drama.

Tuesday, October 21 (Moon in Gemini) Even though your intuition is working on high now, you are wise to go slowly and to attend to routine matters. A patient, receptive attitude will win in the long run. An older person could easily have the answers you are looking for; why not ask? The lucky number is 2.

Wednesday, October 22 (Moon in Gemini) Accept the fact that you could easily be careless with details today; leave them to someone else. Instead, spend your time spreading cheer and good humor. If you warm up and are sociable, you will find that those who share your daily concerns welcome you with open arms. A Sagittarian or a Gemini could play a key role.

Thursday, October 23 (Moon Gemini to Cancer 12:37 a.m.) Someone could be testing you now. The question is—are you willing to settle down and carry your share of the load? You may have to be willing to review and revise. It's possible the structure of something is not quite solid enough for future growth. Some Capricorns are going to have to concern themselves with the details of a legal matter. Tread carefully!

Friday, October 24 (Moon in Cancer) Leave the first move to someone else today, and you may be delighted with the results. Shared affections are very much indicated, but you are wise to take the more passive role. However, you should also remain flexible and ready to change plans at a moment's notice. In some cases, that could include a brief trip. The lucky number is 5.

Saturday, October 25 (Moon Cancer to Leo 1:02 p.m.) Try to throw off the cares of the workweek and devote yourself to the person closest to you. A lot of pretty routine domestic matters may be up for discussion, but by discussing them in an affectionate way, you can do a lot for the relationship. In some cases, you may simply find yourself shifting around furniture. But it really means a lot more than that. Your charming devotion will be the key for greater harmony.

Sunday, October 26 (Moon in Leo) Sometimes even Capricorns can be too idealistic about trusting other people. Realize you are not necessarily wise to do that now. Someone with a rather smooth line and a very believable story could be attracted to you now; keep your wits about you. And count all your change.

Monday, October 27 (Moon Leo to Virgo 11:20 p.m.) You may have to think seriously about what your return will be on a long-term investment—either in money or in love. If you are willing to build up a stable relationship, it probably is worth it. Love, power, and money are prime topics now. You should be able to prove yourself in more ways than one, and another Capricorn could help you do so. The lucky number is 8.

Tuesday, October 28 (Moon in Virgo) Jump at an opportunity that comes your way to get a lot smarter a lot faster. In some cases, a travel opportunity may be "the ticket." For others, it means spreading your message in some way or another; publishing could even be involved. An Aries or a Libran could be a big factor today.

Wednesday, October 29 (Moon in Virgo) Many Capricorns could easily receive a "love letter" today. Even if it comes in some kind of disguise. Don't hesitate to put across your ideas today, and to express some rather bold opinions. You could be starting a shift in direction, and the more exposure you get to an enlarged view of the world, the better. The lucky number today is 1.

Thursday, October 30 (Moon Virgo to Libra 6:04 a.m.) You could be rather surprised when someone in a higher position shows some real personal warmth and caring today. It should give you a pleasant "family feeling" within your professional or work atmosphere. However, resolve not to take advantage of this closer rapport to further your personal ambitions. Take a wait-and-see attitude.

Friday, October 31 (Moon in Libra) If your first idea does not work today, try another—and possibly another. It is vital to be versatile now, and to show just how many different facets there are to your abilities. You should be brimming with optimism, and hopeful for the future. Don't overlook any contact you make now, no matter how casual it seems. A Sagittarian or a Gemini could be the key.

NOVEMBER 1986

Saturday, November 1 (Moon Libra to Scorpio 9:19 a.m.) No matter how insignificant the day's activities seem, there is much more than meets the eye. For one thing, someone with a lot of experience is watching you, and with great admiration. You could be taking a step toward greater recognition now. Don't hang back or be modest; and don't overlook the fact that someone in your immediate circle could easily be involved in your success.

Sunday, November 2 (Moon in Scorpio) Open up and discuss your hopes and dreams with people around you who share common memories. It's okay to be a bit sentimental now. You may get an absolute brainstorm now, and it could have to do with your sensing the mood of the public. Don't dismiss it, because it could be extremely helpful in getting a return from some past efforts.

Monday, November 3 (Moon Scorpio to Sagittarius 10:19 a.m.) Your cheerful lighthearted mood could make you extremely popular today. However, others may not take you seriously enough, unless you project a down-to-earth image as well. But that should not be difficult for you. By asking questions, you will come in contact with some really interesting new people—some of whom could become very staunch allies. The lucky number is 3.

Tuesday, November 4 (Moon in Sagittarius) You may not be feeling quite so happy or lucky today, but you probably will accomplish a lot more than you did yesterday. Some may find themselves involved in some kind of investigation or working with confidential information. It will be very absorbing, but don't let it completely overtake other important matters.

Wednesday, November 5 (Moon Sagittarius to Capricorn 10:49 a.m.) You could get a real lift when someone who seemed to have dropped off the face of the earth suddenly reappears, and you two pick up where you left off. The exchange may give you some new insights and information that could influence your future decisions. In many ways, it could be a banner day. The lucky number is 5.

Thursday, November 6 (Moon in Capricorn) Now you should really swing into your "lunar high," and feel as if you are in the driver's seat. You are! You will gain through any kind of self-expression, use of your artistic talents, and tactful handling of a rather sticky situation. No matter what happens, remember that you are in charge—and take charge.

Friday, November 7 (Moon Capricorn to Aquarius 12:29 p.m.) Others could find you rather unapproachable today, so you should try to unbend a little. If you must, spend some time alone, and resolve to get to know yourself better. No matter how much you may wish to hide today, a situation may force you to show how sensitive you can be when it is necessary. It is good for you! The lucky number is 7.

Saturday, November 8 (Moon in Aquarius) You can successfully buy and sell today, no matter what activities you are actually involved in. You've got a good reputation for handling finances, and it will come in handy today. There is nothing like good credit to help you get credit. Another Capricorn could play a key role.

Sunday, November 9 (Moon Aquarius to Pisces 4:30 p.m.) Be charitable toward someone who comes to you for help, most likely of the financial variety. However, draw the line at making someone more dependent than he/she already is. Some Capricorns will be tying up the loose ends of a commercial transaction and moving on to bigger and better things. Now's the time to take the long-range rather than the short-range view. The lucky number is 9.

Monday, November 10 (Moon in Pisces) You definitely need a new way to approach some old problems. However, it should be easy for you to be original and independent now. In fact, it's okay to be a little daring. Some Capricorns will find that they attract a very warmhearted individual they meet rather casually. Don't be afraid to speak up and say what you think.

Tuesday, November 11 (Moon Pisces to Aries 11:14 p.m.) Now's the time to catch up on correspondence and to get back in touch with people you haven't seen for a while, In some cases, it will be parents and siblings. With the holiday approaching, you could be getting very sentimental about family celebrations of the past. That older person who's been waiting to hear from you would especially welcome a call. Corny as it sounds, it's time to "reach out and touch someone."

Wednesday, November 12 (Moon in Aries) No matter where you go today, you will find yourself bumping into upbeat, intelligent people. Don't miss any opportunity to expand your mental horizons now. Some Capricorns may be getting a lot more knowledgeable about their family roots. Some may even be considering travel to track them down even farther. The lucky number is 3.

Thursday, November 13 (Moon in Aries) The time has come to catch up on some really basic chores you've been putting off. In many cases, they will be right on your own home ground. You are going to have to discipline yourself in order to follow through on details; don't let anyone distract you—particularly an Aquarian who wants you to go out and "play." There will be time for that later on.

Friday, November 14 (Moon Aries to Taurus 8:24 a.m.) You should be feeling a lot less restricted today, and more able to enjoy the surroundings that you yourself have created. You could be very much in the mood for romance—with or without mental stimulation. Invite someone interesting to dinner. For many, your rebeautified residence will be the perfect backdrop.

Saturday, November 15 (Moon in Taurus) It's a perfect day to go on a "sentimental journey"—real or imagined. Family happenings, children, and other "sweet" things will be very much on your mind. For some, it is very possible to go overboard on some form of indulgence or another. Watch yourself! The lucky number is 6.

Sunday, November 16 (Moon Taurus to Gemini 7:26 p.m.) The full moon could easily create a romantic conflict, and possibly a serious misunderstanding with someone who means a lot to you. Before you go off the deep end, be sure to learn the story behind the story. You may be very much offbase. If you expect protection from others now, you will surely be disappointed. It's also wise to be cautious about any kind of speculation today.

Monday, October 17 (Moon in Gemini) Good for you! Some kind of promotion or praise for good work is definitely in order. Even if it doesn't come from someone else, be sure to congratulate yourself. If you take a leading role, you will prove that your experience means more than someone else's smart talk. Compare notes with another Capricorn. The lucky number is 8.

Tuesday, November 18 (Moon in Gemini) Your health may be suffering from some rather poor work habits. Could it be that you are turning into a compulsive workaholic? Get rid of any conditions that are putting a strain on you—including even a piece of furniture that is tiring you unnecessarily. Let someone with much more savvy than you help you overhaul what needs overhauling.

Wednesday, November 19 (Moon Gemini to Cancer 7:46 a.m.) Get set to be a lot more visible on your job. That means you should take particular attention in dressing today. Also, you may come to the conclusion that your weight needs some watching. However, for the most part, you should enjoy being in the spotlight. A Leo or an Aquarian could share it with you, and will be a lot of fun.

Thursday, November 20 (Moon in Cancer) Today you may learn the meaning of the word "compromise." You are going to have to be willing to take a backseat, and to act as a morale booster to someone else. In the long run, it will do a lot for your public image. Be charitable and take a wait-and-see attitude toward almost anything now. The lucky number is 2.

Friday, November 21 (Moon Cancer to Leo 8:25 p.m.) It will be very clear to you today that you are part of the team, not an independent entity. Curb your eagerness to dash ahead on impulses. Also make sure you are able to laugh at your own little foibles—others will laugh with you. It could prove to be a real safety valve. Keep your eye on a Sagittarian.

Saturday, November 22 (Moon in Leo) Okay, it's time to review expenses and balance the budget. You can cut your losses and you can build a more solid foundation for the future. However, if your finances are involved with someone else's, expect to take on a major portion of the load. Deal with it in a practical, businesslike manner.

Sunday, November 23 (Moon in Leo) Your spirits should definitely lift today and you should feel a lot freer to move around. In fact, you will be doing a lot of that. A rather exciting member of the opposite sex will show that he/she is deeply devoted, and also feels a strong physical attraction toward you. Are you prepared to deal with it? For some, an out-of-town visit is on the schedule. The lucky number is 5.

Monday, November 24 (Moon Leo to Virgo 7:46 a.m.) Holiday plans are really beginning to shape up, and a luxury purchase may definitely be on the agenda. Money may also suddenly become available for travel to visit relatives at a distance. Some are going to have to deal with a sudden change in schedule that threatens to be disruptive; you can restore harmony by being diplomatic. Your day will come!

Tuesday, November 25 (Moon in Virgo) You can lift yourself out of your current routine with your own imagination. In fact, it may not be possible for you to go anywhere. Indulge your urge to get away from it all by plunging into a good novel, seeing a good film, or simply spending your time contemplating the cosmos and listening to good music. The lucky number is 7.

Wednesday, November 26 (Moon Virgo to Libra 3:59 p.m.) Today your ambition should return with a vengeance, and lead you to expand your expectations beyond the current moment. You should realize that you are in line for bigger things, and that your life is going to have larger scope soon. You are wise to contact someone who seems to have all the answers; this is one time he/she really does have some. Be willing to let go of a rather limiting past situation.

Thursday, November 27 (Moon in Libra) Now's the time to complete something that has been hanging fire, and to follow through with a vengeance. You know it is the way to expand your opportunities. So you shouldn't let it scare you. It's also a good time to advertise yourself and influence others. Look on the bright side today, even if it is a bit difficult. The lucky number is 9.

Friday, November 28 (Moon Libra to Scorpio 8:15 p.m.) If you did what needed to be done yesterday, today you will really shine! As the honors and recognition come flowing in, you should stand tall and emphasize the fact that you are a leader rather than a follower. For many, someone will show admiration, and it could lead to something a lot more intense. Remain open to it.

Saturday, November 29 (Moon in Scorpio) Now you can relax a bit and let your guard down—particularly with close family and friends. Most should be looking forward to a weekend of simple pleasures, some of them possibly involving children. Another Capricorn or a Cancer could figure prominently today.

Sunday, November 30 (Moon Scorpio to Sagittarius 9:08 p.m.) Now the pace picks up and your popularity should zoom upward. Many Capricorns will be taking a real pleasure trip today, and should be looking forward to it immensely. You should, because you are going to meet a lot of interesting people who will stimulate you. One could be a Sagittarian or a Gemini.

DECEMBER 1986

Monday, December 1 (Moon in Sagittarius) The week will start out on a rather quiet note, and you will probably want to seek seclusion rather than the spotlight. Someone who once was very important in your life may reappear on the scene; consider whether or not you want to renew the attention. Some fairly mundane things need to be done today, but you will find comfort in everyday routine. The lucky number is 2.

Tuesday, December 2 (Moon Sagittarius to Capricorn 8:26 p.m.) This may be a day of rather mixed emotions. Realize that you have a choice between gloom and doom or joy and happiness. If you allow your own fears and self-doubts to get to you, you will do yourself a real disservice. You do have a lot to offer, and if you are willing to laugh at yourself, it could save the day. Accept an invitation.

Wednesday, December 3 (Moon in Capricorn) Now your cycle is going on high, and you should be able to focus your considerable energies. A really big road block can be overcome through both some intuitive insight and attention to practical matters. You are generally good at budgeting your time, and today is one day you should really do that. That way you'll be able to cut through a lot of red tape. The lucky number is 4.

Thursday, December 4 (Moon Capricorn to Aquarius 8:23 p.m.) A relationship will be up for review now, but you are in the driver's seat. If you want to make changes, you will be able to; discuss in a rather intense conversation you have. For most Capricorns, it will be easy to get the other person to bow to your wishes now. The lucky number is 5.

Friday, December 5 (Moon in Aquarius) Many are beginning to shop for the holidays, and today you could drop a bundle on a very lavish gift for a very special person. However, it is worth it if it means reestablishing harmony and cementing a relationship. The lucky number is 6.

Saturday, December 6 (Moon Aquarius to Pisces 10:48 p.m.) Today you should definitely pull in the reins where spending is concerned. Watch your cash and count your change, and don't expect to get something for nothing. Capricorns could be hazy in several respects today, and poor judgment is a real danger. Try to spend some time with a hobby or something beautiful. It will help you get through this time.

Sunday, December 7 (Moon in Pisces) Someone could get very sentimental on you today, and even vow undying affection. Someone will have to decide whether they are ready for a long-term commitment. If you are interested in sealing an important agreement, it can be done today—with great sincerity. Most of you will be more concerned with security than excitement today.

Monday, December 8 (Moon in Pisces) You may be doing some rather deep thinking today, and you are not in the mood for trivia. If you don't find satisfaction in the day-to-day world around you, try reading something that will really stimulate your mind. Or perhaps going to a lecture or a new class. Something is happening to you, and you really want to get involved. The lucky number is 9.

Tuesday, December 9 (Moon Pisces to Aries 4:49 a.m.) You really would rather soar above the clouds today, but most likely you are going to be mired down in rather mundane matters. There are a lot of demands on you, but if you take the creative approach to problems and come up with new solutions, you will surprise everyone, including yourself.

Wednesday, December 10 (Moon in Aries) It's okay to follow someone else's lead today; take a backseat and be happy about it. You really need a change of pace to relax from recent tensions. However, someone will remind you of more carefree days, and it will provide a good escape hatch for your feelings. Bake a cake or do something else comforting.

Thursday, December 11 (Moon Aries to Taurus 2:10 p.m.) You should be in the mood for fun today, but one of the things you've got to be willing to laugh at is your own goof-up. However, it is a small one, and you shouldn't let it ruin your day. Think about getting in shape now or otherwise improving your appearance. Something big is coming up. The lucky number is 3.

Friday, December 12 (Moon in Taurus) You are going to have to revise and rebuild to put things on a more solid foundation; someone you like a lot has great praise for your ability to complete what you started. It is one of your best traits. A practical approach is the best today, although you will have an opportunity to be creative.

Saturday, December 13 (Moon in Taurus) If you relax and let your hair down today, you will be able to charm someone thoroughly. In fact, for many of you, this is a red letter day where love and romance are concerned. A relationship may be undergoing a major change. Others may find a short trip an excellent change of pace. The lucky number is 5.

Sunday, December 14 (Moon Taurus to Gemini 1:41 a.m.) In one way or another, you are going to find yourself taking on extra duties today, and backing up other people. However, good teamwork is indicated, and it should be thoroughly enjoyable. Some will get some excellent decorating tips from a Libra or a Taurus.

Monday, December 15 (Moon in Gemini) Your need to get away from it all may interfere with the work that must be done today. Somehow or other, find a way to indulge your need for fantasy. It could be as simple as a walk in the woods, or a romantic novel. A Pisces will be particularly appealing to you today.

Tuesday, December 16 (Moon Gemini to Cancer 2:09 p.m.) This full moon could easily cause some waves at your place of employment. Realize that there are added tensions in the air, particularly in this sphere. One way to handle things is to show that you are willing to pitch in and help with the workload; it is important to show that you mean business now.

Wednesday, December 17 (Moon in Cancer) Be willing to give more than you get today, because it will pay off in the long run. Most Capricorns will find themselves having to concentrate on the needs of others, including people much less fortunate than they are. This should be a "selfish" day in every way. The lucky number is 9.

Thursday, December 18 (Moon in Cancer) You will want to be the center of attention today, but someone else will want the same thing. Be willing to compromise and to share. Someone around you is very susceptible to flattery now, and you could be rather manipulative. Don't be.

Friday, December 19 (Moon Cancer to Leo 2:44 a.m.) Use your head when it comes to money today—particularly a joint money problem. You may be in a very saving frame of mind, but realize that not everyone is as frugal as you are. Put the accent on warmth and tenderness rather than criticism. A Cancer could play a key role.

Saturday, December 20 (Moon in Leo) The accent is on travel and investigation now. Some may even find themselves looking into psychic or occult matters. You could easily decide that something has to be done about your weight, and it is a rather good time to think about your body image. A Sagittarian could prove to be a delight today.

Sunday, December 21 (Moon Leo to Virgo 2:30 p.m.) Now's the time to put the accent on teamwork and the pulling of resources. You can get a lot of routine jobs out of the way in no time if you get in the right spirit. Some may be accepting visitors from a distance; get a lot of details out of the way so that you can spend time with those who really interest you. The lucky number today is 4.

Monday, December 22 (Moon in Virgo) A change of scenery is on the agenda now. For some, it happens in a rather surprising and sudden way when plans are revised. It is an excellent time to catch up on news of family and friends; you could spend a lot of time on the phone today. With great satisfaction.

Tuesday, December 23 (Moon in Virgo) Resolve not to tangle with someone who takes a hard line with you today; he/she is simply being stubborn and there is little you can do about it. Turn your attention to getting ready for the holiday, and possibly a big family celebration. Many could be cooking up a storm.

Wednesday, December 24 (Moon Virgo to Libra 12:05 a.m.) Someone could really hurt you today, but realize that you are being particularly sensitive. Do not feel sorry for yourself; you can be an inspiration to others by showing how understanding you can be. Your best course is to forgive and forget. The lucky number is 7.

Thursday, December 25 (Moon in Libra) This could be an especially significant day for Capricorns—one that will be remembered long after the season is passed. Someone very important in your life becomes even more important now, and so does a possible gift of money. It could mean all the difference to your plans for the immediate future. However, you are going to have to show how responsible you can be.

Friday, December 26 (Moon Libra to Scorpio 7:06 a.m.) Take a charitable approach today, no matter what mood others are in. For some Capricorns, there is the real possibility of getting involved in some kind of humanitarian cause. Even though your motives are altruistic, you should realize you can expand your influence this way. The lucky number is 9.

Saturday, December 27 (Moon in Scorpio) You should have a lot of hope now and be looking forward to the coming year as one in which you can really score. For some, that means romance will add new meaning to your life. You give off a special glow now and should be able to "charm the birds out of the trees."

Sunday, December 28 (Moon Scorpio to Sagittarius 8:20 a.m.) You may experience some kind of letdown today, but it is only natural after all this activity. Simply relax and enjoy the relaxed mood—which should include some good food and good talk. A rather doting older person will want to give you advice; he/she really does have wise answers. The lucky number is 2.

Monday, December 29 (Moon in Sagittarius) You could feel a little shaky today and be experiencing some self-doubts. Use those particularly "sensitive feelings" to investigate new opportunities. They are out there. It is an excellent time for a "fact-finding mission." A Sagittarian or a Gemini could play a very prominent role.

Tuesday, December 30 (Moon Sagittarius to Capricorn 7:54 a.m.) It is unlikely that you are going to feel like starting anything new today, and you are better off following your instincts. Instead, catch up on a lot of small details and give yourself some breathing room. You are also wise to say no to an early holiday invitation. Stick with what you've got to do.

Wednesday, December 31 (Moon in Capricorn) End the year on a high note with the moon in your own sign. This should be and could be a spectacular New Year's Eve. You will be especially personable and in a mood to communicate. Your date for the evening should find you absolutely fascinating. In fact, you could be the central figure in the gathering of some quite scintillating people. Enjoy! The lucky number is 1.

About This Series

This is one of a series of
Twelve Day-by-Day Astrological Guides
for the signs in 1986
by Sydney Omarr

About the Author

Born on August 5, 1926, in Philadelphia, Omarr was the only astrologer ever given full-time duty in the U.S. Army as an astrologer. He also is regarded as the most erudite astrologer of our time and the best-known, through his syndicated column (300 newspapers), and his radio and television programs (he is Merv Griffin's "resident astrologer"). Omarr has been called the most "knowledgeable astrologer since Evangeline Adams." His forecasts of Nixon's downfall, the end of World War II in mid-August of 1945, the assassination of John F. Kennedy, Roosevelt's election to a fourth term and his death in office ... these and many others ... are on record and quoted enough to be considered "legendary."

SIGNET Books of Special Interest

(0451)

☐ **THE COMPLETE ART OF WITCHCRAFT by Sybil Leek.** Now the world's best-known witch reveals what it takes to be a good witch and how to avoid bad ones. Packed with colorful anecdotes and information, her rich, enticing portrait of witchcraft covers its engrossing, fiery history and presents the remarkably inspiring religion at its core that kept it alive through horrifying persecutions. (127145—$2.95)*

☐ **THE LOVER'S GUIDE TO SENSUOUS ASTROLOGY by Marlowe and Urna Gray.** Your love sign will show you how to meet, seduce and erotically pleasure the playmate of your dreams. (123646—$2.95)

☐ **THE SEXUAL KEY TO THE TAROT by Theodore Laurence.** Let the strange and beautiful symbols of the tarot reveal your path to gratifying love and sexual fulfillment. Learn all about your erotic potential. Fully illustrated. (133013—$3.50)*

☐ **THE TAROT REVEALED by Eden Gray.** This book can unlock the secrets of the tarot for you, for it provides a fascinating and authoritative introduction to the ancient art of the occult. (119657—$3.50)

☐ **MASTERING THE TAROT: Basic Lessons In An Ancient, Mystic Art by Eden Gray.** Now, with the help of one of the most authoritative instructors writing in the field today, even a novice will quickly learn to recognize all the 78 cards and to recall their meanings readily when he encounters them in a layout. (123204—$3.50)

*Prices slightly higher in Canada

Buy them at your local bookstore or use this convenient coupon for ordering.

NEW AMERICAN LIBRARY,
P.O. Box 999, Bergenfield, New Jersey 07621

Please send me the books I have checked above. I am enclosing $_____
(please add $1.00 to this order to cover postage and handling). Send check or money order—no cash or C.O.D.'s. Prices and numbers are subject to change without notice.

Name_____

Address_____

City_____ State_____ Zip Code_____

Allow 4-6 weeks for delivery.
This offer is subject to withdrawal without notice.

COUPON

PROF. LALLEMEND
Dept SO-8 • POB 252
BROOKLYN, N.Y. 11204

516 Fifth Ave., NY., NY. 10036

Dear Reader,

You do not have to 'merely believe' Professor Lallemend, the renowned astrologer, because he will **PROVE** to you how he can help you make your life better!

Just fill out this form and mail it. Professor Lallemend will prepare **YOUR HOROSCOPE** and predict—without charge **TWO ESSENTIAL EVENTS IN YOUR LIFE.** You will be thoroughly convinced by the precision of the forecast and will also learn how you can gain success and inner contentment, as well as avoiding everything which can be an obstacle in the path of your happiness. You will receive his advice absolutely free of charge. All you have to do is, answer the questions below, and mail the coupon TODAY.

Please send me free of charge and without any obligation on my part my horoscope and two predictions in an unmarked envelope.

My Birthdate ....
Time .... Place ....

Please let me know as well, my lucky numbers. I enclose here a number between 0 and 9 which suddenly comes to my mind:

_____

NAME....................
ADD. ....
....
CITY....................
STATE :........ ZIP ....

How well do you know yourself?

This horoscope gives you answers to these questions based on your exact time and place of birth...

How do others see you?
What is your greatest strength?
What are your life purposes?
What drives motivate you?
How do you think?
Are you a loving person?
How competitive are you?
What are your ideals?
How religious are you?
Can you take responsibility?
How creative are you?
How do you handle money?
How do you express yourself?
What career is best for you?
How will you be remembered?
Who are your real friends?
What are you hiding?

Many people are out of touch with their real selves. Some can't get ahead professionally because they are doing the wrong kind of work. Others lack self-confidence because they're trying to be someone they're not. Others are unsuccessful in love because they use the wrong approach with the wrong people. Astrology has helped hundreds of people with problems like these by showing them their real selves.

You are a unique individual. Since the world began, there has never been anyone exactly like you. Sun-sign astrology, the kind you see in newspapers and magazines, is all right as far as it goes. But it treats you as if you were just the same as millions of others who have the same Sun sign because their birthdays are close to yours. A true astrological reading of your character and personality has to be one of a kind, unlike any other. It has to be based on exact date, time, longitude and latitude of your birth. Only a big IBM computer like the one that Para Research uses can handle the trillions of possibilities.

A Unique Document Your Astral Portrait includes your complete chart with planetary positions and house cusps calculated to the nearest minute of arc, all planetary aspects with orbs and intensities, plus text explaining the meaning of:

★ Your particular combination of Sun and Moon signs.
★ Your Ascendant sign and the house position of its ruling planet. (Many computer horoscopes omit this because it requires exact birth data.)
★ The planets influencing all twelve houses in your chart.
★ Your planetary aspects.

Others Tell Us "I found the Astral Portrait to be the best horoscope I've ever read."—E.D., Los Angeles, CA
"I could not put it down until I'd read every word. It is like you've been looking over my shoulder since I arrived in this world!"—B.N.L., Redding, CA
"I recommend the Astral Portrait. It even surpasses many of the readings done by professional astrologers."
—J.B., Bristol, CT

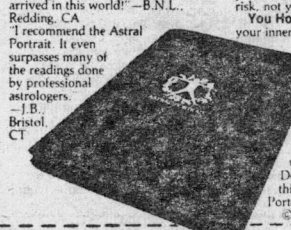

Low Price There is no substitute for a personal conference with an astrologer, but a good astrologer charges $50 and up for a complete chart reading. Some who have rich clients get $200 and more. Your Astral Portrait is an analysis of your character written by some of the world's foremost astrologers, and you can have it not for $200 or $50 but for only $22. This is possible because the text of your Astral Portrait is already written. You pay only for the cost of putting your birth information into the computer, compiling one copy, checking it and sending it to you within two weeks.

Permanence Ordinarily, you leave as astrologer's office with only a memory. Your Astral Portrait is a thirty-five-page, fifteen-thousand-word, permanently bound book that you can read again and again for years.

Money-Back Guarantee Our guarantee is unconditional. That means you can return your Astral Portrait at any time for any reason and get a full refund of the purchase price. That means we take all the risk, not you!

You Hold the Key The secrets of your inner character and personality, your real self, are locked in the memory of the computer. You alone hold the key: your time and place of birth. Fill in the coupon below and send it to the address shown with $22. Don't put it off. Do it now while you're thinking of it. Your Astral Portrait is waiting for you.
© 1977 Para Research, Inc.

Para Research, Dept. BT, P.O. Box 61, Gloucester, Massachusetts 01930 I want to read about my real self. Please send me my Astral Portrait. I understand that if I am not completely satisfied. I can return it for a full refund. ☐ I enclose $22 plus 1.50 for shipping and handling. ☐ Charge $23.50 to my Master Card account. ☐ Charge $23.50 to my VISA account.

Card number		Good through Mo.		Day	Yr.
Mr/Ms		Birthdate Mo.		Day	Yr.
Address		Birthtime (within an hour)			AM/PM
City		Birthplace City			
State	Zip	State		County	

Know in advance the changes in your life

Wouldn't it be useful to know when important events in your life are going to happen? How would you respond? What will you experience emotionally, intellectually and psychologically? And how will these experiences affect your life?

Your transits can provide valuable clues to various trends or stages of personal growth. This is especially true for the slower moving outer planets—Jupiter through Pluto. The transits for these planets are long lasting and profound in their psychological consequences. Many occur only once in a lifetime. The Astral Forecast is all about the outer planets.

This horoscope provides a reliable tool for astrological forecasting. The Astral Forecast will show you how the outer planets affect your sense of timing, that is, the times that are appropriate for you to take certain kinds of actions and inappropriate for others. This horoscope includes every significant transit to your outer planets that occurs in a twelve-month period. You can use your Astral Forecast to better understand how the outer planets affect such important life issues as career, child rearing, love, marriage and more.

For example, when Jupiter is in the first house, this transit represents a major growth cycle in your life. This is the best time for you to explore who you really are as an individual. Under this transit, you will feel more secure about yourself and the impression you make on others. Therefore, understanding yourself and your influence on others can make this transit an especially powerful and

important time in your life. This is also a time for learning and gaining new experience. All this is part of your present need for personal growth, which affects not only yourself, but also the way you deal with the world as a whole. This is one time when persons and resources are likely to be drawn to you, and you should take constructive advantage of them.

You can find out in advance what your transits are going to be. But if you do it on your own, you will have to consult several astronomical tables to find the positions of each of the transiting planets every day and then compare them mathematically to the positions of the planets at the time of your birth.

There's an easier way to learn of your transits. Our IBM System/36 computer will handle all the calculations and provide you with information on all your outer transits based on your exact time and place of birth. With the Astral Forecast you not only receive the most accurate calculation of your personal transits for the next twelve months, you will also receive an extensive printout interpreting the character and significance of your individual transits.

Your Astral Forecast is the most accurate and authoritative guide to the outer transits that you can receive. It is based on the work of Robert Hand, one of America's most famous astrologers, and the author of several astrology books.

Like all Para Research horoscopes, the Astral Forecast is inexpensive. For just $16.00 you can have the same kind of advice that would otherwise cost you hundreds of dollars. This low price is possible because the astrological data is stored in our computer, and can be easily formatted and printed. Also, the mathematical calculations can be done in a matter of minutes. Your only cost is the cost of putting your personal information into the computer, producing one copy and then mailing it.

When you order your Astral Forecast, you receive an unconditional money-back guarantee. This means you can return your Astral Forecast at any time and get a full refund of the purchase price. We take all the risk.

Order your Astral Forecast today. Discover how the transits can bring energy to each part of your personality, fulfill your potential and help you gain more control over your own life.
© 1983 Para Research, Inc.

Para Research, Dept. BT, P.O. Box 81, Gloucester, Massachusetts 01930 Please send me my Astral Forecast. I understand that if I am not completely satisfied, I can return it for a full refund. ☐ I enclose $16 plus $1.50 for shipping and handling. ☐ Charge $17.50 to my MasterCard account. ☐ Charge $17.50 to my VISA account.

Card number		Good through Mo.	Day	Yr.
Mr/Ms		Birthdate Mo.	Day	Yr.
Address		Birthtime (within an hour)		AM/PM
City		Birthplace City	State	
State	Zip	Start calendar with Mo.	Yr.	

Don't Let A TERRIBLE THING HAPPEN TO YOU!

SECRET KNOWLEDGE REVEALED THAT HAS BEEN HANDED DOWN THROUGH HISTORY- TO <u>HELP GIVE YOU A RICHER, LOVE FILLED, HAPPIER LIFE.</u>

Will The POWER Of The OCCULT DOLL Work For YOU?

- **OCCULT SUPPLIES**—For centuries it was and still is a tradition that in Secret Ancient Rituals and Magic of Haiti, Africa, and Latin America, dolls and spells were used to carry out every purpose desired. Used for Love, Luck, Riches to gain power. These ancient rituals were rare a constant source of comfort and hope to those who pratice.

We have been making these OCCULT DOLLS and RITUALS for certain customers with Special Problems to see if they were able to help. We are happy to tell you that we feel they have been a great success. Each Doll is made of a certain color with Amulets, Charms, and Herbs sewn in. Believed to attract WHAT YOU WANT. Each Doll is handmade with Great Care by one who knows and believes. Comes with full instructions.

- **LOVE DOLL**
We feel the Most Powerful Love Occult Ritual is done with Red, and special items sewn in. Use to bring a love back to you to get your relationship back to the love and excitement you once had we believe. Comes with special Red tipped pin, powerful instructions
D300 . . . . 5.98

- **MONEY DRAWING DOLL**
Green Doll handmade with coins and herbs sewn inside. We believe that Green has the power of attracting money to one in need. Strong money directions included.
D500 . . . . 5.98

- **OCCULT RITUAL HANDBOOK**
Everything you always wanted to know about Occult Rituals and Magic—songs, chants, spells for every purpose. Use of Roots, Herbs, Oils plus ceremonial rites and more. The secrets are here.
Bk120 . . . . 4.98

Triple Win BINGO BAG

Did you ever wonder why some people always win at BINGO? Do they have a secret? Now you can have your own secret! Your own BINGO BAG to carry with you.

NOW YOU CAN WIN TOO!
When your numbers are called, you be the one to shout BINGO! You get Bingo Oil, Gemstone, Charm, Seal plus Green Bag and full instructions.
KK795 All 7 items 7.95

LOVE RUB

Rub on your hands or body — or on the body of the one you love. Get what you want and use it wisely.

K371-Red-Passionate Love
K372-Pink-Win love and conquer Evil
K373-Green-Money Drawing
K374-Light Blue-Power to Find a Job

3.98 Any 3 for 11.50

FOLLOW ME COLOGNE

Comes with "LUCKY FORTUNE" A Few Drops Does the Trick. To attract your love, wear this whenever you go out. Sprinkle in your draws also.
K297 Large 4 oz. size
4.98

SPIRITUAL OILS

Used by many thousands of satisfied people because the fragrance charms the senses. Try them today!

Save 77¢
2.25 Order any 3
Only 5.98

K-4 — Attraction	K-14 — Lady Luck
K-100 — Commanding	K-11 — Lodestone
K-2 — Compelling	K-112 — Lovers
K-101 — Concentration	K-113 — Lucky Money
K-102 — Crossing	K-114 — Lucky Hand
K-103 — Dragon Blood	K-9 — Money Drawing
K-16 — Fast Luck	K-7 — Power
K-104 — Finance	K-117 — Protection
K-105 — French Love	K-121 — Spirit
K-106 — Good Luck	K-8 — Success
K-107 — High Conquering	K-122 — Uncrossing
K-109 — Holy Spiritual	K-123 — Van Van
K-110 — Jinx Removing	
K-111 — King Solomon	

SPECIAL INCENSE

2.25
Save 77¢
Order any 3
Only 5.98

Burn incense to attract, to dispel wicked odors. Best incense available, attracting fragrances, satisfying results.

NUMBER IN EVERY BOX
People are used to buying incense with a number. And considering it lucky. We don't claim these numbers as such.

K-77 — Commanding	K-48 — Success
K-42 — Compelling	K-34 — Jinx Removing
K-78 — Concentration	K-84 — Lady Luck
K-97 — Crossing	K-66 — Lovers
K-80 — Dragon Blood	K-87 — Lucky Hand
K-41 — Fast Luck	K-88 — Lucky Money
K-33 — Finance	K-91 — Masters
K-81 — French Love	K-47 — Money Drawing
K-82 — Good Luck	K-39 — Power
K-83 — High Conquering	K-43 — Van Van
	K-35 — Uncrossing

Write to: **ANN HOWARD DEPT.SY1 200 West Sunrise Highway, Freeport, N.Y. 11520**

$5 Dollar Deposit on all C.O.D. Orders! Prepaid Orders Please Add $1.95 for Postage.
FREE- Latest Catalog-Candles, Oils, Incense, Spells, More. Just Write. No claims are made.
These alleged powers are gathered from writings, books, folklore & occult sources.
Sold as curios.

"Next to my mother, you have been the greatest inspiration of my life."

You'll be amazed!

When you read what Marguerite Carter has to say about your life in the year ahead you'll be amazed. She delves into the most important areas of your life: romance, money, goals, and significant changes. You'll find out all the wonderful ways you can live a better life when you have your Unitology Forecast prepared for you by Marguerite Carter.

She'll help you.

Marguerite Carter has counseled thousands of enthusiastic followers around the world for decades. She has been the guiding light and helping hand for people from all walks of life: business leaders, hollywood stars and just everyday folks. There is a good reason why they seek her services year after year. They get the help they need in the most important areas of their lives!

'... it was amazing.'

People write all the time telling about how Marguerite Carter has helped them.

"... it was amazing. I just can't believe it." W.C., Canada

MARGUERITE CARTER

"... could not put it down until I read it cover to cover." M.L., Illinois

"Without a doubt, next to my mother, you have been the greatest inspiration of my life. Many others could probably say the same thing." M.A., PA

In letter after letter people comment on the realistic guidance they've received for getting what they want from life. They've found the help they need in times of decision or resolving personal problems. These are judgments by a caring counselor, not some impersonal computer.

Hidden Opportunities

The things you want most may not be out of reach. Marguerite Carter says, "Many people are completely unaware that the opportunities for money, love or advancement are passing them by almost daily . . ." Without knowledge of when the conditions are favorable or unfavorable, the chances for success and happiness are greatly diminished.

Get your Unitology Forecast with special notations by Marguerite Carter. It will be prepared to your specific birthdate information. Remember that you will receive a full year of guidance, regardless of when your request is received, and you'll know that your forecast has come from one of the world's most highly respected astrologer-counselors.

O-6

Marguerite Carter • P.O. Box 807 • Indianapolis, Indiana 46206

☐ Yes Miss Carter, Please send me my Unitology Forecast for the year ahead. Enclosed is my remittance of $9.95 plus $1.00 for postage and handling. (First Class $1.30) Make all checks payable in U.S. funds. Allow 4 weeks for delivery.

Name _____

Address _____

City _____ State _____ Zip Code _____

Birthplace _____

Month _____ Day _____ Year _____

Place _____ Hour _____

ASTROLOGY QUESTIONNAIRE

Help us bring you even better astrology guides by filling out this survey and mailing it today.

A. Book Title (Sign): _____

B. Using the scale below how would you rate this astrological guide? (Place one rating from 0–10 in the space provided.)

Poor	Not So Good	O.K.	Good	Excellent
0 1	2 3	4 5 6	7 8	9 10

Rating

Overall Opinion of book

Essay On:
1. Defining Terms _____
2. Your House of The Sun _____
3. The Geometry of Relationships _____
4. Twelve Places at the Table _____
5. Moods of the Moon _____
6. Venus and Mars _____
7. Venus Sign Position Chart _____
8. Mars Sign Position Chart _____
9. The Planets as "Stars" _____
10. Astrotrivia _____
11. Sun Sign Changes _____
12. Your Sign: The Big Picture _____
13. Your Sign: Objectives and Obstacles _____
14. Pairing Off With Your Sign _____
15. Your Sign's Sex Role Dilemma _____
16. Your Sign: Female _____
17. Your Sign: Male _____
18. Your Sign: Help Wanted _____
19. How "Pure" a _____ are you? _____
20. Find Your Rising Sign _____
21. Your Sign: Astro-Outlook for '86 _____
22. 15 Months of Day-By-Day Predictions _____

C. In total about how many astrology guides have you purchased for yourself in the past 12 months?
# of books _____

D. What topics would you be interested in having Sydney Omarr write about in the 1987 Astrology Guide?

_____

_____

E. What is your education?

1( ) High School   3( ) 4 yrs college
2( ) 2 yrs college   4( ) Postgraduate

F. What is your occupation? _____

G. What is your marital status?

1( ) Single   3( ) Divorced   5( ) Widowed
2( ) Married   4( ) Separated

H. Age: _____   **I.** Sex: 1( ) Male
                                       2( ) Female

Please Print Name: _____

Address _____

City _____ **State** _____ **Zip** _____

Phone # ( ) _____

Thank you. Please send to New American Library, Research Dept., 1633 Broadway, New York, NY 10019